the Adobe® Photoshop®

Lightroom™

book

for digital photographers

Scott Kelby

The Adobe Photoshop Lightroom Book for Digital Photographers Team

CREATIVE DIRECTOR
Felix Nelson

TECHNICAL EDITORS
Cindy Snyder
Kim Doty

TRAFFIC DIRECTOR
Kim Gabriel

PRODUCTION MANAGER
Dave Damstra

COVER DESIGNED BY
Jessica Maldonado

COVER PHOTOS
COURTESY OF
Scott Kelby

Published by
New Riders

Composed in Cronos and Helvetica by Kelby Publishing

Trademarks
All terms mentioned in this book that are known to be trademarks or service marks have been appropriately capitalized. New Riders cannot attest to the accuracy of this information. Use of a term in the book should not be regarded as affecting the validity of any trademark or service mark.

Photoshop Lightroom is a registered trademark of Adobe Systems, Inc.
Photoshop is a registered trademark of Adobe Systems, Inc.
Windows is a registered trademark of Microsoft Corporation.

Warning and Disclaimer
This book is designed to provide information about Adobe Photoshop Lightroom for digital photographers. Every effort has been made to make this book as complete and as accurate as possible, but no warranty of fitness is implied.

The information is provided on an as-is basis. The author and New Riders shall have neither liability nor responsibility to any person or entity with respect to any loss or damages arising from the information contained in this book or from the use of the discs or programs that may accompany it.

ISBN 13: 978-0-321-49216-6
ISBN 10:   0-321-49216-1

9 8 7 6 5 4

www.newriders.com
www.scottkelbybooks.com

For the cutest little baby
in the whole wide world,
Kira Nicole Kelby.

ACKNOWLEDGMENTS

First, I want to thank my amazing wife Kalebra. We've been married nearly 18 years now, and just looking at her still makes my heart skip a beat, and again reminds me how much I adore her, how genuinely beautiful she is, and how I couldn't live without her. She's the type of woman love songs are written for, and I am, without a doubt, the luckiest man alive to have her as my wife.

Secondly, I want to thank my 10-year-old son Jordan, who spent many afternoons pulling me away from writing this book so we could play *Dragon Ball Z: Budokai Tenkaichi 2* (where I finally got my three wins!). God has blessed our family with so many wonderful gifts, and I can see them all reflected in his eyes. I'm so proud of him, so thrilled to be his dad, and I dearly love watching him grow to be such a wonderful little guy, with such a tender and loving heart. (You're the greatest, little buddy.)

I also want to thank my newborn daughter Kira Nicole Kelby for being such a little sweetie. My wife and I knew we were having a baby girl, we just didn't realize that she would in fact be "the cutest little baby in the whole wide world."

I also want to thank my brother Jeffrey for being such a positive influence in my life, for always taking the high road, for always knowing the right thing to say, and just the right time to say it, and for having so much of our dad in you. I'm honored to have you as my brother and my friend.

My heartfelt thanks go to the entire team at KW Media Group, who every day redefine what teamwork and dedication are all about. They are truly a special group of people, who come together to do some really amazing things (on really scary deadlines), and they do it with class, poise, and a can-do attitude that is truly inspiring. I'm so proud to be working with you all.

Thanks to my layout and production crew. In particular, I want to thank my friend and Creative Director Felix Nelson for his limitless talent, creativity, input, and just for his flat-out great ideas.

A heartfelt thanks goes to my Tech Editor Kim Doty, who worked harder on this book than a person should be allowed to work, and yet she kept her trademark upbeat attitude and warm smile throughout the entire process. I truly couldn't have done this book without you. Also, a big, big thanks to Cindy Snyder, who helped put all the techniques through rigorous testing and caught lots of little things others would have missed. Also, thanks to "The Michigan Layout Machine" Dave Damstra and his amazing crew for giving the book such a tight, clean layout, and for letting me make changes up to the last possible minute. We got truly lucky when we found you!

Thanks to my best buddy Dave Moser, whose tireless dedication to creating a quality product makes every project we do better than the last. Thanks to Jean A. Kendra for her support, and for keeping a lot of plates in the air while I'm writing these books. A special thanks to my Executive Assistant Kathy Siler for all her hard work and dedication, and for arranging things so both the Bucs and Redskins would have bad seasons this year so we wouldn't fight.

Thanks to my Publisher Nancy Ruenzel, and the incredibly dedicated team at Peachpit/ New Riders. You are very special people doing very special things, and it's a real honor to get to work with people who really just want to make great books. Also many thanks to the awesome Ted "XL Shirt Connection" Waitt, Glenn "The New Kid" Bisignani, and to marketing maverick Scott Cowlin.

I owe a special debt of gratitude to George Jardine, photographic evangelist at Adobe, for all his help and for caring enough to listen, and to Lightroom Product Manager Tom Hogarty for answering my late-night emails. Also, a big thanks (and a big hug) to the amazing Jennifer Stern, who now has many loyal fans at NAPP HQ (and count me as #1!). And a hearty congratulations to everyone on Adobe's Lightroom team for creating a tool that photographers so desperately need, so they can spend more time focusing on the photography instead of the process.

Also thanks to Kevin Connor and John Nack at Adobe for their help, and for hearing my pleas, and to the wonderful Deb Whitman and Mala Sharma for all your continued support.

Also thanks to my "Photoshop Guys" Dave Cross and Matt Kloskowski, for being such excellent sounding boards for the development of this book. You guys are the best! A special thanks to Debbie Stephenson for leading our seminar team to another amazing year, and for being such an important part of my first U.S. Lightroom Tour.

Thanks to my friends at Adobe Systems: Terry White, Addy Roff, Cari Gushiken, Russell Brady, Julieanne Kost, and Russell Preston Brown, and thanks to John Loiacono for letting me do his intro (...and here he is...Johnny L!). Gone but not forgotten: Barbara Rice, Rye Livingston, Bryan Lamkin, and Karen Gauthier.

I want to thank all the talented and gifted photographers who've taught me so much over the years, including: Bill Fortney, Moose Peterson, Joe McNally, George Lepp, Anne Cahill, Vincent Versace, David Ziser, Jim Divitale, Helene Glassman, and Monte Zucker.

My thanks to Matt Kloskowski, Ashley Gellar, Susan Hill, Kleber Stephenson, Rod Harlan, Scott Cowlin, Sarah Crist, Debbie Stephenson, and Susie (from Paradise portraits) for lending me their wonderful faces for the book.

I would like to dedicate the Develop module section of this book to beloved color expert, brilliant author, and tireless educator Bruce Fraser, who passed away last year after battling cancer. Bruce's contributions to the digital imaging community, to Photoshop, and even Lightroom, are countless, and I hope you'll take this moment to reflect on both his many contributions to our industry, and a life spent helping people around the world in their understanding and enjoyment of something that means so much to so many of us.

Thanks to my mentors whose wisdom and whip-cracking have helped me immeasurably, including John Graden, Jack Lee, Dave Gales, Judy Farmer, and Douglas Poole.

Most importantly, I want to thank God, and His son Jesus Christ, for leading me to the woman of my dreams, for blessing us with two amazing children, for allowing me to make a living doing something I truly love, for always being there when I need Him, for blessing me with a wonderful, fulfilling, and happy life, and such a warm, loving family to share it with.

OTHER BOOKS BY SCOTT KELBY

The Digital Photography Book

The iPod Book

The Photoshop CS2 Book for Digital Photographers

The Photoshop Channels Book

Photoshop Down & Dirty Tricks

Photoshop CS2 Killer Tips

Photoshop Classic Effects

InDesign CS/CS2 Killer Tips

Mac OS X Tiger Killer Tips

Getting Started with Your Mac and Mac OS X Tiger

ABOUT THE AUTHOR

Scott Kelby

Scott is Editor and Publisher of *Photoshop User* magazine, Editor-in Chief of *Darkroom* magazine (the new magazine for Adobe Photoshop Lightroom users), and is Editor and Publisher of *Layers* magazine (the how-to magazine for everything Adobe).

Scott is President and co-founder of the National Association of Photoshop Professionals (NAPP) and is President of the software training, education, and publishing firm KW Media Group.

Scott is a photographer, designer, and an award-winning author of more than 40 books, including *Photoshop Down & Dirty Tricks, The Photoshop Book for Digital Photographers, The Photoshop Channels Book, Photoshop Classic Effects*, and *The Digital Photography Book.*

Since 2004, Scott has been awarded with the distinction of being the world's #1 best-selling author of all computer and technology books, across all categories. His books have been translated into dozens of different languages, including Chinese, Russian, Spanish, Korean, Polish, Taiwanese, French, German, Italian, Japanese, Dutch, Swedish, Turkish, and Portuguese, among others, and he is a recipient of the prestigious Benjamin Franklin Award.

Scott is Training Director for the Adobe Photoshop Seminar Tour and Conference Technical Chair for the Photoshop World Conference & Expo. He's featured in a series of Adobe Photoshop training DVDs and has been training Adobe Photoshop users since 1993.

For more information on Scott, visit scottkelby.com.

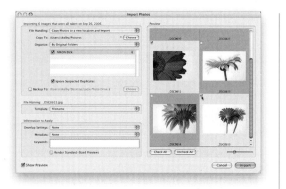

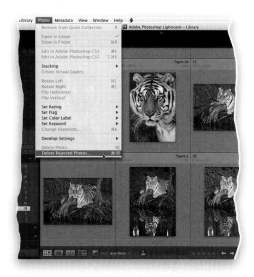

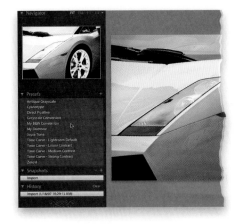

TABLE OF CONTENTS

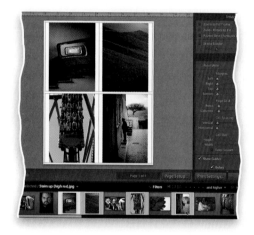

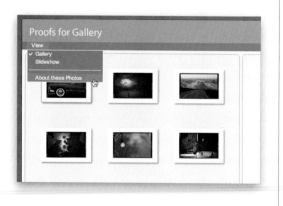

AN UNEXPECTED Q&A SECTION

Q. I didn't expect to see the book start with a Q&A section. Don't Q&A sections normally come after a chapter, rather than before the first chapter?
A. Normally they do. That's why this one is so unexpected. But there is a reason it's here. It's here to take up pages. You see, authors are paid on how many pages they write, regardless if the pages are actually necessary or if they even relate to the topic of the book. So, I thought I'd just pick up a few extra bucks right up front and add a Q&A.

Q. Really?
A. Of course not. That's not the way book publishing really works. It's unfortunate, because us authors could really cash in, but sadly, you don't get paid on how many pages you write. You get paid on how many books you sell, and how many books you sell is dependent on three factors: (1) how many times you can work naughty double-entendre phrases into your text, (2) how many times you can work French words into your text, like "double-entendre," but mostly it's (3) how useful people actually find your book.

Q. So how useful is this book going to be?
A. That depends on whether the person who bought the book (that's you by the way), takes the time to read the introduction. You see, the introduction of the book is where the author bares the soul of the book—where he (or she) shows how to get the most out of the book, so readers really maximize their experience. The author addresses common concerns, gives helpful tips and ideas on how readers should best use their time, and generally tries to help readers connect with the book.

Q. But this book doesn't have an introduction. Why not?
A. It's because no one reads the introduction of books anymore. No, they'd rather turn right to the first chapter and fumble around on their own, stumbling from project to project, rather than spending just two minutes to find out how the book was written, why it was written that way, what to look out for, and what to avoid.

Q. Are people really that shallow?
A. Yes. But not you. You're not like that. You know why? Because you're reading the introduction right now. Oh sure, it's called "An Unexpected Q&A Section" but come on, have you ever heard of an unexpected Q&A section? Especially one that comes before the first chapter? You knew this was a ruse to get you to read the introduction but you kept on going. I like you, kid. You've got moxie.

Q. What exactly is moxie?
A. Moxie is an industrial-strength abrasive cleaner that removes lime, rust, and scale from a variety of surfaces.

Q. I have that? I have moxie?
A. I'm not 100% sure.

continued

Q. Is the rest of the book like this?

A. Thankfully, no. The rest of the book is pretty much step-by-step, without straying too much from the path. That's why, in this unexpected Q&A, I stray quite a bit from the path. You see, when you write step-by-step books, there's no room for your own writing style to come through. It's pretty much "Go under this menu for this" and "click on that button for that." It's just so "to the point." So, in a step-by-step book like this, I only get two real writing outlets which keep me from climbing into a tower with a high-powered rifle and picking off pedestrians. They are: (1) this unexpected Q&Atroduction, and (2) the chapter intros for each chapter, which by the way, have little to do with what's actually in said chapter.

Q. But the rest of the book is regular?

A. Absolutely. Thanks to my strict regimen of high fiber. Sorry, that was lame.

Q. Okay, I've been pretty patient now, where are those "helpful tips" you were talking about earlier?

A. Oh those. Well, here's one: If you go to this book's website (www.scottkelbybooks.com/lightroomphotos) you can download many of the key photos used here in the book so you can follow along using the same images that I used. See, this is one of those things I was talking about that you'd miss if you were a little short of moxie (which I'm 97.1% sure, you're not) and jumped right to Chapter 1. Here's another tip: Read this book in order, starting with Chapter 1. That might seem like kind of a "duh" tip, but if you've read any of my other books, you know I generally write books that are "jump in anywhere" types of books. It's different with Photoshop books, because many people buy them to learn a specific technique, like image sharpening, so they buy it and jump straight to the sharpening chapter, and that's perfectly okay in Photoshop books.

Q. But this isn't a Photoshop book, right?

A. Right. Adobe Photoshop Lightroom is a workflow tool. It's designed to take you through the process of importing your photos, sorting them, processing them (in your digital darkroom), viewing them in their final version, and then printing them. Photoshop Lightroom has been designed that way, as a workflow tool, from the very beginning. So, I recommend that you learn it that way—in order, starting with Chapter 1 and working through the book in order.

Q. But what if I bought the book specifically just to learn the Slideshow features?

A. Too bad, you have to read Chapters 1 through 6 first.

Q. Are you serious?

A. Of course not. These are just guidelines, not steadfast rules carved into stone. So, if you're kind of loose with money, and getting a good value by learning in the manner the author suggests isn't of interest to you, then just jump in anywhere. Again, I'm kidding (kind of). However, I do recommend learning Photoshop Lightroom's workflow in order. It's the way the program was designed, and if you learn it that way, you'll have a better understanding, but hey—it's your book—if you decide to hollow out the insides to safely store your valuables, I'll never know. You'll feel somewhat guilty, but again, I'll never know.

Q. I hate that word "workflow."

A. Everybody does, but that's not a question. Can you restate it in the form of a question?

Q. Okay, whatever. Don't you hate that term workflow?
A. Not at all.

Q. I thought you said everybody hates it?
A. You can't believe everything you read. Okay, I do hate that term, because it makes things sound like work. Workflow just means: the order in which you do things. Since there are no officially-sanctioned guidelines for what a proper workflow is, then workflow is just a personal preference. It's the order in which a particular photographer has chosen to manage and process his or her photos. Almost every photographer has his or her own workflow method. So, you're probably wondering: who's workflow is right? I can answer that: Mine!

Q. Really? You've got the right workflow?
A. Well, it is for me, but it might not be for you. By the way, if it's not right for you, that's okay—it just makes you wrong (kidding). Actually, it's true—everyone's workflow is different, but with Photoshop Lightroom, Adobe went a long way toward helping photographers by leading us through what they, and many photographers around the world, feel is a sensible and quick way to work with digital images. That's what Photoshop Lightroom is all about, and I'm here to help you through that process as best I can. So, from here on out, I'm Mr. Serious, but I do appreciate you taking the time to read this unexpected Q&A and hope you'll join me for some unexpected chapter intros between all the Step One, Step Two stuff. See you there!

Q. I've heard a lot about the last two chapters. Is it okay if I jump over to them now?
A. Nope. To really get anything out of them, you'd need to read the rest of the book first. If you just jump to the end now, without "paying your dues" or "wood shedding" or "riding the pony" (riding the pony?), I have to be honest with you—I'm not sure you're mature enough to handle this explosive of a book. Maybe you should wait until you're in your thirties—they're that special.

Q. What makes them so special?
A. They're special because they're different, and being different makes you special (my mother always said that so it must be true). Anyway, those last two chapters are where it all comes together, as I take you on two live photo shoots and we follow the entire process, from the moment of capture to final output, and you see every step along the way. It's where "it all comes together;" it's where "the rubber meets the road;" it's where "insert your own cliché saying here."

Q. One last thing, Scott. You did an eBook version of this book. How different is this printed edition from the eBook?
A. I'm glad you asked that (actually, I'm glad I asked that). It's 100% new—I rewrote the whole entire book from scratch, adding 200 more pages, plus three additional chapters, and all new photos and projects. In short, I threw away a good chunk of my life.

Q. So we're pretty much done here?
A. Yup. Now turn the page, before I start tearing up.

Exposure: 1/20 | Focal Length: 18mm | Aperture Value: ƒ/3.5

Importing
getting your photos into photoshop lightroom

Now, do we really need an entire chapter just on importing photos? Nope. We could just skip it, but then the book would start with Chapter 2, and you'd be sending emails to the book's publisher complaining that your book is missing Chapter 1. See, that's the key word there—missing. You wouldn't think I intentionally skipped it—you'd think that there must have been some mix-up at the printing plant, and your copy accidentally wound up without a Chapter 1. So, you'd take it back to the bookstore and you'd ask for a replacement copy. You'd get home and find out that, once again, Chapter 1 was missing. Then you'd start to think that this is no coincidence. It must be some sort of a printing conspiracy (orchestrated by a covert government agency), and that right now, somewhere in the Midwest,

there's an unmarked warehouse chock full of Chapter 1s. You'd then start to call me names. Unspeakable names. Names that would make you feel ashamed and dirty, but you'd do it anyway because you'd feel so certain that this was all part of a carefully crafted strategy designed to keep you from knowing the contents of Chapter 1. Obviously, there's something in Chapter 1 that "they" don't want you to know. Suddenly that missing Chapter 1 is worth fighting for. You deserve a Chapter 1, and to know exactly what's in it. So, because I care about you, my reader, the way I do, I stood up to "the man" on your behalf and demanded that this book have a Chapter 1, and that it would be on importing photos, because there's more to it than it first seems. See, it all makes perfect sense once you look at it calmly and logically.

Getting Your Photos Into Photoshop Lightroom

At its heart, Photoshop Lightroom is a very slick photo database, and one of the coolest things about it is it keeps track of all the photos you import, even if they're not on your computer any longer. For example, if you imported photos that you keep on an external hard drive, even when you unplug that drive, their thumbnails are still in Lightroom's database, so you can still work with those photos, and when you reconnect the drive, it reconnects to the real photos. Not too shabby. But this all starts with getting your photos into Lightroom, so let's get to it.

Step One:
The photos you bring into Photoshop Lightroom are probably coming from either your camera (well, your camera's memory card), or they're already on your computer (everybody's got a bunch of photos already on their computer, right?). We'll start with importing photos from your camera's memory card. If you have Lightroom open, and you connect your memory card reader to your computer, the Import Photos dialog you see here appears. (*Note:* If you don't actually want to import the photos from your memory card right now, just click the Cancel button and this dialog goes away. At the end of this chapter, I'll show you how to stop that Import Photos dialog from showing up automatically if it's driving you crazy.) If you cancel the Import Photos dialog, you can always get back to it by clicking on the Import button (found at the bottom of the left side Panels area in Lightroom's Library module) or pressing Command-Shift-I (PC: Ctrl-Shift-I). If your memory card reader is still connected when you do either, the smaller Import dialog (shown at the bottom here) appears. Click the top button to import photos from your memory card, click the bottom button if you want to choose files already on your computer. In our case, click the top button.

Step Two:

I recommend turning on the Show Preview checkbox at the bottom left of the Import Photos dialog so you can see a preview of the photos on your memory card. This way, you get to pick and choose which photos you want to import (or you can just import them all, but at least this way you'll have a choice, right?). When you turn on the Show Preview checkbox (shown circled here in red), a Preview section appears on the right side of the dialog (as seen here). The little slider that appears below the right side of that Preview section controls the size of the preview thumbnails, so if you want to see these thumbnails larger, just drag that slider to the right.

Step Three:

By default, every photo in this Preview section has been selected to be imported (that's why there's a marked checkbox in the top-left corner of every thumbnail). If you see one or more photos you don't want imported, just turn off their checkboxes. Now, what if you have 300+ photos on your memory card, but you only want a handful of these imported? You just click the Uncheck All button at the bottom of the Preview section (which unchecks every photo), and Command-click (PC: Ctrl-click) on just the photos you want to import. Then, turn on the checkbox for any of these selected photos and all the selected photos become checked, and will be imported. One more tip: if the photos you want are contiguous, then click on the first photo, press-and-hold the Shift key, scroll down to the last photo, and click to select all the photos in between at once.

Continued

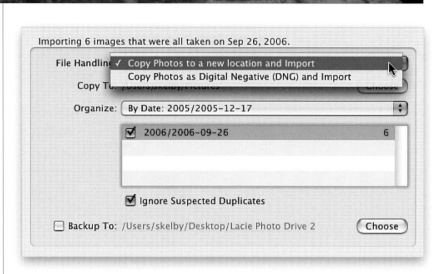

Step Four:

On the top left of this same Import Photos dialog, go to the File Handling pop-up menu (shown here) and choose how you want Lightroom to handle the photos on your memory card. There are two File Handling choices when importing from a memory card: (1) Copy Photos to a New Location and Import (as shown here), or (2) Copy Photos as Digital Negative (DNG) and Import (DNG is an open source archival format for RAW images developed by Adobe to ensure that years from now we'll still be able to access our RAW photos. For more on DNG, visit www.adobe.com/products/dng).

Step Five:

Both Copy or Copy as DNG just make a copy of the selected photos on the memory card, and then write those copies to your computer. Neither moves your originals off the card, so if there's a serious problem during import (hey, it happens) those originals on the card can act as your backup (at least, for now). By the way, by default Lightroom puts these copies into your Pictures (PC: My Pictures) folder. If you want them saved elsewhere, click the Choose button (as shown here) to pick a different location—but here's a tip: put all the photos you import into Lightroom in one main folder (you can have as many subfolders as you want). This will keep your file structure simple and backing up much easier.

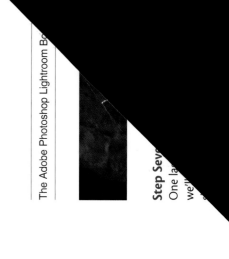

Step Sev
One la
we'll

this, select all your JPEGs and put them in a separate folder before importing.

ANOTHER TIP: You can convert any photo into DNG (Digital Negative) format by clicking on the photo(s) you want to convert, going to the Library menu, and choosing Convert Photo to DNG (you can convert JPEGs, TIFFs, etc., to DNG, but I only convert RAW files). This DNG replaces the RAW file in Lightroom, but the RAW file remains in the same folder on your computer (you have the option of deleting the original RAW file when you make the conversion). I erase the original once I have a DNG.

Step Six:
You also get to choose how to organize those files once they're imported. The default choice is By Date: 2005/2005-12-17, which means your photos will appear in a separate folder within your Pictures folder labeled with the year taken, then in a subfolder labeled with the actual date taken. There are other date choices, but if you don't want them sorted by date, you can (a) change the imported folder's name by double-clicking directly on it in the list below the Organize pop-up menu (the 2006/2006-09-26 folder in Step Five's capture), or (b) choose Into One Folder from the Organize pop-up menu, which tosses your imported photos loose into your Pictures folder, so turn on the Put in Subfolder checkbox, and give this folder a descriptive name.

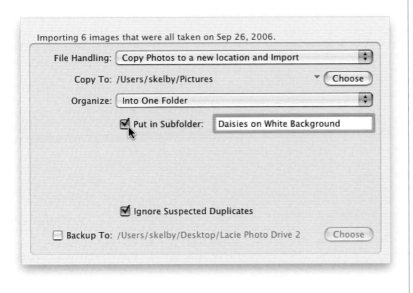

Continued

en:

...st thing about organization, then ...n move on. If you start out with a ...imple plan for managing your thousands of photos, your life will stay simple and easy. I've included a capture here of how I have my Lightroom managed photos organized on my computer. From left to right: Everything is in one main folder named Pictures. Inside of that, I have folders for shots taken in 2005, 2006, and 2007, plus my Lightroom library database folder (Lightroom puts it in your Pictures or My Pictures folder by default). Inside my 2007 folder, you can see the subfolder Daisies on a White Background, which I just created in the previous step, and inside of that are the photos that I imported off my memory card. This is the simple kind of file structure that makes managing your photo collection dramatically easier.

Step Eight:

Now, at the bottom of the File Handling section of the dialog is what I consider to be one of the best timesaving, good-sense features of this dialog. It's a checkbox called Backup To and when you turn on that checkbox, Lightroom will automatically back up the photos you're importing to a second location at the same time (click the Choose button, as shown here, to choose the location of your external hard drive). For example, if I'm importing photos from a memory card to my computer, I use Backup To to automatically copy those same photos to an external hard drive (which I named LaCie Photo Drive 2). This way, I have two copies of each imported photo— one on my computer, and one on my external hard drive—and this gives me much more peace of mind.

Now, for the long-term archiving of these photos, I recommend that after Lightroom backs up your imported photos to that second hard drive, you immediately burn that folder of photos to a DVD (using archival-quality blank DVDs), and store these DVD archives off site (at your home, office, etc.). Hey, these are your digital negatives and can't be replaced—if your studio burns down, or is robbed, or is hit by a hurricane or flood, your entire irreplaceable photo collection will be gone forever. But if you have off-site DVD backups, all is not lost. By the way, the hard drives I've been using are LaCie hard drives designed by F.A. Porsche (high-speed USB 2.0 or Firewire versions). They're small, have never let me down, and Amazon.com was selling the 500-GB model for about $180 (as of this writing).

Step Nine:
The next most important thing you can do for organizing your photos (in this same Import Photos dialog) is to give them usable names that describe the subject or location where they were taken. (*Note:* This File Naming option is only available when you copy or move files while importing—if you're importing photos on your computer in their current location, it imports them with their current names instead.) In our case, since we're copying from a memory card, we chose to copy the photos from the card and import them, so it allows us to rename the files we're copying. By default, Lightroom uses a file naming template called "Filename" (shown here) which leaves the cryptic filenames assigned by your camera untouched (in other words, it keeps the lame "_DSC0610.jpg" name intact). Is it just me, or is that not a particularly good name for a photo of a daisy?

Continued

Step Ten:

To rename the photos, as they're imported, with a more descriptive name, you can either: (a) choose one of the built-in naming templates from the File Naming Template pop-up menu, or (b) create your own custom File Naming preset, which when saved will appear in the File Naming Template pop-up menu (I did a step-by-step tutorial on how to create these later in this chapter). In this case, we'll just choose the built-in template Custom Name – Sequence (shown here) from the pop-up menu.

Step Eleven:

When you choose the Custom Name – Sequence template (as shown), a Custom Text field appears beneath the pop-up menu (as seen here). Type in a more descriptive name in the Custom Text field (in this example, since they're photos of daisies, I chose [wait for it...wait...] "Daisies." Hey, it's not the most creative name, but it is descriptive). This template also automatically adds a sequential number right after your new name, so my first file would now be "Daisies–1," followed by "Daisies–2," and so on. (*Note:* If you're importing an entire shoot from multiple cards, you can choose to start your sequence with a particular number. That way, if the first card you imported brought in photos named Daisies–1 through Daisies–178, you could then enter 179 in the Start Number field to start the sequential numbering for your next card's import at 179.)

File Naming: Daisies-1.jpg

Template: Custom Name – Sequence

Custom Text: Daisies   Start Number: 1

Information to Apply

Develop Settings: Grayscale Conversion

Metadata: None

Keywords:

☐ Render Standard-Sized Previews

New Metadata Preset

Preset Name: Untitled Preset

☐ Basic Info
Caption
Rating · · · · ·
Label

☐ IPTC Content
Headline
IPTC Subject Code
Description Writer
Category
Other Categories

☑ IPTC Copyright
Copyright   © Scott Kelby 2007   ☑
Rights Usage Terms   No usage authorized with prior written permission   ☑
Copyright Info URL   http://www.scottkelby.com/copyright   ☑

☐ IPTC Creator
Creator
Creator Address
Creator City
Creator State / Province
Creator Postal Code
Creator Country
Creator Phone

(Check All) (Check None) (Check Filled)   (Cancel) (Create)

Step 1[...]

The nex[...] Apply, wh[...] to three di[...] applied to y[...] ed. First is De[...] ...ch lets you apply diffe[...] ...t-in tonal adjustments created in the Develop module. For example, if you knew you were going to convert all of these imported photos to black and white, you could choose the built-in Grayscale Conversion Develop preset (as shown here), and as they're imported, they'll all be automatically converted to black and white. You can also create your own presets. For example, if you knew you had completed a shoot using the wrong white balance setting in your camera, you could create a preset with the proper white balance setting, and as each photo was imported, the white balance would be fixed. Not bad, eh? (See Chapter 4 to learn how to create your own Develop presets.)

Step Thirteen:

The next menu down is where you embed your copyright info, contact info, usage rights, captions, and loads of other information right into each file as it's imported. This info is known as metadata, and rather than adding it manually each time you import, you should create your own metadata preset now. Just choose New from the Metadata pop-up menu, and a blank New Metadata Preset dialog appears (shown here). First, click the Check None button at the bottom of the dialog (so no blank fields will appear when you view this metadata in Lightroom—only fields with data will be displayed). Now, in the IPTC Copyright section, type in your copyright information (as shown here).

Continued

Step Fourteen:

Next, go to the IPTC Creator section and enter your contact info (after all, if someone goes by your website and downloads some of your images, you might want them to be able to contact you to arrange to license your photo). Now, you may feel that the Copyright Info URL (Web address) that you added in the previous step is enough contact info, and if that's the case, you can skip filling out the IPTC Creator info (after all, this whole metadata preset is to help you protect your copyright, and help potential clients get in contact with you, but it is not mandatory, just recommended). Once all the metadata info you want embedded in your photos is complete, go up to the top of the dialog, give your preset a name (I chose "My Copyright and Contact"), and then click the Create button as shown.

New Metadata Preset

Preset Name: My Copyright and Contact

IPTC Content

Headline	
IPTC Subject Code	
Description Writer	
Category	
Other Categories	

IPTC Copyright

Copyright	© Scott Kelby 2007
Rights Usage Terms	No usage authorized without prior written permissi
Copyright Info URL	http://www.scottkelby.com/copyright

IPTC Creator

Creator	Scott Kelby
Creator Address	333 Douglas Road E.
Creator City	Oldsmar
Creator State / Province	FL
Creator Postal Code	34677
Creator Country	USA
Creator Phone	813-433-5000
Creator E-Mail	skelby@photoshopuser.com
Creator Website	http://www.photoshopuser.com/lightroom
Creator Job Title	Owner

IPTC Image

Check All   Check None   Check Filled   Cancel   Create

Step Fifteen:

Now, in the Import Photos dialog, when you click on the Metadata pop-up menu you'll see your metadata preset in that menu (as shown here). All you have to do is choose that preset, and it does the rest.

File Naming: _DSC0610.jpg

Template: Filename

Information to Apply

Develop Settings: None

Metadat: ✓ None
    My Copyright and Contact
Keyword
    New...

✓ Show Preview

Step Sixteen:

As easy as it is to create a metadata template, deleting one is a different story. You have to find the folder on your computer that contains your Lightroom metadata presets, and drag the preset you want to delete into the Trash (or the Recycle Bin on a PC). On a Mac, to find this Metadata Presets folder, start in your Home folder in Finder, then look in your Library folder for a folder called Application Support. Inside that folder is a folder called Adobe, and if you look inside that you'll find a folder named Lightroom (you're almost there), and inside that folder you'll see the Metadata Presets folder. (Whew! The path to that folder on my own computer is shown here.) Here's how to find that folder if you use a PC: Start in your C drive in Windows Explorer, then look in your Documents and Settings folder for the Application Data Folder. In that folder is the Adobe folder, and if you look inside it, you'll see the Metadata Presets folder. All right, back to our Information to Apply section.

Step Seventeen:

The Keywords field at the bottom is another critical step in setting up an efficient digital workflow. Words you type in this field are embedded into your photos, and they become keywords that help you later when you're searching for a particular type of photo. For example, for these daisy photos, click in the Keywords field and type in some generic keywords like flowers, white background, petals, daisy, and studio (plus any other words you think describe these photos, as shown here). Put a comma between each search word or phrase, and just make sure the words you choose are generic enough (in other words, don't use "yellow daisies" because they're not all yellow).

Continued

SCOTT KELBY

Step Eighteen:

Now, here's where the few seconds you spend adding keywords really pays off. Let's say next month a client calls and needs a flower shot for a print ad. Because you've been diligently adding keywords to your photos as you import them, instead of digging through thousands of photos in folder after folder, trying to locate and gather all your flower shots, now you can just go to the Keyword Tags panel in the Library module, click on "Flowers," and every single flower photo you've taken appears instantly (no matter which folders or collections they're in). If you click on the keyword "Daisy," it narrows the results to just shots of daisies. If you want only daisies that were shot on a white background (as seen here), you can add "White Background" as a keyword child of "Daisy." This is very powerful stuff, and you'll see this next level of keyword power in the next chapter. But now, back to the Import Photos dialog.

Step Nineteen:

The final option in the Import Photos dialog lets you choose the quality of the thumbnail previews Lightroom will display. This is truly a speed vs. quality issue. Personally, I like to see my imported photos appear in Lightroom as quickly as possible. I hate to wait, so I leave the Render Standard-Sized Previews checkbox turned off (as shown here). That way, the images come in lickity-split and if I want to see a higher-quality preview for a photo, I just click on its thumbnail and it renders the high-quality version (which can take a few seconds). However, if you don't mind waiting around while Lightroom renders high-quality previews for every image you import, then turn on the Render Standard-Sized Previews checkbox and go grab a cup of coffee. Or two. And a sandwich. Maybe catch a movie.

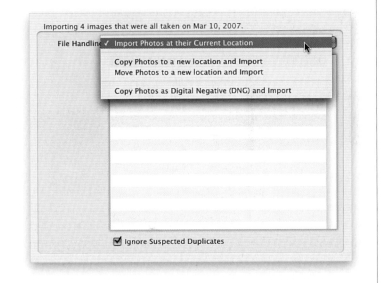

Step Twenty:

Now, before you click the Import button, there's one more thing I need to mention. Thus far, we've been talking about importing photos from a memory card. What about importing photos that are already on your computer? You follow the same steps you just learned, except for one simple thing: at the top of the dialog, under File Handling, you choose Import Photos at Their Current Location so it doesn't move or copy them (after all, they're already on your computer, right?), it just lets you now manage them in Lightroom. Also, when you choose to import them from their current location, Lightroom doesn't let you rename them—they keep their existing names, but you'll learn later on how to change the names of photos that were already on your computer. The rest is the same.

Step Twenty-One:

At last, you can click the Import button found at the bottom right of the Import Photos dialog, and your photos will begin importing. A progress bar will appear in Lightroom's upper-left corner so you can see how things are progressing. If you change your mind and want to cancel the import process, just click on the little X that appears at the far right end of the progress bar. The X will turn red, to let you know you've cancelled the import.

Continued

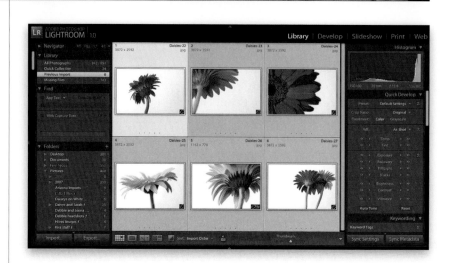

Step Twenty-Two:

Once imported, your photos will appear in the Library module's Grid view (as shown here). As you can see, these images have been renamed (notice they no longer have those _DSC0610.jpg names), and the little tag icon that appears in the bottom-right corner of each thumbnail is your indication that at least one keyword has already been assigned to those photos. Although it took us 21 steps before we actually got to click the Import button here in the book, in real life (once you've set up your metadata preset, file naming presets, etc.), you'll only spend literally about a minute in this dialog. But that minute (spent choosing your folder name, choosing your metadata and file naming presets, and adding keywords) will save you hours of time and loads of frustration. At the end of this chapter (just a few pages away), I'll show you some importing preferences that can speed up the process even more.

You just learned the manual way to import photos into Photoshop Lightroom, but there's also an automated way to import that many users absolutely love. Here's the basic idea: you choose a folder on your computer to be a "watched" folder (which just means Photoshop Lightroom keeps an eye on that folder), and any photos that you put into that watched folder will be automatically imported into Photoshop Lightroom without you lifting a finger. I know—pretty sweet! The official name for this is Auto Import and here's how to set it up step-by-step:

How to Automate the Importing of Photos by Using a Watched Folder

Step One:
The first step is to create an empty folder in a convenient location on your computer that will act as your watched folder (I created mine on my Desktop, so I wouldn't have to go digging around for it). Go ahead and create that new blank folder now (I named mine "Import Into Lightroom," just so it's clear at a glance what that folder is for).

Step Two:
Now go under the File menu, under Auto Import, and choose Auto Import Settings. This brings up the dialog you see here. The first thing you choose here is which folder you want to be your watched folder. So, click the Choose button, then choose that new folder you created on your Desktop in the previous step (the one you named "Import Into Lightroom"). Next, under Destination, click the Choose button and choose where you want any auto-imported photos to be stored on your computer (in my case, I chose my Pictures folder). Luckily, Auto Import doesn't just toss your imported photos randomly into the Pictures folder—it puts them in their own separate folder. You can choose the name it gives that folder in the Subfolder Name field (I left my subfolder named Auto Imported Photos, as seen here).

Continued

Step Three:

The rest of this dialog is pretty much like (okay, exactly like) the standard Import Photos dialog you just learned about in the previous tutorial, so I'm not going to go through all that again. Here's what I did in the rest of the dialog: Under File Naming, I chose to rename my imported files as "Tigers–1," "Tigers–2," and so on. In the Information section, I didn't add any Develop Settings, but I did choose to have my copyright metadata embedded into each imported photo, and I added keywords to help make searching for these photos of tigers easier in the future. I also left the Render Standard-Sized Previews checkbox turned off because I want faster-drawing previews. Now that your settings are in place, you can click OK, but there's one more thing to do.

Step Four:

You've configured the Auto Import settings, but you haven't turned it on yet. You do that by going under the File menu, under Auto Import, and choosing Enable Auto Import (as shown here). That's it—now any photos you put in that folder will automatically be imported into Lightroom, with the settings you chose applied. *Note:* If days later you're working on an architectural shoot, you'll want to go back to the Auto Import Settings dialog and choose a different filename (instead of Tigers), and some new, more fitting keywords.

TIP: We also use Auto Import to let us shoot tethered—where you connect your digital camera to your computer and your shots go straight into Lightroom, so you can see them at full-screen size while you're shooting. For a step-by-step on shooting tethered, see Chapter 10.

Staying organized is critical when you have thousands of photos, and because digital cameras generate the same set of names over and over, it's really important that you rename your photos with a unique name right during import. A popular strategy is to include the date of the shoot as part of the rename. Unfortunately, only one of Photoshop Lightroom's import naming presets includes the date, and it makes you keep the camera's original filename along with it. Luckily, you can create your own custom file naming template just the way you want it. Here's how:

Save Time By Creating Your Own File Naming Templates

Step One:
Using a file naming template is easy— finding where to create one is the tricky part. Don't look up in the menu bar (that would make it too easy), instead this option is found inside three different dialogs: Import, Export, and Auto Import Settings. It doesn't matter which one you choose, so press Command-Shift-I (PC: Ctrl-Shift-I) to bring up the Import Photos dialog. From the File Handling pop-up menu at the top, choose Copy Photos to a New Location and Import, and then the File Naming section will appear. In that section, click on the Template pop-up menu and chose Edit (as shown here).

Continued

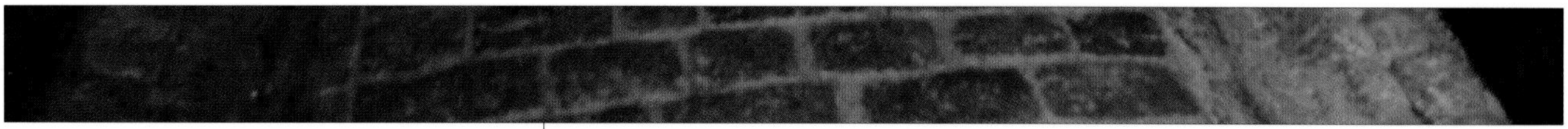

Step Two:

This brings up the Filename Template Editor (shown here). At the top of the dialog, you'll see a large field where you put together the elements that you want to make up your new file naming template. In my dialog here, my last chosen preset (from the pop-up menu at the top) was Custom Name – Sequence, so the field shows the two blue tokens (that's what Adobe calls them; on a PC, the info appears within braces) that make up that preset (your dialog may show a different preset and set of tokens, depending on your last chosen preset). Go ahead and click on the tokens to select them and then press the Delete (PC: Backspace) key on your keyboard to remove them, so you can start from scratch.

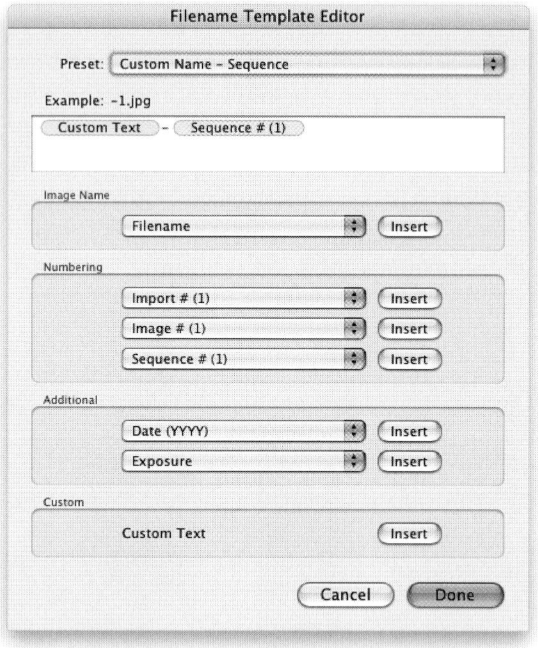

Step Three:

I'm going to show you the setup for a popular file naming system for photographers, but this is only an example—you can create a custom template later that fits your studio's needs. We'll start by adding the year first (this helps keep your filenames together when sorted by name). To keep your filenames from getting too long, I recommend using just the last two digits of the year. So go to the Additional section of the dialog, click on the first pop-up menu, and choose Date (YY) as shown here (the Y lets you know this is a year entry, the YY lets you know it's only going to display two digits). The Date (YY) token will appear in the naming field and if you look above the top-left side of it, you'll see a live example of the name template you're creating. At this point, your new filename is 07.jpg, as seen here.

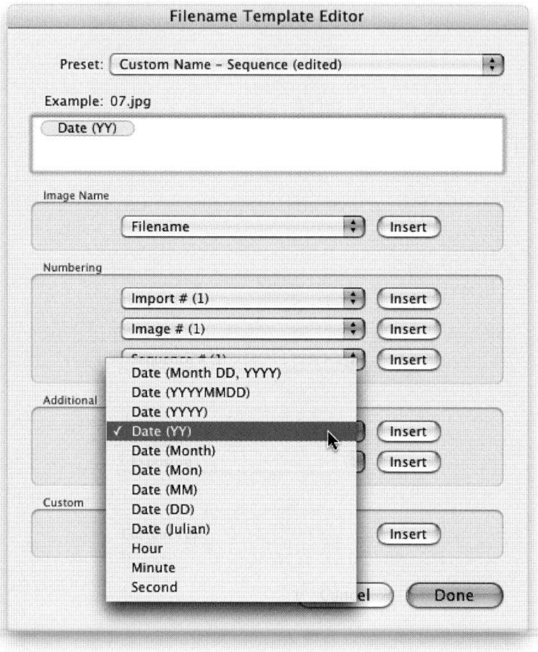

Step Four:

After the two-digit year, we add the two-digit month the photo was taken by going to the same pop-up menu, but this time choosing Date (MM), as shown here. (Both of these dates are drawn automatically from the metadata embedded into your photo by your digital camera at the moment the shot was taken.) By the way, if you had chosen Date (Month), it would display the entire month name, so your filename would have looked like this: 07February, rather than what we want, which is 0702.

Step Five:

Before we go any further, you should know there's a rule for file naming, and that's no spaces between words. However, if everything just runs together, it's really hard to read. So, after the date you're going to add a visual separator—a thin flat line called an underscore. To add one, just click your cursor right after the Date (MM) token, then press the Shift key and the Dash key to add an underscore (seen here). Now, here's where I differ from some of the other naming conventions: after the date, I include a custom name that describes what's in each shoot. This differs because some people choose to have the original camera-assigned file-name appear there instead (personally, I like to have a name in there that makes sense to me without having to open the photo). So, to do that, go to the Custom section of the dialog and to the right of Custom Text, click the Insert button (as shown here) to add a Custom Text token after your underscore (this lets you type in a one-word text description later), then add another underscore (so it looks like _Custom Text_. No text will appear in your example up top, though, until you add it).

Continued

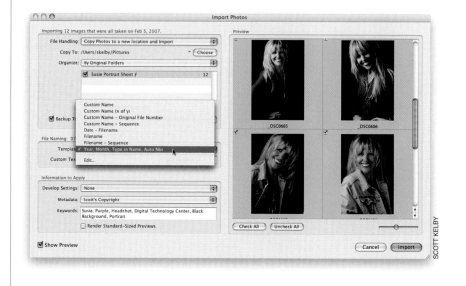

Step Six:

Now you're going to have Photoshop Lightroom automatically number these photos sequentially. To do that, go to the Numbering section and choose your numbering sequence from the third pop-up menu down. Here I chose the Sequence # (001) token, which adds three-digit auto-numbering to the end of your filename (you can see the example above the naming field).

Step Seven:

Once the little naming example looks right to you, go under the Presets pop-up menu, and choose Save as New Preset. A dialog will appear where you can name your preset. Type in a descriptive name (so you'll know what it will do next time you want to apply it—I chose "Year, Month, Type in Name, Auto Nbr") and click Create. Then, when you go to the Import Photos dialog and click on the File Naming Template pop-up menu, you'll see your custom template as one of the preset choices (as shown here).

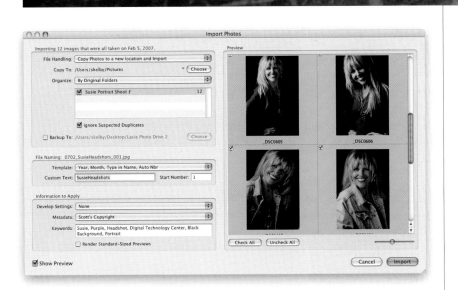

Step Eight:
Now, after you choose this new naming template from the Template pop-up menu, click below it in the Custom Text field (this is where that Custom Text token we added earlier comes into play) and type in the descriptive part of the name (in this case, I typed in "SusieHeadshots," all one word—no spaces between words). That custom text will appear between two underscores, giving you a visual separator so everything doesn't all run together (see, it all makes sense now). If you look at the File Naming example (right above the Template pop-up menu), you'll see a preview of how the photos will be renamed. Once you've chosen all your Information to Apply settings at the bottom of the dialog, you can click the Import button.

Choosing Your Preferences for Importing Photos

I put the import preferences at the end of the Importing chapter, because I figured that by now, you've imported some photos and you know enough about the importing process to know what you wish was different. That's what preferences are all about (and Photoshop Lightroom has preferences controls because it gives you lots of control over the way you want to work).

Step One:

The preferences for importing photos are found within two different tabs in the Preferences dialog. To get to that dialog, go under the Lightroom menu on a Mac or the Edit menu on a PC, and choose Preferences (as shown here).

Step Two:

When the Preferences dialog appears, first click on the File Management tab up top (shown highlighted here). The first preference lets you tell Photoshop Lightroom how to react when you connect a memory card from your camera to your computer. By default, it opens the Import Photos dialog. However, if you'd prefer it didn't automatically open that dialog each time you plug in a card reader, choose Do Nothing from the pop-up menu (as shown here). The next section you need to know about is the Preview Cache section. It lets you choose (1) the size of your high-resolution previews (smaller is faster), (2) the quality of the high-res previews (high quality is much slower), and (3) when to have Lightroom throw away the higher-res previews it stores in its database (you normally only need them while you're first working on the files, and maybe for a few weeks more, but after 30 days I have Lightroom discard them. The default settings for this section are pretty decent.

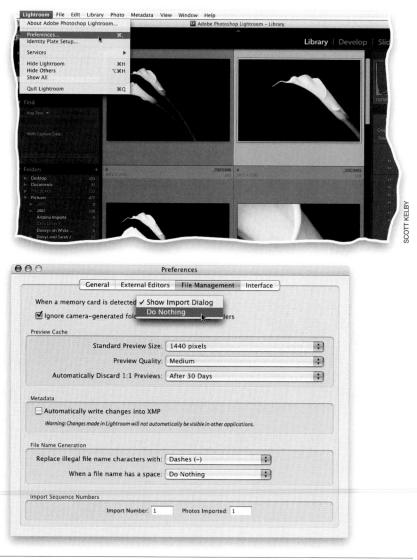

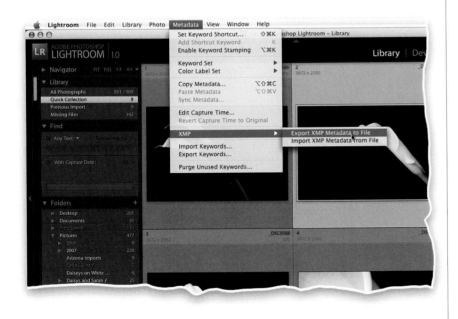

Step Three:

The next section, determine whether metadata you add to right, keywords, etc.) and to a totally separate file, so photo you'll have two files—o contains the photo itself and a se file (called an XMP sidecar) that con that photo's metadata. Now, why woul you ever want to do this? Well, normally Lightroom keeps track of all this metadata you add in its database file—it doesn't actually embed the info until your photo leaves Lightroom (by exporting a copy over to Photoshop, or exporting the file as a JPEG, TIFF, or PSD—all of which support having this metadata embedded right into the photo itself). However, some programs can't read embedded metadata, so they need a separate XMP sidecar.

Step Four:

I used to leave this on, until a conversation I had with Lightroom insider Jeff Schewe, who pointed out that writing all those XMP sidecars takes time, and thus slows Lightroom down. So now, if I'm sending a file to a friend or client and I want the metadata written separately to an XMP sidecar file, first I go to the Library module and click on the file to select it. Then I go under the Metadata menu, under XMP, and choose Export XMP Metadata to File (as shown here). This writes any existing metadata to a separate XMP file (so you'd need to send both the photo and the XMP sidecar together). The rest of the default Preferences settings are pretty decent (like which character to insert when you import a photo whose filename contains a character Lightroom doesn't recognize. I mean, you could edit this, but...come on).

Continued

...er Standard-Sized
Previews, chances are you won't even be in the same building by the time Lightroom's finished importing. So, you would want to choose either "Air Raid Siren" or "Fog Horn," so you can hear it wherever you might be in the city. You knew I was kidding, right?

Step Six:
While you're right there, directly below the menu for choosing an "importing's done" sound is another pop-up menu for choosing a sound for when your exporting is done. I know, this isn't an importing preference, but since we're right there, I thought…what the heck. I'll talk more about some of the other preferences later in the book, but since this chapter is on importing, I thought I'd better tackle it here. So, now you know: (a) How to import photos from a memory card or from your computer, and (b) how to rename your photos as they're imported, embed your copyright and contact info, and add keywords. You also learned (c) how to set up an automated import system, and (d) how to apply some of your own preferences to the process. You're ready to get down to work (actually, this was work—it's time to get to more fun stuff).

Exposure: 1/80 | Focal Length: 70mm | Aperture Value: ƒ/4.8

Library
organizing your photos

The first module you wind up using in Adobe Photoshop Lightroom is usually the Library module—it's where you go to sort and organize your photos. Now, here's the thing. While what you're supposed to do here is organize your photos, very few people have the intestinal fortitude to actually do it—to actually go through all their images, and tag each and every one with keywords and custom metadata. My hat's off to these meticulous people (freaks), but I'm not one of them. That's because as soon as I import my photos, I take a quick look at 'em, separate the good from the bad, and then start messing with the good ones in the Develop, Slideshow, Print, and Web modules. Those are the party modules. That's where the fun is, so I hang out there (it's kind of like the Rain® Nightclub in Vegas, only without all the celebrities, flashing lights, music, and liquor. Okay, there's some liquor, but not all that much). You know who uses the Library module to its fullest extent? People who have a metabolic predisposition to become serial killers—them and molecular biologists. I don't know why. Anyway, maybe I'm just speaking for myself here, because honestly, I couldn't keep track of all my photos if they had my name and phone number embedded in them with a microchip tracking device. I guess it's because I don't care about my bad photos. I only care about my good photos so I don't want to waste my time tagging photos I'm probably never going to use for anything other than my work in molecular biology.

The Best Way to View Your Photos

Well, technically there is no "official" best way, but Photoshop Lightroom has so many different (and often clever) ways to view your imported photos, that once you see them all, you'll definitely find one or more methods that you like best. Although our main goal in this chapter is to sort our photos and separate the winners from the losers, learning the ins and outs of Photoshop Lightroom's view modes and viewing options is critically important to helping you make the most informed decisions possible about which photos make it (and which ones don't).

Step One:

Sorting takes place in the Library module, so if you're not already there, press Command-Option-1 (PC: Ctrl-Alt-1). There are four parts to the Library module: (1) the panels on the left side, which are for organizing your photos; (2) the panels on the right side, which are for adding info and making quick edits to your photos; (3) the middle section, which shows thumbnails (or close-ups) of the photos you're currently working with; and (4) the filmstrip, which runs across the bottom of every module so you always have access to all the photos in your folder, no matter where you are in Photoshop Lightroom. Now that you know the layout, let's start sorting: go to the Folders panel on the left side, and click on one of the folders of photos you've imported (as shown here) to display the photos in that folder.

SCOTT KELBY

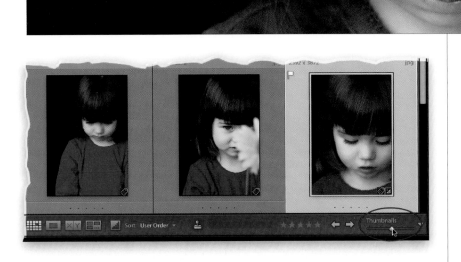

Step Two:
Our goal at this point is to find the very best photos from this group, but it's hard to make informed decisions about your photos with the thumbnails displayed at this small size. You can increase the size of the thumbnails by clicking-and-dragging the Thumbnails slider to the right. It's found on the right side of the toolbar located at the very bottom of the middle Preview area (it's circled here in red).

Step Three:
Because the center Preview area (where the photos are displayed) is kind of narrow, you can only get your thumbnails so big. (By the way, if you don't see the Thumbnails slider, click on the down-facing arrow at the right end of the toolbar and choose Thumbnail Size from the pop-up menu.) Luckily, you can hide any one, or all, of the side panels and the filmstrip so you can not only get larger previews, but so there's less onscreen distraction. For example, to hide the left column of panels, you just click on the little Show/Hide icon (it looks like a sideways-facing arrow, and is circled here in red) and the panels are hidden from view (look how much more room you now have to see your thumbnails). However, if you move your cursor over that area, the panels temporarily pop back out so you can make a quick adjustment, and when your cursor moves away from that area, they automatically hide themselves again. So, go ahead and try that just to see how it works.

Continued

Step Four:

Now that you have more room to see your photos, go back to that Thumbnails slider, drag it to the right (as shown here), and look at how much bigger you can get your thumbnail previews. Also, notice how much less distracting it is when even just that one Panels area is hidden from view. By the way, this view—where you see thumbnails displayed in the center Preview area—is called the Grid view, and when working in the Library module (or any module, actually) you can always jump to this thumbnail Grid view by pressing the letter G on your keyboard.

Step Five:

Now, for an even bigger thumbnail view, go ahead and hide the right side panels by clicking on the Show/Hide arrow on the far right (shown circled here), then click-and-drag the Thumbnails slider to the right a bit more until your row of four thumbnails across gets even larger, as shown here. *Note:* The number of thumbnails that appear in a row is determined by the thumbnail size you choose. As you make the thumbnails larger, Lightroom automatically reduces the number in each horizontal row, so as you increase the size, you'd go down to a row with only three across, then two across, and so on. If you make the thumbnails smaller (by dragging the slider back to the left), then you'll get more thumbnails per row.

TIP: Want an easy way to hide any individual panel without clicking the little Show/Hide arrow? Press the F5 key on your keyboard to show/hide the top taskbar. F6 hides the filmstrip, F7 hides the left side panels, and (big surprise coming up) F8 hides the right side panels.

S...

If ...
ca...
na...
ru...
se...
drag the scroll bar on the right down to move that bottom row of thumbnails into full view. However, it's probably just easier to hide the filmstrip. You do that by clicking on its Show/Hide arrow, which is at the bottom center of your screen (it's shown circled here). Now you can fully see both rows of thumbnails, plus the focus is all on your photos—there are no side panels or filmstrip to distract you while you're trying to find the best photos from your shoot. Personally, I love this uncluttered, large-thumbnail Grid view, and it's what I use when I'm trying to find the best photos from a particular shoot.

Step Seven:
You can also collapse the top taskbar (the area above your thumbnails with the Library, Develop, etc., links on the right and the Lightroom logo on the left) by clicking its Show/Hide arrow (at the top center). Now, if it seems like a pain to have to close these all one-by-one (and it is), use these shortcuts instead:
(1) To hide just the side panels, simply press the Tab key on your keyboard.
(2) To hide the side panels and the film-strip at the bottom, and even the taskbar across the top, press Shift-Tab.
One thing that doesn't get hidden is the toolbar across the bottom of the Preview area. To hide the toolbar too, just press the T key. So, to get the extra-uncluttered look you see here, you'd press Shift-Tab, then T.

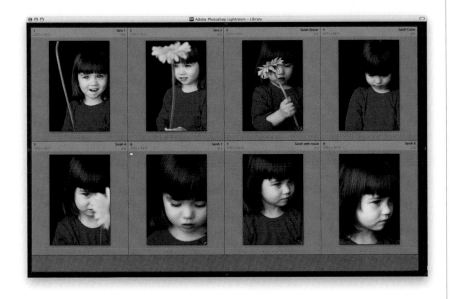

Continued

Step Eight:

If you want to enjoy the immeasurable pleasure of distraction-free viewing (and I know you secretly do), then add one more key. Press the F key on your keyboard twice. The first time you press F, it hides the window title bar directly above the black area of Lightroom's interface, then the second F actually hides the menu bar at the very top of your screen, so now you just see your photos on a solid top-to-bottom black background (as shown here). I know you might be thinking, "I don't know if I find those two thin bars at the top really that distracting." So, try hiding them once and see what you think. Luckily, there's an easy shortcut to jump to the "super-clean, distraction-free nirvana view," you see here. You press Command-Shift-F (PC: Ctrl-Shift-F), then T. To return to regular mode, use the same shortcut.

Step Nine:

Before we leave the wonderful world of hiding panels, there's an option you'll want to know about. As I mentioned earlier, when you hide a panel it will automatically pop back into view if you move your cursor over that edge of the screen. This is called Auto Hide, and although some folks love it, it annoys the living daylights out of some others. Luckily, you can turn Auto Show/Hide off by Control-clicking (PC: Right-clicking) on any one of those Show/Hide arrows. This brings up a contextual menu (shown here) where you can choose your panel poppin' options. The default is Auto Hide & Show. If you choose Auto Hide, then to open a hidden panel you have to click on its Show/Hide arrow, but when your cursor moves away from that panel, it automatically hides. If you choose Manual, then there's no auto anything—you use the arrows to show and hide every time.

Step Ten:

Believe it or not, there are a couple of other viewing options you'll want to know about. I know it seems like a lot of options, but that's what I love about Lightroom—it gives you lots of choices about how you work, and if you try them all at least once, you'll quickly find the ones that suit you best. So, press Shift-Tab and T to return to the normal "all panels" view and return the Preview area toolbar. Now press the letter L to enter Lights Dim mode, in which everything but your photos are dimmed (kind of like you turned down a lighting dimmer). Also in this mode, a thin white border appears around your thumbnails so they really stand out. Perhaps the coolest thing about this dimmed mode is the fact that the panels and filmstrip all still work—you can still make adjustments, change photos, etc., just like when the "lights" are all on.

Step Eleven:

The last viewing mode is Lights Out (you get Lights Out by pressing L a second time), and this one really makes your photos the star of the show because everything else is totally blacked out, so there's nothing (and I mean nothing) but your photos onscreen (to return to regular Lights On mode, just press L again).

TIP: You have more control over Lightroom's Lights Out mode than you might think: just go to Lightroom's preferences (under the Lightroom menu on a Mac or the Edit menu on a PC) and click on the Interface tab, and you'll find pop-up menus that control both the Dim Level and the Screen Color when you're in full Lights Out mode.

Continued

Step Twelve:

Now that you know that trick, are you ready for the ultimate viewing experience? I call this "super mondo blackout view," and although it takes a few keystrokes to get there, it's worth it. This shortcut hides the panels, the filmstrip, the top taskbar, the title bar, the menu bar, the toolbar, and it blacks out everything but your photos. Ready? Type in this: Command-Shift-F (PC: Ctrl-Shift-F), then T, L, L. I know, it's a lot of letters, but look at the result (shown here).

Step Thirteen:

Okay, now let's return to the regular view (with everything visible), and let's start our search for the best photos from this particular shoot. If you see a photo in the thumbnail grid that you'd like to see larger, you can click on it and press the letter E on your keyboard. But it's quicker to just double-click directly on the thumbnail and it jumps to Loupe view (where you see one photo at a time, zoomed in), and by default the entire photo fits within the Preview area.

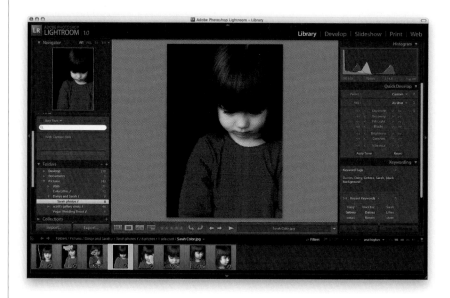

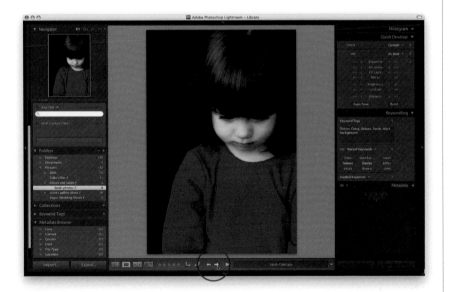

TIP: If you've imported the photos from a shoot and you have to break for lunch, or run an errand, or do anything that's going to take you away from Lightroom for a little while, before you step away select all the photos in your shoot, then go under the Library menu, under Previews, and choose Render Standard-Sized Previews. That way, when you return—no more waiting for higher-resolution previews to draw.

Step Fourteen:
If you want to see the entire photo at as large a view as possible within Lightroom, hide the filmstrip and the top taskbar, and the photo will automatically resize to fill that extra space. Look how much larger the photo is now, with the top and bottom areas hidden. (*Note:* If this shot had been taken in landscape orientation—wide rather than tall—then instead of hiding the top and bottom areas, you'd press the Tab key to hide the left and right Panels areas.) While you're in this Loupe view, you can view the other photos in this folder by using the Select Previous Photo and Select Next Photo buttons in the toolbar (shown circled in red here).

TIP: To return to the thumbnail Grid view, just press G on your keyboard, or go to the toolbar and click on the first icon on the far left, which is the Grid View button. The next button over is the Loupe View button. You can toggle back and forth between the Grid and Loupe views by pressing the Tilde key (~) on your keyboard.

Continued

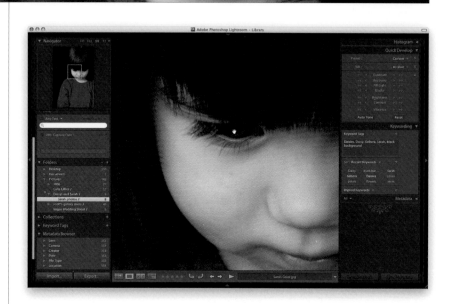

Step Fifteen:

If you want to zoom in even closer, click your cursor on the spot where you want to zoom into, and your image instantly zooms in to give you a 1:1 view (that's the default zoom setting) of that area. You can then click, hold, and drag to move around your zoomed-in photo. You can also use the same keyboard shortcuts as Photoshop for zooming in/out, which are Command–+ (PC: Ctrl–+) for zooming in and Command–– (minus; PC: Ctrl––) for zooming out. If you're in Loupe view and need to zoom in tight for just a moment or two, try this: don't just click with the Magnifying Glass—click-and-hold with it. It will stay zoomed in tight as long as you hold the mouse button down. When you're done, release the mouse button to zoom back out. If you're in the Grid view and you want to zoom in and check something quickly on the selected photo, just press-and-hold the letter Z. If instead you want to open the photo in Loupe view, press the Spacebar once. Want to zoom in tighter? Press it again. Press it a third time to return to the Fit in window Loupe view.

TIP: Once you're zoomed in, you can also pan around your photo in the Navigator panel (at the top of the left side panels). This panel has a small preview of your entire photo, and in that preview is a small white zoom square that you can click-and-drag around. The area that appears inside the white zoom square is displayed full size in the middle Preview area.

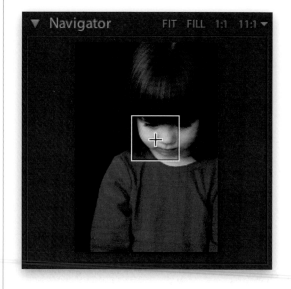

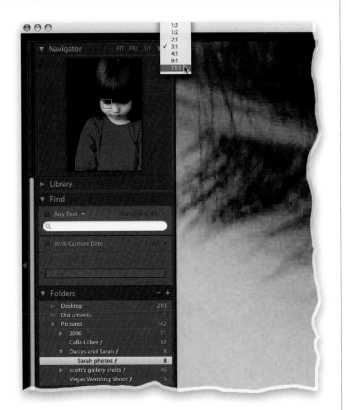

Step Sixteen:

If you want other magnifications, you have two choices: (1) Use the one-click zoom buttons in the Navigator panel where you can jump between Fit within the Preview area, Fill the Preview area, show in a 1:1 view, or zoom in really close with a 3:1 ratio, which is the view you're seeing here. You can also jump between these four views by pressing Command–+ (plus; PC: Ctrl–+) to jump to the next higher magnification, or Command–– (minus; PC: Ctrl––) to go to the next lower one. Or (2), you can use the pop-up menu in the upper-right corner of the Navigator panel (as shown here) to choose even tighter magnifications, up to 11:1 (by the way, whatever you choose in this pop-up menu becomes the zoom amount when you double-click on the photo). To zoom back out to the standard Fit view, click once anywhere on the photo.

Step Seventeen:

So, now you know how to zoom, but what do you do when you have two photos you want to compare side-by-side, so you can choose the best of the two? In the Grid view (or the filmstrip—it doesn't matter which), click on the first of the two photos you want to compare, then Command-click (PC: Ctrl-click) on the second image so they're both selected. Now press C to jump to Compare view, which puts your two photos side-by-side for comparison, as shown here. After I pressed C, I then pressed Shift-Tab to hide all the panels so I'd have a much larger Compare view. (*Note:* Once you have two photos selected, you can also jump to Compare view by clicking the Compare View button, which is the third button from the left in the toolbar.)

Continued

Step Eighteen:

If you look at the top center of the Preview area, you'll see one photo is noted as "Select" and one is noted as "Candidate." Basically, what this means is that one photo is currently selected, and any view changes you make in the toolbar will only affect the Select photo if the Lock icon in the toolbar (next to the word "Compare") is unlocked (it is locked by default). Try this and you'll see what I mean: click on the Lock icon to unlock your two images, then click-and-drag the Zoom slider to the right (to zoom in tighter), and you'll see that only the Select image actually zooms in, and the Candidate stays at the same magnification (as shown here). If you want the Candidate to now match the magnification of the Select photo, just click the Sync button (circled here in red). If you drag the Zoom slider again, it still only affects the Select image (so you'd have to click the Sync button every time you move the slider).

Step Nineteen:

Now, if you want both photos (the Select and the Candidate) to magnify together each time you move the Zoom slider, then just click the Lock icon again (circled in red here). As soon as you click that Lock icon, the Candidate image jumps to the same magnification as the Select image, because now they're both linked to each other (zoomwise, anyway), so when you move the Zoom slider, they zoom in and out in tandem. Of course, you can unlock or lock the two any time by clicking on the Lock icon.

TIP: Want to zoom in tight just for a few seconds to check some details? Just press-and-hold the Spacebar, and as long as you hold it down, it stays zoomed in. When you release it, your photo returns to normal view. This is particularly handy when you're in Compare view.

Step Twenty:

Here's something important to note: Lightroom considers the Select photo as "the one you selected," which means other photos you're comparing it to are the Candidates to win the hypothetical photo showdown. So, if you click the Select Previous Photo or Select Next Photo buttons (the left and right arrows) on the bottom right of the toolbar (shown circled here), it replaces the current Candidate with a new Candidate (basically, the previous or next photo in your folder, as shown here). This lets you quickly compare new photos to your Select photo.

Step Twenty-One:

Okay, so what happens if you bring up a new Candidate image, and you like it better than the Select image? Then you click the Swap button on the right side of the Preview area toolbar (it's circled in red here), and now the Candidate image becomes the Select image (insert your favorite "The student becomes the master" cliché here). So, if you were to press the Select Previous/Next Photo buttons in the toolbar, then your new Select photo will stay in place, and the new Candidate photos rise up to try and topple it (I just inserted my own cliché. What is even more amazing is that I remembered the keyboard shortcut that puts the accent above the "e" in "cliché").

Continued

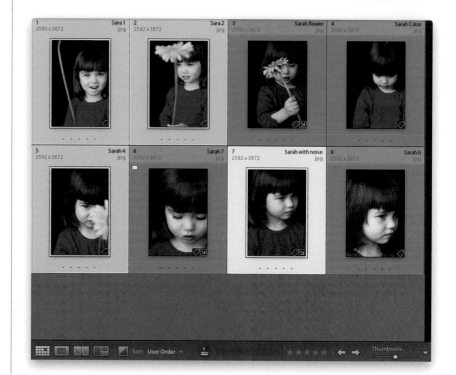

Step Twenty-Two:

Let's take things up a notch (you were afraid I was going to say that, weren't you?). So, what if you want to compare more than two photos onscreen at the same time? Let's say you have four photos you like, but you only need three photos for your project. Well, here's what you do: First, return to the regular view (press Shift-Tab), and then press G to return to the Grid view. Now, click on the gray Grid view background or press Command-D (PC: Ctrl-D) to deselect your previous photos. Then, click on one photo, press-and-hold the Command (PC: Ctrl) key, and click on three other photos (their cells become lighter to show that they're selected, as shown here). By the way, while we're here, did you notice that the cell of the first photo I selected (photo #7) is brighter than the rest of the cells? That shows that #7 is the "most selected" of the four. As you'll see later, what that means is that if you were to edit this photo (fixing the color, exposure, etc.), once you selected the other photos, Lightroom would use this photo as the source photo whose settings or metadata you want to have the other photos sync with.

TIP: Want to deselect everything but the "most selected" photo? Press Command-Shift-D on a Mac or Ctrl-Shift-D on a PC.

Step Tw...

To comp...
onscreen ...
the letter ...
Survey view ... view button—it's the fourth button from the left in the toolbar (by the way, I have no idea why they named this Survey view. Maybe they ran out of names that make obvious sense. How about Compare Multiple view, or Compare More view, or Review mode? But I digress). When they appear in Survey view, if you want them larger onscreen, press Shift-Tab to hide all the panels and the filmstrip (as seen here). If you look at the photos being "surveyed," you can see that the Most Selected photo (the one I selected first) has a white border around it, whereas the other photos being reviewed have no border. They all have an X in the bottom-right corner. Those X's are about to come in handy.

Step Twenty-Four:

So, how do you remove one of the photos under review when it doesn't make the cut? You can do it one of two ways: (1) click on the tiny X that appears in the photo's lower right-hand corner, or (2) press-and-hold the Command (PC: Ctrl) key and just click on the photo you want to remove. After doing that, now I'm down to just three photos (as shown here), and the photos zoom up to fill in the empty space.

Continued

Step Twenty-Five:

So, that's the process—to remove a photo in Survey view, Command-click (PC: Ctrl-click) on it. To add more photos to the ones you're already reviewing, move your cursor down to the bottom of the screen so the filmstrip pops up (as shown here), then Command-click on any photo(s) you want to add. In the example shown here, I added three more photos to my Survey view group by Command-clicking on them in the filmstrip.

TIP: This really isn't a step, it's more like a tip that needs a screen capture. The tip is this: while you're in Survey view, you can actually reorder the images onscreen by simply dragging-and-dropping them right into the order you'd like. In the example shown here, I dragged the fourth photo over to the sixth spot, and while you're dragging, it changes into that tiny little thumbnail you see here, to let you know you're reordering the photo. *Note:* You must be in the bottom-most subfolder or subcollection for this to work.

Step Twenty-Six:

One last thing about Survey view—while you're in this view there are going to be times when you need to take a closer look at one of the photos you're surveying. No sweat, just click on that photo, press the letter Z (for Zoom), and it takes you to a zoomed Loupe view of the photo. Once you've seen what you needed to see, press the letter Z again, and you'll return to Survey view with the same photos selected. Pressing the letter Z is the shortcut for toggling between a zoomed Loupe view and the previous view—in this case you toggled between Survey view and a zoomed Loupe view.

Step Twenty-Seven:

Okay, we're winding up our section on viewing our photos, but there's still one little thing that you might want to use to temporarily give you a quick, uncluttered view. You already learned that pressing the letter T on your keyboard hides the toolbar, or makes it visible if it was hidden. However, this particular shortcut has a hidden feature. Instead of just pressing T, hold it down instead, and it temporarily hides the toolbar for as long as you hold T down (as shown here, where it is temporarily hidden). When you release the T key, the toolbar returns. So the next time you want it out of the way for a quick moment or two, just press T and holddddddddddddd (give this one a try and you'll see what I mean). See, I told you you'd want to know this one.

Making Your Own Custom Loupe View in the Library or Develop Module

When you're in the Library Grid view, if you double-click on a photo (or click on the Loupe View button in the toolbar), your photo enters the Loupe view, which is a zoomed-in view of your photo. Besides just displaying your photo really big, the Loupe view also can display as little (or as much) information about your photo as you'd like as text overlays, which appear in the top-left corner of the Preview area. You'll be spending a lot of time working in Loupe view, so let's set up a custom Loupe view that works for you.

Step One:
Go to the Library module's Grid view, click on a thumbnail, and press E on your keyboard to jump to the Loupe view (of course, there are five ways to Sunday to get to the Loupe view in Photoshop Lightroom: you can press E, you can click on the Loupe View button, you can choose Loupe from the View menu, you can double-click on the photo, you can click on one of the zoom ratios in the Navigator panel, you can go under the Photo menu and choose Open in Loupe, or you can just mentally focus on the words "Loupe view," and before long it will appear).

Step Two:
Press Command-J (PC: Ctrl-J) to bring up the Library View Options dialog and then click on the Loupe View tab. At the top, turn on the Show Info Overlay checkbox. The pop-up menu to the right lets you choose from two different info overlays. Info 1 overlays the filename of your photo (in larger letters), in the upper-left corner of the Preview area (as seen here). Below the filename, in smaller type, is the photo's capture date and time, and its cropped dimensions (good news, we may have a winner of the "bad default settings" contest). Info 2 also displays the filename, but underneath it displays the exposure, ISO, and lens settings.

Step Three:

Luckily, you can choose which info is displayed for both info overlays using the pop-up menus in this dialog. So, for example, instead of having the filename show up in huge letters, here for Loupe Info 2 you could choose something like Common Photo Settings from the pop-up menu (as shown here). By choosing this, instead of getting the filename in huge letters, you'd get the same info displayed under the Develop module's histogram (like shutter speed, f/stop, ISO, and lens setting) even though you're in the Library module. You can customize both info overlays separately by simply making choices from these pop-up menus. (Remember: the top menu in each section is the one that will appear in really large letters.)

Step Four:

Any time you want to start over, just click the Use Defaults button and the default Loupe Info settings will now appear. Personally, I find this text appearing over my photos really, really distracting most of the time. The key part of that is "most of the time." The other times, it's handy. So, if you think this might be handy too, here's what I recommend: Either (a) also turn on the Show Briefly When Photo Changes checkbox below the Loupe Info pop-up menus. This makes the overlay temporary—when you first open a photo, it appears for around 4 seconds, and then hides itself again. Or, you can do what I do: (b) leave those off, and when you want to see that overlay info, press the letter I to toggle through Info 1, Info 2, and info overlay off. At the bottom of the dialog, there's also a checkbox that lets you turn off those little messages that appear onscreen, like "Working" or "Assigned Keyword," etc.

Sorting Your Photos

Every time you come in from a shoot, there's always that exciting moment when you first get to see your photos in Photoshop Lightroom and see if you really got "the shot." Sometimes it happens right away, and sometimes you have to do some serious paring down to get to the shot you're really looking for, and having a solid strategy for sorting, organizing, and managing your images is the first step to creating a workflow that works for you, and not against you. Here's where to start, how to make smart sorting choices, and how to let Photoshop Lightroom make it all easy.

Step One:

When you import photos into Photoshop Lightroom, by default they're displayed in order by the time and date they were taken (Adobe calls this sorting by Captured Time), so the first photo you took on this shoot appears first, in the top-left corner of the Grid view, followed by the next most recent, and so on. If you'd prefer to see the last photo you took appear first, then the second to last, etc., just click the little Sort Direction (stairstep) button in the toolbar (it's shown circled in red here). There are other sorting options, like sorting your photos by when they were last edited, or by their aspect ratio (landscape or portrait), or a number of other methods, which you can choose from the Sort pop-up menu (also shown here).

TIP: If you see three little dots appear above your thumbnail in the grid or the filmstrip for a few moments, don't sweat it—it just means the thumbnail is still being rendered.

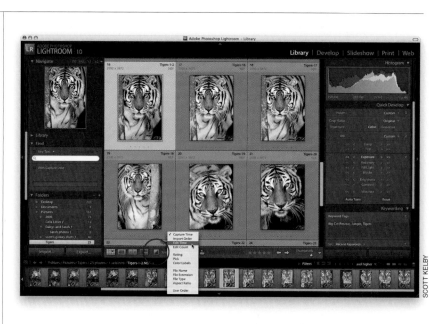

SCOTT KELBY

Step Two:

In each shoot, there are some photos you really like, some photos you think are just okay, and sometimes a few that are so messed up that even with just a quick glance at those tiny thumbnails, you can still see how messed up they are. These last ones are just taking up space on your computer, and since you've got a backup of all the originals, I recommend trashing them as soon as possible. So, when you see one of these hopeless shots, click on it, and then press the Delete (PC: Backspace) key on your keyboard.

Step Three:

When you press the Delete key, a dialog appears, asking you how badly you hate this photo. If you click Remove, it just removes it from Lightroom, but that bad photo still lives on your computer, wasting the same amount of space. That's why I recommend you click on Delete (as shown here), so not only is it removed from Lightroom, it's removed from your computer, freeing up space for more photos. Not only do you free up space by getting rid of photos you're never going to use, but it also makes the sorting and organizing process easier, because you won't be managing photos you don't care about. The fewer photos you have to manage, the faster that process becomes, so get rid of your lame photos now, and your sorting life gets better in many ways.

Continued

TIP: In the Expanded Cell view, information about that photo is displayed at the top of the cell. However, if you click directly on any of that info, a pop-up menu of other data, including camera data and IPTC metadata, can be displayed there instead—just choose the data you want displayed there from the list. To hide all the visible extras in Expanded Cell view—badges, rating stars, etc.—press Command-Shift-H [PC: Ctrl-Shift-H].

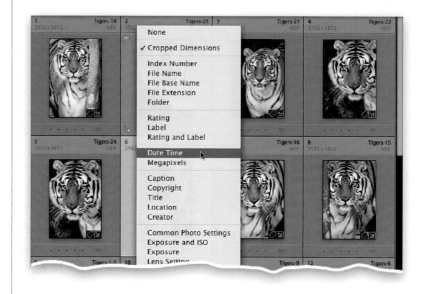

Step Four:

Now that the lame shots are gone, it's time to find the shots from this just-imported shoot that you really care about. Now, there is a manual way of sorting in Lightroom—you just click-and-drag the thumbnails (right there in the Grid view) into the order you want them. The problem is, this is a very slow, tedious way of sorting, and worse—you're not taking advantage of Lightroom's powerful filtering features. So, the only time I manually sort my thumbnails is after I've used the filtering features, and I'm now working with just the results. If I want one of them to be in the first position, then I'll drag it over there (as shown here). Outside of that, it's too slow and inefficient, and if you're using Lightroom, I imagine one of the things that attracted you to it was its ability to help you work faster and smarter, so manual sorting isn't for you.

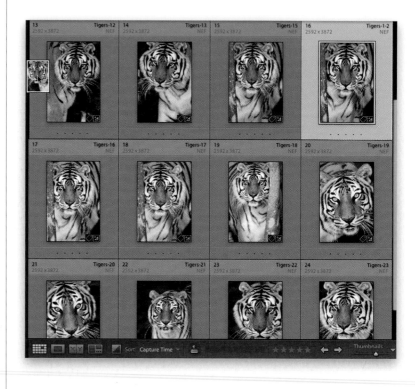

SCOTT KELBY

Step Five:

Instead of manually dragging-and-dropping to sort our photos, there are two more efficient methods, but the one you choose has to do with how in-depth you like to go with your sorting (photo editing) process. For example, when I come in from a shoot and start sorting, I'm only concerned with three things: (1) finding the best shots and separating those so I can develop them, (2) finding the unusable shots and deleting them, and (3) pretty much ignoring the rest. That's why I like Lightroom's Pick flags. To see these flags as you apply them, make sure they'll be visible by going under the View menu and choosing View Options. In the Library View Options dialog, make sure the checkbox for Include Pick Flags (shown circled here) is turned on.

Step Six:

So, if this simple good/bad form of editing appeals to you, here's how to use the Pick flags. I recommend starting by getting rid of the stinkers first. Not only is it easier (lame shots usually stand out pretty well), but getting them out of the way lowers the number of photos you'll need to search through to find your "keepers." So, when you come across a photo that's totally messed up (like the out-of-focus shot shown here), press the letter X on your keyboard, which flags that photo as Rejected. If you're in the Loupe view (as we are here), the words "Flag as Rejected" will appear briefly on the bottom third of the photo (as shown). If you're in the Grid view, a little black flag with an X on it will appear just outside the top-left side of your photo (as shown here circled in red), letting you know the photo has been flagged as Rejected.

Continued

Step Seven:

You can also apply Pick flags in Survey view and Compare view the same way—just click on the photo and use the keyboard shortcut. In Grid view, Survey view, or Compare view, when you flag a photo you get two forms of feedback: (1) you get the onscreen text "Flag as Rejected," and (2) you see the flag icon added to one of the corners of your photo's cell (it is in the bottom-left corner of the cell in Compare view, and is shown circled here in red). By the way, if you flag a photo and then change your mind (you want to "unflag" it), just press the letter U on your keyboard. Now press G to return to the Grid view.

Step Eight:

Now that you've gone through and flagged all the bad photos as Rejected, you're ready to find the best photos from the shoot and flag those as Picks. First, let's hide the Rejected ones from view (after all, the decision has already been made on those, so let's get them out of our way). Go to the Filters section of Lightroom (which is located on the top right of the filmstrip. I've zoomed in on it here so you can see it better). Right after the word "Filters," you'll see three flag icons (they're circled here in red). These are clickable filter buttons that let you separate your photos based on how (or if) they are flagged.

Step Nine:

Rather than clicking on these individual flags (which you could do, but each flag has two functions, so you wind up clicking a number of times), it's easier if you just Control-click (PC: Right-click) on any

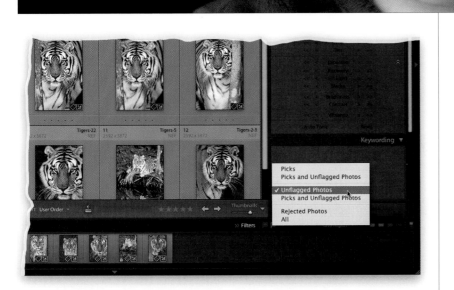

of those flags and a contextual menu will appear. From this menu, choose Unflagged Photos (as shown here). Now all your photos flagged as Rejected are hidden, and just the photos you haven't flagged one way or the other are still visible. The search for the best photo from your shoot just got narrower, and faster. *Note:* You can toggle this filtering feature off any time, so you instantly see all the photos in your folder, collection, etc., without any filtering for ratings, flags, or labels by turning off the Filters switch at the far right end of the Filters section of the filmstrip. Try this first if the photos you're working on are suddenly gone (chances are they're just being filtered, and turning the filters off will bring them all back. Well, at least if filtering is the problem).

Step Ten:
You'll use the exact same process for finding your Picks, and can work in any view you'd like (Grid, Survey, Compare, or Loupe). Personally, I like to use the Loupe view when I'm looking for my Picks because when looking at the small thumbnails in the Grid view, pretty much everything looks in focus. In the Loupe view, because it's zoomed in, I can better evaluate the sharpness of my photos, which keeps me from accidentally flagging an out-of-focus photo as a Pick. So, let's get started. From the Grid view, click on the first photo (in the top-left corner), and then press the E key to jump to the Loupe view (the photo shown here is in Loupe view). Now, click the Select Next Photo button (the right arrow icon) on the toolbar (or the Right Arrow key on your keyboard) to view each unflagged photo in your folder. When you find a shot you want to flag as a Pick, press the letter P on your keyboard.

Continued

Step Eleven:

Here's the thing: the second you flag this photo, it disappears. Why? Because now it's flagged, and back in Step Nine you turned on the Unflagged Photos filter to see only your unflagged photos. Ahhhhh. That's why it's instantly hidden from view (because it's no longer unflagged) and so the next unflagged photo in your folder is now displayed in the Loupe view. Now you can continue to use the Right Arrow key (or the Select Next Photo button in the toolbar) and work on finding, and flagging, your Picks.

Step Twelve:

Before we go on, I want to mention three other ways to flag photos (I think the X and P shortcuts are the quickest, but I want to show you other ways to flag in case you prefer another method). If you prefer clicking on flags, here are your options: (1) You can add Pick buttons to the toolbar, and then click on the Flag as Pick or Flag as Rejected icons. To make these flag icons visible, go to the toolbar's pop-up menu (click on the down-facing arrow at the right end of the toolbar), and choose Pick (as shown here), which adds the two flag icons (circled in red). (2) In the Grid view you can move your cursor over a thumbnail cell, and a grayed-out flag icon appears. If you click on that icon, it's a Pick. If you Option-click (PC: Alt-click) on the icon, it's flagged as Rejected. To remove either flag, just click on it. (3) Control-click (PC: Right-click) on any thumbnail in the filmstrip, and in the contextual menu, go under Set Flag and choose Pick or Rejected. Give all three a try and see if you don't think the keyboard shortcuts are quicker.

TIP: If you press-and-hold the Shift key while you assign a rating, Lightroom jumps to the next unrated photo automatically. Don't want to hold the Shift key? Then turn on the Caps Lock key on your keyboard (as long as it's on, it's like you're holding the Shift key, so…get to ratin'!).

Step Thirteen:
Okay, so at this point you've flagged some photos as Rejected, flagged others as Picks (hopefully you have more Pick photos than Rejected), and everything else is shots that were just okay—not good enough to be a Pick, but not bad enough to be Rejected, so we're just going to ignore them. Now, back to the Rejected photos: why waste space on your hard drive storing photos that are rejects? So, go to the Photo menu (up top) and choose the very last menu item in the list: Delete Rejected Photos (as shown here). Now, only the photos you flagged as Rejected are visible.

Continued

Step Fourteen:

So, Lightroom is displaying only your Rejected photos (just to give you one last brief look before you kiss them goodbye forever), and it brings up the dialog shown here. This is where you decide whether to just Remove them from Lightroom (they'll still take up space on your hard drive), or to Delete them, which is what I recommend (assuming you backed them up somewhere). This removes them from both Lightroom and your computer's hard drive. When you hit the Delete button in that dialog, those photos are headed for the Trash (PC: Recycle Bin), and the only photos left visible in Lightroom are your unflagged ones, because you had filtered down to Unflagged Photos only.

Step Fifteen:

Go back and Control-click (PC: Right-click) on those three little flags in the Filters section, and choose Picks from the contextual menu (as shown here). Now just the photos you like best from that shoot appear onscreen. Okay, so the job of finding the best photos and getting rid of the worst photos is done. Now what? Well, I'll show you what I do next in just a moment, but before I do that, I need you to think back to Step Five, and the beginning of this whole "Sorting Your Photos" process. Remember when I wrote "…there are two other methods that are much more efficient, but the one you choose has to do with how in-depth you like to go with your sorting (photo editing) process"? Well, I showed you the first one, flagging (the method I prefer), but the other method, star ratings, gives you more control because you can rate photos anywhere from zero to five stars, but because just about every photo gets a rating, it can take much longer.

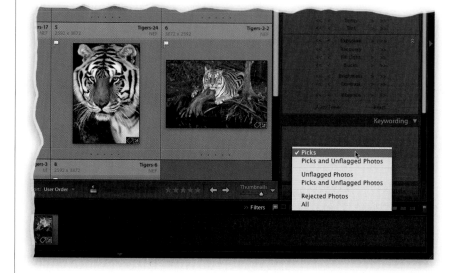

Step Sixteen:

Now, applying star ratings is easy, and you can try this on the same photos you're already using. Go back and Control-click (PC: Right-click) on the three little flags in the Filters section, and choose All from the contextual menu to show all your photos. Like flagging, you can apply ratings in all the different views (Grid, Compare, Survey, and Loupe). We'll start with the Grid view, so press G to show your photos in Grid view. Then, click on a photo and press a number (1 through 5) on your keyboard. Here I pressed 4 and it set the photo's rating to four stars. A confirmation appears briefly onscreen, as seen here, and you can see the 4-star rating under the thumbnail itself (shown circled in red here). You can increase the current rating of a photo by pressing the Right Bracket (]) key on your keyboard, or decrease it using the Left Bracket ([) key. To remove a rating for a selected photo, press 0 (zero) on your keyboard.

Step Seventeen:

There's four other ways to add star ratings: (1) Click on one of those five little light-gray stars on the toolbar (if you don't see them, choose Rating from the toolbar's pop-up menu). Click on a photo (or select multiple photos), then click on the fifth star for a 5-star rating, the fourth star for a 4-star rating, and so on. (2) You can click directly on the five little dots under each thumbnail (even in the Loupe, Compare, or Survey views). Or (3), you can Control-click (PC: Right-click) on any photo (in Grid view or in the filmstrip), go under Set Rating in the contextual menu, and choose the star rating you'd like (as shown here). Lastly, (4) you can assign star ratings in the Metadata panel in the right side panels.

Continued

Step Eighteen:

So, what makes this a bit more tedious is that you have to choose a rating for each photo. I know what to do with 5-star photos (the best ones), and I know not to throw away 4-star photos, but what do I do with 3-star photos? And why would I waste my time rating any photos with two stars? This is why I don't like star ratings. Anyway, you filter these like you filter flags—in the Filters section of the filmstrip. There you'll see five small dots that represent the five stars. To see just the photos you rated with four stars, click on the fourth dot, and only 4-star photos and higher are visible. Ah, but it doesn't end there.

Step Nineteen:

How are you seeing 4-star photos and higher (you see the 4- and 5-star rated photos at the same time)? You choose that from the pop-up menu to the right of the star dots (as shown here). You can also choose to see just four stars and lower or four stars only. By the way, your photos can have both star ratings and flags. Even worse, you can also add color labels (press 6 for Red, 7 for Yellow, 8 for Green, or 9 for Blue), and sort those using the color rectangles in the Filters section. So you could use the filters to just see your Picks, then rate those picks with one to five stars, and then color label them, too. (If this sounds like you, organizing photos probably shouldn't be your biggest concern.) Once your ratings are in place, you can filter down to your 1-star photos and delete them, and then filter again to show just your 5-star photos. So, once I've got just my Picks (or 5-star rated photos) onscreen by themselves, what would I do next? It's a feature we haven't talked about, so in the next tutorial, we'll pick-up where we left off.

Creating Descriptive Names for Your Color Labels

Besides ratings and Pick flags, another way to rank photos is with color labels. Some use color labels to further refine their flagged or rated photos (for example, flagged photos are keepers, within those keepers are a few 5-star photos, and the best of those are labeled green, the next best yellow, and so on). However, by default there are no descriptions for what these colors mean (is a purple label good or bad, and what about blue?). That's why creating your own descriptive names comes in handy, plus Photoshop Lightroom's menu even displays your custom names.

Step One:
The default set of label names is simply their colors (Red, Yellow, Green, Blue, Purple), so to create your own custom label sets, go under the Metadata menu, under Color Label Set, and choose Edit (as shown here).

Step Two:
This brings up the Edit Color Label Set dialog (shown here) with the default set of names, which aren't too descriptive (even I knew that the red dot meant Red). There's a little note at the bottom of the dialog that tells you if you're going to be moving photos back and forth between Photoshop Lightroom and Adobe Bridge, make sure the color label names in both applications are consistent (if you name the red label "Cancelled by client" here in Lightroom, give the red label the same custom name in Bridge).

Continued

Step Three:

Now you just highlight each field and type in the name you want to assign to each color label (as shown here). The numbers to the right of the first four color labels are the shortcuts you'd use to apply those labels. Purple doesn't have a shortcut (my guess is that's because the star ratings already used the number 0—it's the shortcut for a 0-star rating). Once you're happy with your new color label names, go up to the Preset pop-up menu, choose Save as New Preset, and give your preset a name (as shown here). By the way, if you created a custom label set and later need to make a change to that set, come back to this dialog, choose your preset from the Preset pop-up menu, change the text for the label(s) you want to change, then go back under the Preset pop-up menu and choose Update Preset.

Step Four:

Since you now have multiple color label sets (well, at least two), you'll need to first tell Lightroom which set you want to use. You do that by going under the Metadata menu, under Color Label Set, and choosing the set you want (in our case, it would be the Client Proofing Labels set). Once you've made your choice, you can start labeling (it's possible that you'll create this one set, and that's the only set you'll need from here on out. In that case, you won't have to go to the Color Label Set menu again). You can assign these labels by pressing 6, 7, 8, or 9, but if you need to assign the last one, you'll have to either go under the Photo menu, under Set Color Label, and choose it from the menu (notice how the menu has been updated with your color label set names?), or you can use the color label swatches within the grid cells themselves (if you have this View option turned on).

Think about this: In our previous tutorial, when we imported our tiger photos, they were in their own separate folder named Tigers. But within that folder, we sorted (flagged or rated) our photos. Now we could always go to that folder and filter them again, so it's not that hard to get to our best photos again. But once you've gone through all that trouble, there's a better way to stay organized, and that is to create collections. These are custom collections you create that are separate from your folder, so they are your ultimate organization tool.

Keeping Things Organized by Making Collections

Step One:

Okay, we're going to pick up right where we left off with our tiger photos, but I'm really tired of seeing those tiger photos again and again, so can we switch to some other photos, just for the sake of variety? Great, thanks—I really appreciate it. Here I imported some photos from a photo shoot last fall in a small Vermont town. I went through and flagged them (or if you want to pretend I rated them instead, that's fine by me), and now I have turned on my Picks filter, so just my Picks are visible (as shown here). Now (finally), here's what I'd do next:

Step Two:

I'd press Command-A (PC: Ctrl-A) to select all my Picks, then I'd go to the Collections panel (in the Panels area on the left side), and click on the + (plus sign) to the right of the panel's name, as shown circled in red here. (That little + is the Create New Collection button.) This brings up the Create Collection dialog (shown here) where you enter the name of your new collection (I chose "Vermont Picks"). Make sure the Include Selected Photos checkbox is turned on (as it is here) and then click the Create button. The keyboard shortcut for creating a New Collection is easy to remember—it's Command-N (PC: Ctrl-N).

Continued

Step Three:

If you look at the Collections panel, you'll see your new collection (shown here). You're probably thinking, "How does this collection thing help me?" You can think of collections as traditional photo albums. If you were going to put a photo album together from your Vermont trip, you wouldn't put every photo from the trip in it—just the best ones. That's what you just did—you put your best photos in a collection. These are handy for a variety of reasons. For example, if a few weeks from now you want to see just the best photos from your trip, you'd have to go to the original Vermont folder and use the filters to get back to just your Picks (and that takes too long). Since you've got a collection of your best photos, now you're just one click away. What's nice is that these are copies of your Picks, so you're not wasting hard drive space by adding collections. In fact, add as many collections as you'd like, because they take up virtually no space.

Step Four:

When you create a collection, Photoshop Lightroom takes you straight to that collection, and now you can do things you couldn't do back in your main Vermont folder, like rearrange or delete photos without disturbing the original photos. Plus, you can add photos to your collection any time, from any folder, by just dragging a photo from the grid (or filmstrip) and dropping it onto your collection (as shown here, where I'm dragging a tiger photo into my Vermont Picks collection). The green circle with a plus sign on the thumbnail lets you know you're adding this photo. By the way, the same photo can be in as many collections as you'd like.

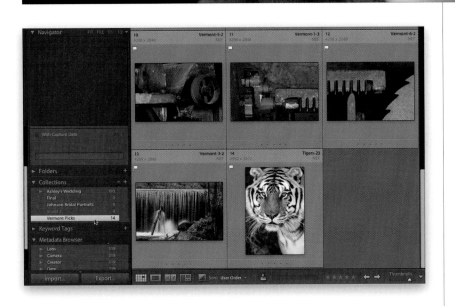

Step Five:

If you click on that Vermont Picks collection again, you'll see that a tiger has been added to this collection. Despite the fact that the tiger looks uncomfortably out of place in Vermont, at least you know it can be done. So, although you probably wouldn't add a tiger to your Vermont Picks collection, you might create a collection of your best shots of the past six months or the past year. Since collections don't take up extra room on your hard drive, you can create as many as you'd like for any reason you'd like. You can have collections of all blue photos, or all portraits, or all of a particular family member, or...well, that's part of the fun—building collections of photos that are always one click away.

Step Six:

Here's another cool thing: collections can have kids (called "subcollections") that are part of the big collection. For example, in our Vermont Picks collection, some of those photos are of a gristmill's waterfall, and some are photos of some old machinery in that gristmill. Well, let's create a subcollection of the machinery. Start by Command-clicking (PC: Ctrl-clicking) on all the machinery shots (as shown here, where I made the thumbnails a little smaller so you could see them all), and once they're all selected click on the Create New Collection plus sign button (as shown here).

Continued

Step Seven:

This brings up the Create Collection dialog where you can name your subcollection "Machinery," but look closely at the dialog. This time, because you were already working within a collection, there's a new checkbox under Collection Options. It's called Create as Child of "Vermont Picks." Go ahead and turn that checkbox on (as shown), and leave the Include Selected Photos checkbox turned on as well, then click the Create button.

Step Eight:

When you click that Create button, those machinery photos—and just those machinery photos—are put into their own subcollection. By the way, if the whole subcollection thing is a bit confusing, when you look in the Collections panel, you'll totally get it. Look at your Vermont Picks collection. If you look to the left of it, you'll see a right-facing "disclosure" triangle (I call them "flippy" triangles because they flip up or down). So, click on the flippy triangle and it reveals the Machinery subcollection that is the child of the Vermont Picks main collection. If you click on your Machinery subcollection, you'll see just the machinery shots you selected earlier. Now, here's the kicker: you didn't remove those machinery shots from the Vermont Picks collection (go ahead, click on the Vermont Picks collection and you'll see that all the same photos you originally put there, including that stupid tiger shot, are still there), but now you have a subcollection with just the machinery shots. Ahhh, now it's starting to make sense. Hey, let's seal the deal by making another subcollection.

Step Nine:

Make sure you've clicked on the Vermont Picks collection, and this time you'll Command-click (PC: Ctrl-click) on the gristmill waterfall shots. Once they're all selected, go back to the Collections panel and click on the plus sign button to create a new collection. The Create Collection dialog will appear again, so name your subcollection "Gristmill Waterfall" and make sure you turn on the Create as a Child of "Vermont Picks" checkbox, then click Create. Look over in the Collections panel, and under Vermont Picks you'll see a new subcollection for your waterfall shots. So, do this: First, click on your Vermont Picks collection to see all the photos, then under Vermont Picks, click on Gristmill Waterfall to see just the waterfall shots (as shown here), then click on the Machinery subcollection to see just those shots. This is very handy stuff.

Step Ten:

In our example, we only had four gristmill waterfall shots, but let's say we had 60 and only five of those are your favorites (and you've selected all five of those). Now, you could create a new collection that would be a child of the Gristmill Waterfall subcollection. You see where this is going? It's organization heaven! By the way, while we're here—if you create a collection and then later want to change its name, you can just double-click directly on the collection's (or subcollection's) name and the field highlights for you to type in a new name (as shown here, where I double-clicked on the Gristmill Waterfall subcollection, and when it highlighted, I typed in the new name "Waterfall shots"). Just press the Return (PC: Enter) key when you're done to lock in your changes.

Continued

Step Eleven:

Another nice thing about collections is that you can delete any photos within them without deleting the original photos, which are still safe and untouched in your Vermont folder. In fact, if you delete an entire collection, it still doesn't disturb the originals in your Vermont folder. In case you were wondering, to delete a photo within a collection, just click on it and press the Delete (PC: Backspace) key on your keyboard. When you do this, you don't get a warning dialog—it's just gone—immediately. If you delete a photo from a collection and change your mind, just press Command-Z (PC: Ctrl-Z) to Undo the deletion. To delete an entire collection, you can either Control-click (PC: Right-click) on the collection and then when the contextual menu appears, choose Delete (as shown here), or just click on the collection you want to delete, then click on the – (minus sign) at the top-right side of the Collections panel.

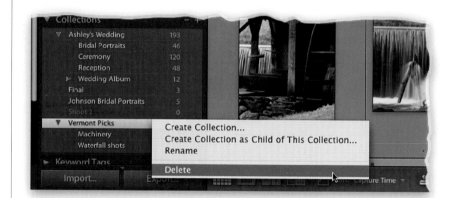

Step Twelve:

If you do go to delete an entire collection, you will get an "Are you sure you want to do this?" dialog (like the one shown here), which is not only warning you that you're deleting a collection, but it's also letting you know that this collection has additional collections tied to it (subcollections) that will be deleted as well. You can hit Cancel (rather than Delete as shown here), because in real life you wouldn't just create a collection and then delete it. And besides, once you create a collection, there's another very important thing you should do for the long-term organization of your photo collection. However, that's a different technique, and it starts on the next page, where we'll pick up again.

Staying Organized by Assigning More Keywords

One of the biggest challenges you're going to face in managing your library of perhaps thousands of photos is being able to quickly find the exact photo (or photos) when you need it. The key to staying organized like this is applying the next level of keywords to your photos now that you've created a collection of your best photos. Since you applied the basic keywords when you first imported these photos into Photoshop Lightroom, now it takes just a few minutes to assign these more precise keywords, but that little bit of time now will save you hours of frustration later.

Step One:
Go to the Vermont Picks collection. Now, look down in the toolbar and you'll see the Keyword Stamper tool, which looks like a rubber stamp (if you don't see the tool, then choose Keyword from the toolbar's pop-up menu to make it visible). Click in the text field to the immediate right of that tool to highlight it. Now, type in a keyword that further describes a key element in your photo. For example, in our collection there are four waterfall shots, so type in the word "Water" (as shown here), then press the Return (PC: Enter) key. Now that word is assigned to the Keyword Stamper tool.

TIP: Besides heading down to the toolbar to get the Keyword Stamper tool, you can get it temporarily by simply Command-Option-clicking (PC: Ctrl-Alt-clicking) on the photo you want to stamp. If you're going to be doing some serious stamping, then press Command-Option-K (PC: Ctrl-Alt-K) and you'll actually switch to the tool. When you're done, either click back on its gray circular home in the toolbar or just press the same keyboard shortcut again.

Continued

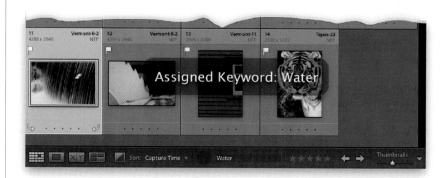

Step Two:

Click on the tool, and then click once directly on a photo in your collection that contains water. When you do this, three things happen: (1) a message appears onscreen confirming that you've assigned the keyword Water to it, (2) your cursor turns into an eraser, so if you clicked the same photo again, it erases the keyword you just assigned, and (3) when this photo is selected, if you look at the Keywording panel in the right side panels, you'll see Water appears as a keyword tagged to this photo along with the keywords you assigned during import.

TIP: To assign multiple keywords with the Keyword Stamper tool, simply separate each word with a comma in the tool's text field in the toolbar.

Step Three:

Another way to assign keywords is to go to the Keyword Tags panel in the left side Panels area, and click the + (plus sign) icon (shown circled here in red). A dialog appears where you can type in the keyword you want to add, then you can select the photos you want to have that keyword, and then drag-and-drop them on that keyword in the Keyword Tags panel. Personally, I think the Keyword Stamper does a faster job, because it takes less clicks—you just click on a photo and you're done. If you want to apply the same keyword to 30 photos, just select all 30, then stamp any one of those 30, and they're all stamped with that keyword instantly. So, let's use the Keyword Stamper to apply "Water" as a keyword to the other photos in our collection that have water somewhere in the photo. (*Note:* When you're done stamping, just click that tool on its gray circle home on the toolbar.)

SCOTT KELBY

TIP: When you click on a thumbnail, take a look over in the Keyword Tags panel, and every keyword assigned to that photo will have a checkmark beside it.

Step Four:

Now, let's put those keywords to use. Go to the Keyword Tags panel in the left side Panels area, and click on the word Water (by the way, any keyword you add with the Keyword Stamper is automatically added to this Keyword Tags panel). Now only our water photos are visible. It's like a one-word search. But since we only applied this keyword to photos in our Vermont Picks collection, we're only going to see water photos from Vermont, which really limits the power of keywords. But in the next step, we'll expand that power.

TIP: If you decide you need to remove a keyword from a photo, click on the keyword in the Keyword Tags panel, then Control-click (PC: Right-click) on the photo and choose Remove Keyword from the contextual menu.

Step Five:

Remember back when we were working on those tiger photos? There were some photos in that folder that had the tiger reflecting in the water, right? Well, they should have the Water keyword applied to them as well. So, go to the Folders panel, click on Tigers, then get the Keyword Stamper again, and click once on the photos with water in them (as shown here).

Continued

Step Six:

Now go back to the Keyword Tags panel in the left side Panels area, click on the keyword Water, and look at the results. You're getting all the shots with the keyword Water assigned to them from both the Vermont and the tiger shoots. So, going forward—whenever you make a collection, go ahead right then and create keywords that describe the photos, and assign them to your photos. Then, if months later you need a photo with water in it to use as a background for a project you're working on, you just go to the Keyword Tags panel, click on Water, and every photo in your entire Photoshop Lightroom library database tagged with the keyword Water will appear in an instant. That's the goal. That's where you want to be—where everything is tagged with a keyword, and getting right to the photos you want is just one click away.

Step Seven:

Now, you've no doubt noticed that I waited until I created a collection before I applied that second level of keywords (the keywords that are more descriptive of what's in each particular photo). That's just how I choose to do it in my own personal workflow, because I need to keep things moving at full speed. I don't have the time to look at each of those 600+ shots to see if they have water, or someone wearing a sweater, or a bird flying in the sky, etc. However, my collections contain just a fraction of each shoot (the best or most usable shots), so taking a couple of minutes to add these more precise keywords is no problem. So, that's my workflow, but if you want to tag each and every photo from every shoot (including ones you're going to delete minutes later), that's between you and Lightroom. Now, back

to our story: As you can imagine, it doesn't take very long for your list of keywords to get really long, but there's a couple of ways to deal with this. One is to use a hierarchical technique, like we did with collections, where you create new keywords that are children of a main keyword. The advantage to doing this is not just that your keyword list will be shorter and more organized (as shown here), but more importantly, it gives you more sorting power. For example, if you create the keyword Water and then create related child keywords like H20, Liquid, Soaked, Splash, and Wet, here's how it helps: If you click on H20, of course it will just show you all the files in your entire library tagged with H20. But if you click on Water (the top-level keyword), then it will show you every file tagged with either Water, H20, Liquid, Soaked, Splash, or Wet. A huge timesaver.

Step Eight:
To set up these extra keywords as children of a main keyword, go to the Keyword Tags panel (in the left side Panels area) and Control-click (PC: Right-click) on the word you want as a top-level word. Then, from the contextual menu that appears, choose Create Keyword Tag as Child of This Keyword Tag (as shown here). This will bring up a dialog where you can type in your new keyword. Click the Create button and this new keyword will appear as a hierarchical keyword under your main keyword Water. In our example (seen in the previous step), the words we added as children could be tucked away (hidden from view in the Keyword Tags panel) by clicking on the flippy triangle to the left of our main keyword. To access those keywords again, just click the flippy triangle again. So, they're there when you need them, tucked away when you don't.

Continued

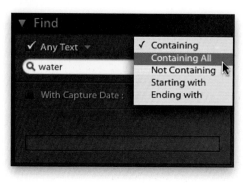

Step Nine:

Besides clicking on keywords to find the photos you want, you can also use the Find panel (shown here), which appears above the Folders panel in the left side Panels area. Here, you can just type a keyword in the text field to locate any word associated with a file (so it could be a keyword, a filename, etc.). You can control what Find searches for using the pop-up menu on the left directly above the text field (Filename, Keywords, etc.). To narrow your search, you can use the pop-up menu on the right side (as shown here), which is not only useful for keywords, but for narrowing any search you're doing using text. Now, I mentioned earlier that there was a second way to organize your keywords, and that is by using keyword sets.

Step Ten:

Keyword sets are just what they sound like: a group of related keywords you put together, so when you need quick access to them they're right there. You create a keyword set in the Keywording panel in the right side Panels area. You first have to click on a photo to activate this panel, and then you'll see a field at the top called Keyword Tags. You could type in the words you want in your set there, but I think it's easier to go right below that, where to the immediate right of where it says Set, you can choose Custom Keyword Set from the pop-up menu, then click on the word Edit (circled here in red) to bring up the dialog you see here. Now you can simply type in the words you'd like in your set. Don't click the Change button yet—instead choose Save as New Preset from the Preset pop-up menu at the top of this dialog, give your new keyword set a name (I chose Vermont 2), and then click Change.

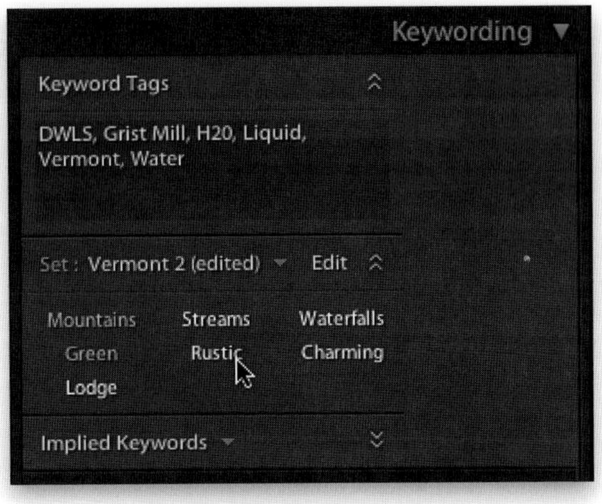

Step Eleven:
Now, in the future when you go to the Keywording panel and choose Vermont 2 from the Set pop-up menu, all those words will appear right there. You can click on a photo (or multiple photos) and then just click right on the word in that set you want to apply to your selected photo(s) (as shown here). Now that I've shown you that, I have to admit that personally, I'm not a big fan of these keyword sets. To me, it's still just too manual and requires too many clicks. That's why I use the first method (the hierarchical keywords) almost exclusively for organizing and applying my keywords. But hey, that's just me.

TIP: If you have a number of keywords in your Keyword Tags panel that are grayed out, those are not being used by any photos in your database. So, you can have Lightroom delete those orphaned keywords (which makes your tags list cleaner and shorter) by going under the Metadata menu and choosing Purge Unused Keywords.

ANOTHER TIP: If you want to export your keywords so you can (a) load them into a different Lightroom library, (b) load them into a copy of Lightroom on a different computer, or (c) if you want everyone in your office to use the same set of keywords, go under the Metadata menu and choose Export Keywords. This creates a text file with all your keywords. To import these keywords into another user's copy of Lightroom, go under the Metadata menu and choose Import keywords, then locate that keyword file you exported earlier.

When To Use a Quick Collection Instead

When you create collections, they're a more permanent way of keeping your photos organized into separate albums (by permanent, I mean that when you relaunch Photoshop Lightroom months later, your collections are still there—but of course, you can also choose to delete a collection so they're never really that permanent). However, sometimes you want to just group a few photos temporarily, and you don't actually want to save these groupings long term. That's where Quick Collections come in, which are temporary and go away on their own.

Step One:

Before we get started, I'm beginning to get tired of seeing those Vermont shots, so I'm going to use a different batch of photos here that I never get tired of seeing—photos of my 11-month-old baby daughter Kira (taken by my sister-in-law Heidi). So, I imported these photos (they were already on my hard drive), added keywords in the Import Photos dialog, etc. Let's say that I want to show my wife just the shots of Kira playing her little toy keyboard. I don't need to separate these permanently, just long enough to show my wife. That's when I'd use a Quick Collection.

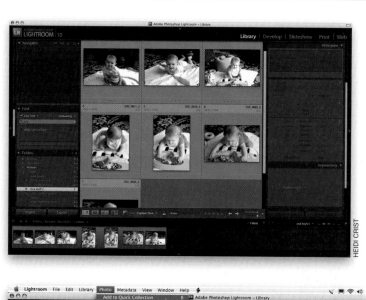

Step Two:

Creating a Quick Collection couldn't be easier. Just select the photos you want in your Quick Collection, then you can either go under the Photo menu and choose the very first menu item, Add to Quick Collection, or just press the letter B on your keyboard (which is much faster). Or there's a third way, which is absolutely annoying as heck because it actually adds a round gray circle (called a Quick Collection Marker) to the upper right-hand corner of each photo (not just outside the photo in the surrounding cell, like in earlier Beta versions of Photoshop Lightroom—I'm talkin' right smack dab on the photo itself. Nice).

Step Three:

To turn this annoying option on, go to the Library View Options (this is where you customize what is visible within your Grid view cells and your Loupe view) by pressing Command-J (PC: Ctrl-J). When the dialog appears, to turn on/off these distracting gray dots, click on the Grid View tab up top, and then turn on/off the checkbox for Include Quick Collection Markers (as shown here). I've included a close-up of a cell here, so you can see the little gray dot I'm talking about—you'd just click on that dot (either in the Grid view, or in the filmstrip) to add it to your Quick Collection. It doesn't look too bad here, but that's only because the gray dot happens to appear over a very dark part of the photo. If the photo had been framed so the white blanket was in that corner, you'd say what everyone else says, "Why is there a gray dot on your photo?"

Step Four:

To see the photos you put in a Quick Collection, go to the Library panel (in the left side Panels area), and click on Quick Collection (as shown here). Now just those photos are visible, and if you like, you could do a quick Impromptu Slideshow by pressing Command-Return (PC: Ctrl-Enter). To remove a photo from your Quick Collection, just click on it and press the Delete (PC: Backspace) key on your keyboard (it doesn't delete the original, it just removes it from this temporary Quick Collection). If you decided you wanted the photos in your Quick Collection to be saved as a regular collection, just press Command-A (PC: Ctrl-A) to select them all, then go to the Collections panel and click on the plus sign button to save them as a collection.

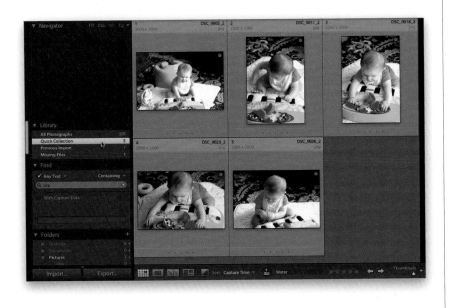

Stay Organized By Grouping (Stacking) Similar Photos

Let's say you've just shot a wedding, and in the Grid view you now see thumbnails of literally hundreds of photos. Finding the "keepers" seems pretty daunting, but you can reduce clutter and work more efficiently by grouping (stacking) similar photos. For example, if you have 12 shots of a particular pose, stack them together. That way, just one photo thumbnail of that pose will represent all 12 shots of that pose. You can collapse and expand these photo stacks in just one click, plus Photoshop Lightroom can even do your stacking automatically, based on time intervals.

Step One:

Here, we've imported images from a wedding shoot, and you can see what I was talking about above, where there are numerous shots that include the same pose. Seeing all these photos at once just adds clutter, and makes finding your "keepers" that much more of a task. So, we're going to group similar poses into a stack with just one thumbnail show- ing. The rest of the photos are collapsed behind that photo. Start by clicking on the first photo of a similar pose (as seen highlighted here), then press-and-hold the Shift key and click on the last photo that has the same pose (as shown here) to select them all (you can also select photos in the filmstrip if you prefer).

Step Two:

Now press Command-G (PC: Ctrl-G) to put all your selected photos into a stack (this keyboard shortcut is easy to remem- ber if you think of G for Group). If you look in the grid now, you can see there's just one thumbnail visible with that pose. It didn't delete or remove those other pho- tos—they stacked behind that one thumb- nail (in a computery, technical, you'll-just- have-to-trust-that's-what's-happening kind of way). Look how much more manage- able things are now that those 12 photos are collapsed down to one.

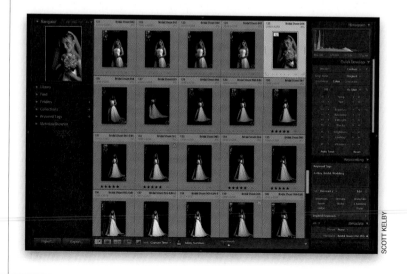

TIP: This is going to sound weird at first, but it makes sense. Kinda. Apparently when your average person sees a portrait of themselves, it looks a little weird to them because they're used to seeing their own image in a mirror (which is reversed to the way a camera, or anyone, sees them). So, if you flip their portrait horizontally before showing it to them, it's more pleasing to them (at least, that's the theory). To do this in Photoshop Lightroom, select the photos you want horizontally flipped, then go under the Photo menu and choose Flip Horizontal.

Step Three:

In the zoomed-in view here, you can see the number 12 in a rectangle in the top left of the thumbnail. That's to let you know two things: (1) this isn't just one photo—it's a stack of photos, and (2) how many photos are in this stack. The view you're seeing here is the stack's collapsed view (where 11 similar photos are collapsed behind the first one).

Note: You can only build stacks with the contents of a folder (in the Folders panel), so if you click on a collection, or filter down photos using keywords, or metadata, or the Find panel, you won't be able to stack them—you have to go to the Folders panel and choose a folder of photos there (and yes, you can only stack photos from the same folder).

Continued

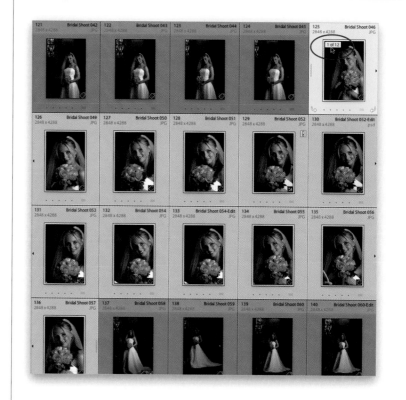

Step Four:

To expand your stack and see all the photos in it, just click directly on that little number 12 in the top-left corner of the thumbnail (the expanded view is shown here), press S on your keyboard, or click on one of the two little thin bars which appear on either side of the thumbnail. (To collapse the stack, just do any of these again.) Of course, if you have more or less than 12 photos, it won't say 12 on your stack. (I really didn't have to mention that, did I? Sorry.) By the way, to add a photo to an existing stack, you can either: (a) Click on the stack first, then Command-click (PC: Ctrl-click) on the photo(s) you want to add to the stack (to select it), then press Command-G (PC: Ctrl-G) to group it with your existing stack. Or my preferred method is to (b) just drag-and-drop the photo you want to add right onto the existing collapsed stack.

Step Five:

Before we go any further, I want to show you how stacks can help you in finding the best shot from the photos of this particular pose. So, go to your stack and click on the little number to expand it. When you expand a stack, all the photos in that expanded stack are automatically selected, which is great because now you can press the letter N on your keyboard to enter Survey view (shown here). After you enter Survey view, press Shift-Tab to hide all the panels and make your thumbnails larger. Now that you're seeing just that pose, you can remove photos from contention by clicking on the little X in the bottom-right corner of each thumbnail until you come up with your single best photo, and you can rate that as a Pick or give it a 5-star rating right there in Survey view.

Step Six:
When you're done choosing your best photo from that pose, press G to return to the Grid view, choose another stack from a different pose, and do the same thing. This is a very efficient way to quickly find the best photos from the entire wedding shoot. Okay, here are a few things that will help you in managing your stacks. The first photo you select when creating a stack (the top photo) will be the one that remains visible when the stack is collapsed. If that's not the photo you want to represent your stack, you can make any photo in your stack the top photo. First, expand the stack, then Control-click (PC: Right-click) directly on the photo you want at the top of the stack. When the contextual menu appears, go under Stacking, and choose Move to Top of Stack (as shown here).

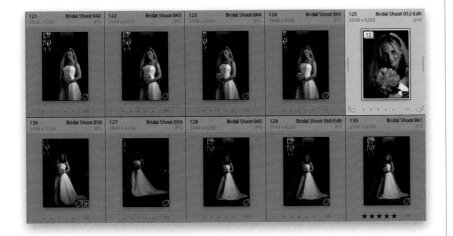

Step Seven:
Here, you can see we've replaced the old top photo with this better photo from our stack. For my personal workflow, I leave the first photo I selected (when I made my stack) as the top photo until I enter Survey view. Once I've narrowed things down to my favorite photo in Survey view, then I Control-click (PC: Right-click) on that photo and use the contextual menu I showed in the last step to make my best-of-that-pose photo the top photo. That way, after I've gone through a number of stacks, I'm only looking at my best photos, with other contenders stacked neatly behind in case I change my mind later.

Continued

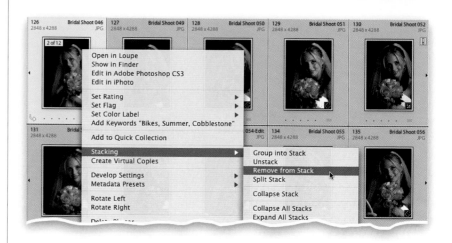

Step Eight:

If you'd like to remove a photo from your stack, first expand the stack, then Control-click (PC: Right-click) directly on that photo, and the contextual menu shown here will appear. This time choose Remove from Stack (as shown here). This doesn't delete it, or remove it from a collection, etc. It just takes it out of this stack. So, for example, if you removed just one photo, when you collapsed the stack again, you'd see two thumbnails in the grid—one representing the 11 photos still stacked, and a second thumbnail of just that individual photo you removed. *Note:* If you want to remove more than one photo from your stack at the same time, first press Command-D (PC: Ctrl-D) to deselect all the photos in your expanded stack. Command-click (PC: Ctrl-click) on the ones you want removed to select them, and then choose Remove from Stack from the contextual menu.

Step Nine:

Before we move on—one more thing on the topic of removing photos from your stack. If you do want to actually delete a photo in your stack (not just remove it from your stack), just expand the stack, then click on the photo and press the Delete (PC: Backspace) key on your keyboard. Okay, here's another tip: if you want all your stacks expanded at once (so every thumbnail from the shoot is visible again), just Control-click (PC: Right-click) on any thumbnail (not just a stack—any thumbnail), choose Stacking, and then choose Expand All Stacks. If you want to collapse all your stacks, instead choose Collapse All Stacks, and now you'll see just one photo representing each pose (as shown here).

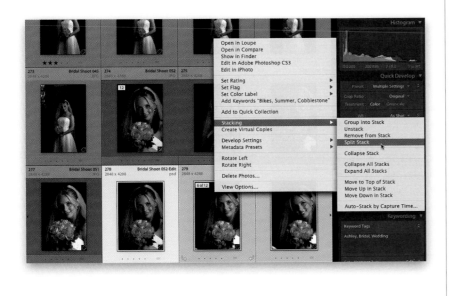

Step Ten:

Lightroom can automatically stack similar photos together based on how much time passed between poses, or a lighting change, or a location change. This works on the premise that while you're shooting, you're shooting fairly continuously. However, when you change poses, or lighting, or location, etc., there's a short (or long) pause while you set up the next shot. You tell Lightroom how long you think your average pause is, and everything with a shorter pause gets stacked (this works better than it sounds). To turn on this auto-stack feature, Control-click (PC: Right-click) on any thumbnail, then from the contextual menu, under Stacking, choose Auto-Stack by Capture Time. The dialog shown here appears, and as you drag the slider left or right, you'll see photos start jumping into stacks in real time. This is one of those you just have to try to see that it usually works pretty darn well.

Step Eleven:

By the way, if you use the auto-stack feature, it's possible that it might stack some photos together that don't actually belong together. Okay, I said it's possible, but in reality it's highly likely. Not every time, mind you, but it will happen. If that happens, it's easy to split a stack and have those other photos separated into their own stack. This is where I use splitting the most (for auto-stack mistakes), but you can also use it any time you want to separate some of the photos in a stack for any reason. To split a stack, just select the photos you want to split out into their own stack, then Control-click (PC: Right-click) on any one of those selected photos, and in the contextual menu that appears, go under Stacking and choose Split Stack (as shown here). Now, you'll have two stacks—in our case, one with nine photos, and one with three.

Continued

Step Twelve:

One last thing about stacks: once photos are in a stack, any edits you apply to your stack while it's collapsed are actually only applied to the top photo in your stack. So if you go to the Quick Develop panel and change the white balance temperature, or add keywords in the Keywording panel (as shown here), it only affects the top photo—not the rest of the photos in the stack. Quick Develop settings, keywords, and any other edit can be applied to the entire stack if you click on the number to expand the stack (then they are all selected) before you change your setting or add your keyword.

When you take a digital photo, the camera automatically embeds a host of information directly into the photo itself, including everything from the make and model of the camera it was taken with, to the type of lens that was on the camera at the time, to the time and date, and even whether your flash fired or not. That can be very handy stuff (and Photoshop Lightroom can even search photos based on this embedded information, called EXIF data). Beyond that, you can embed your own info into the file, and the ability to do that is more important than you might think.

Working With, and Adding to, Your Photo's Embedded Metadata

Step One:
In the Library module, to see a photo's metadata (which includes the info embedded by your camera [called EXIF data], along with info embedded automatically by Photoshop Lightroom, plus any custom info you may have added when you imported the photo into Lightroom), go to the Metadata panel located in the right side Panels area (shown here). As you can see, it lists all the EXIF information about this particular image, including when it was shot, the size, make, and model of the camera, the settings on your camera at the time it was taken, the lens type—you name it.

Step Two:
By default, Lightroom displays all the metadata embedded in this photo, but if you find that you've got information overload, you can choose to display only certain parts of the metadata (like only the EXIF camera data, or only information you've added here in Lightroom or in Photoshop) by choosing which set of info to display from the pop-up menu at the top left of the Metadata panel header (shown here, where I chose Quick Describe, which displays just the first few lines of the camera EXIF data, some info Lightroom embeds, and the basic IPTC data [the stuff you choose to embed]).

Continued

Step Three:

Go to the pop-up menu again, and choose EXIF to show just the info embedded by your camera. This is handy info to have, but the Metadata panel does more than just display info. You see those little arrows that appear to the right of some fields? They're hot-linked to associated functions. For example, near the bottom of the list, you'll see your camera's serial number. Click on the arrow to the right of that field (shown circled here in red), and now any photos taken with the camera bearing that serial number will be displayed in the grid. Same thing for the arrow beside the Lens field—click it and all photos taken with that lens appear. Some arrows have different functions (hover your cursor over an arrow for a few seconds and it will display what that arrow does). For example, the arrow beside the File Path field opens a window showing where that file is on your computer. A very nice feature.

Step Four:

Now go and choose IPTC from the Metadata panel pop-up menu (in case you were wondering, IPTC stands for the International Press Telecommunications Council) to display just the section where you can add your own information to the file (things like your copyright notice, usage rights, your contact info in case someone wants to license your photos, etc.). Ideally, you'd have Lightroom automatically embed all this info during the import process (see the importing tutorial in Chapter 1 for a refresher on creating metadata templates and applying them during import), but if you didn't have it added just click on a field, type in your info (as shown), then hit the Return (PC: Enter) key to lock in your changes.

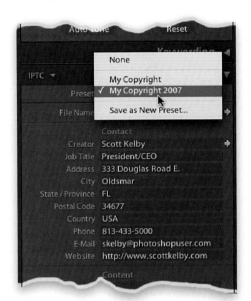

Step Five:

Now, if you did create a Metadata preset (which is basically a template with all of your copyright and contact info already filled in), you can apply that preset in the Metadata panel by choosing it from the Preset pop-up menu at the top of the panel (shown here, where it filled in all the contact info for me. That's the power of metadata presets—you only have to type in all that copyright and contact info once, then you can add it all to other selected photos by either choosing it from that pop-up menu or choosing it during import). Once you create a preset, it will make more sense, so if you didn't create one back in Chapter 1 (the chapter on importing), jump back there and build one (or more) now so you can apply it when you need it. They save loads of time.

Step Six:

When you assign metadata to a photo, it goes into one of three places: (1) If it's a JPEG, TIFF, PSD, or DNG, the information is embedded directly into the file itself, so there's nothing really to deal with. (2) If it's a photo in RAW format, then by default its metadata is stored in Lightroom's database. Or, (3) for RAW photos you can choose to export this metadata to what's called an XMP side-car file. This is a separate file from your original image, and if you were to look in that image's folder on your computer, you'd see your RAW file, then next to it you'd see an XMP sidecar file with the same name, but with the XMP file extension (the two files are circled here in red). These two files need to stay together because one is the photo, and the other is that photo's metadata (so if you were to back up this photo to a disc—or move it—be sure to grab both files).

Continued

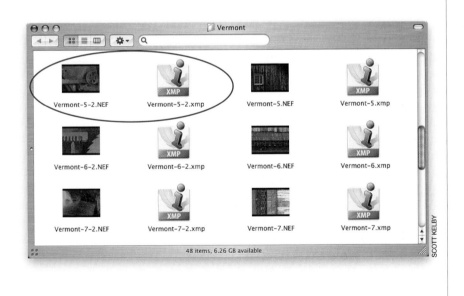

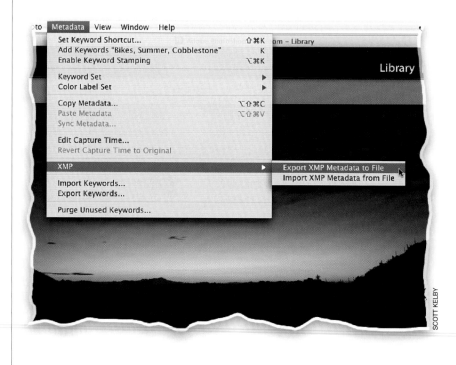

Step Seven:

There are two advantages of saving your metadata changes as XMP sidecar files: (1) Any Develop settings you've applied, all your embedded keywords, ratings, and cropping will be recognized by Adobe's Bridge and Camera Raw 3.7 or higher (both are part of Photoshop CS2/CS3). And (2), if you share your RAW photos with other people, you'll be able to include your metadata. If you'd like to have your RAW photo metadata in separate XMP sidecar files, then press Command-, (PC: Ctrl-,) to open Lightroom's Preferences dialog, click on the File Management tab, and turn on the checkbox for Automatically Write Changes into XMP. Now, your changes to RAW photos (from edits, to cropping, to keywords, to ratings, etc.) will be written to a separate XMP file automatically.

Step Eight:

The downside of always writing the metadata to XMP sidecars (which I learned after talking recently with Lightroom Alpha tester Jeff Schewe) is a speed issue. Each time you make a change to a RAW file, Lightroom has to write that change into XMP, which slows things down a bit, so he (and now I, as well) leave the Automatically Write Changes into XMP checkbox turned off. Instead, when I need to send a RAW file over to Bridge or Camera Raw for additional editing, at that point I go under the Metadata menu, under XMP and choose Export XMP Metadata to File (as shown here). *Note:* Remember, this XMP sidecar issue only relates to RAW files, not JPEGs, or TIFFs, or PSDs, or DNGs, which all embed the metadata directly into the file automatically.

Step Nine:

Here's a tip that could really save you some time: if you manually entered some IPTC metadata for a photo, and you want to apply that same metadata to a different photo, you don't have to type it all in again—you can copy that metadata and paste it on another photo. Start by clicking on the photo where you entered your metadata, then go under the Metadata menu and choose Copy Metadata, or press Command-Option-Shift-C (PC: Ctrl-Alt-Shift-C). This brings up the Copy Metadata dialog (shown here), where you can choose which lines of metadata you want to copy (just turn off the checkbox to the right of any data field you don't want).

Step Ten:

Click the Copy button and that info is stored into memory. Now select the photo(s) you want it applied to, go under the Metadata menu, and choose Paste Metadata. Better yet—that copied metadata stays in Lightroom's memory, so you can paste it tomorrow, the next day, etc. (Basically, it stays there until you copy a different set of metadata.) If you don't need that long-term storage of metadata, then try this: click on the photo that has the metadata you want, then Command-click (PC: Ctrl-click) on those other photos to select them. Now click the Sync Metadata button (at the bottom of the right side Panels area), which brings up the Synchronize Metadata dialog (shown here). It looks and works almost exactly like the Copy Metadata dialog. Turn off the checkboxes for any data you don't want synched, then click the Synchronize button to update those other photos.

Continued

Step Eleven:

If you find yourself doing a lot of this metadata pasting (or syncing), you might as well create a metadata preset. This gives you two advantages: (1) it doesn't get lost if you copy metadata from a different photo, and (2) you'll be able to apply this preset in the Import Photos dialog to save time. To save the currently selected photo's IPTC metadata as a preset, go to the Metadata panel, and from the Preset pop-up menu choose Save as New Preset (as shown here). When the dialog appears, give your preset a name, click the Create button, and you're set! Two things to note: (1) Any time you apply a metadata preset (or copy-and-paste metadata), the preset (pasted) metadata replaces any existing metadata in the photo. And (2), when you copy metadata, it's only copying things like your ratings, copyright, contact info, etc. It doesn't copy camera data (ISO, lens, exposure, etc.).

Step Twelve:

Another piece of metadata you may need to change is the time your photo was taken (well, at least if it's wrong). For example, I live on the East Coast, but I often shoot on the West Coast. Unfortunately, I must have the memory retention of a hamster because I never remember to change my camera's time zone setting to Pacific (three hours earlier). If this should happen, go to the grid, select the photos that need a time zone change, then go under the Metadata menu and choose Edit Capture Time (which brings up the dialog shown here). The top choice in the New Time section lets you enter the correct date and time, the center choice on the right lets you move the hours up or back for a time zone adjustment, and the bottom choice changes the time to reflect the time the file was created.

Admittedly, this particular feature is more of a "Wow, that's cool!" feature than an incredibly useful feature, but…wow, is it cool! If your camera has built-in GPS (which automatically embeds into your photo the exact latitude and longitude of where the photo was shot), then gather your friends around Photoshop Lightroom and prepare to blow them away because it not only displays this GPS information, but one click will actually bring up a map and pinpoint the location where you took the photo. That way…well…well…I dunno—it's just really cool.

If Your Camera Supports GPS, Prepare to Amaze Your Friends

DAVID DENTRY

Step One:
Import a photo into Photoshop Lightroom that was taken with a digital camera that has the built-in (or add-on) ability to record GPS data (camera companies like Ricoh make GPS-enabled digital cameras, and many Nikon dSLRs [like the D200, D2X, and D2Hs for example] have a GPS-compatible connector port, which can make use of add-ons like Sony's GPS CS-1 unit, with a street price of around $120 [at the time of writing]).

Step Two:
In the Library module, go to the Metadata panel in the right side Panels area. Near the bottom of the panel, if your photo has GPS info encoded, you'll see a metadata field labeled GPS with the exact coordinates of where that shot was taken (shown circled here in red).

Continued

Step Three:

Just seeing that GPS info is amazing enough, but it's what comes next that always drops jaws whenever I show this feature live in front of a class. Click on the little arrow that appears to the far right of the GPS field (it's shown circled here in red).

Exposure Bias	0EV
Flash	Did not fire
Exposure Program	Normal
Metering Mode	Pattern
ISO Speed Rating	ISO 125
Focal Length	12 mm
Lens	12.0-24.0 mm f/4.0
Date Time	1/30/07 9:41:05 AM
Date Time Original	6/22/05 12:38:45 PM
Make	NIKON CORPORATION
Model	NIKON D2X
Serial Number	5018727
Artist	
Software	Capture NX 1.1.0 M
GPS	40°47'7" N 73°25'7" W
Altitude	52 m

Step Four:

When you click on that little arrow, if you're connected to the Internet, Lightroom will automatically launch your default Web browser, connect to Google Maps, and it will display a full-color photographic satellite image with your exact location pinpointed on the map (as shown here). Seriously, how cool is that!? Now, in all honesty, I've never had even a semi-legitimate use for this feature, but I've found that despite that fact I still think it's just so darn cool. All guys do. We just can't explain why.

Okay, so we've rated, and ranked, and added metadata, and we've done all of the stuff we're supposed to do to help us locate that one photo that we need in a hurry (by the way, whenever you really need to find a photo, it's never when you have plenty of time—it's always "We need to have that by noon," and it's 11:25 a.m.). Here's where we gather together, in one place, some of the most important techniques for helping you get to those photos fast.

Finding the Photos You Want, Fast!

Step One:
Let's say you're getting ready for a slide presentation to a client and you want to use a shot from one of your trips to Amsterdam (but you're not sure which shot, or which trip you took it on). Go to the Find panel (in the left side Panels area). Since it searches in whichever folder or collection you're working in, to search your entire library, go to the Library panel and click on All Photographs. Now, in the Find panel, from the top-left pop-up menu choose Any Text (as shown) so it searches everything—from the file-names, to keywords, to metadata, and more. Then click in the search field, type "Amsterdam," and press the Return (PC: Enter) key (you can narrow your text search by choosing search options from the pop-up menus, as shown here).

Step Two:
Instantly, all the photos you've taken of Amsterdam over the years appear. Now, do you remember when you might have taken them? If you think they were taken between the spring and fall of 2006, then turn on the With Capture Date checkbox (as shown here), and now you can narrow the search by the exact time frame you think the photos were taken by choosing a time frame from the pop-up menu (here I chose Last Year from the pop-up menu).

Continued

SCOTT KELBY

Step Three:
Last year is a pretty broad time frame (in that menu there are presets for searching just last month's, this month's, this year's, etc.), especially if you were in Amsterdam numerous times during the year. However, if you have an idea of the range of time in which those photos might have been shot (between the spring and fall of 2006, right?), you can click on the date that appears above either end of the timeline, and a dialog will pop up (shown here) where you can enter the date and time (using either the pop-up calendar or by highlighting each number field and just typing in numbers).

Step Four:
When you click OK, the timeline updates to reflect just that time frame, and now only the photos that fall between those two dates are still visible. Now, you can use the timeline sliders to narrow the time frame even more. For example, drag the left slider slowly to the right (going from May to June to July), and as you get into July, now only the photos taken in Amsterdam between July and August are visible (as seen here). This is a great tool to use when you have some idea of the date, but if you go through these steps and you're down to just the shots you took between July and August of 2006, what if the ones you're looking for aren't there? Now what? Next, I'd try the Keyword Tags panel (shown in the next step).

TIP: You can use the timeline by itself to find just the photos from a particular year, or month, or day.

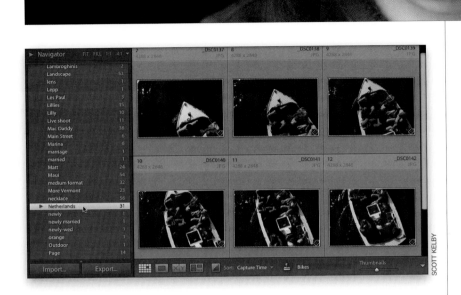

Step Five:

Here's where adding those keywords when you imported your photos really pays off. So, if you can't remember the exact date the shots were taken, maybe you can remember where they were taken. Well, the shots were taken somewhere in the Netherlands (you thought it was Amsterdam, but then again you thought it was last year, too. Do you drink a lot? Because that might be a factor. [Like the way I make up a scenario for you, and then turn it around on you?]). Anyway, go to the Keyword Tags panel (in the left side Panels area), click on the keyword Netherlands, and all your shots from the Netherlands appear.

Step Six:

Although your memory is sketchy, that's okay because you didn't forget to create hierarchical keywords, so clicking on Netherlands brings you all the shots taken in that country. If you click on the flippy triangle to the left of this keyword, it expands to show you all the keywords you created as children of your Netherlands keyword. For example, under the Netherlands, click on Bike, and now only the shots of bikes that you took in the Netherlands appear (as shown here). The difference here is, if you just clicked on the keyword Bike, it shows all your photos, from all over the world, tagged with the keyword Bike. But by using keywords that are children of your main keyword, you're two clicks away from narrowing things down to just the bike shots from the Netherlands. Sadly, upon seeing these, you realize that the shot you're looking for still isn't here. Next stop—the Metadata Browser, which lets you filter things down by metadata.

Continued

Step Seven:

The Metadata Browser is pretty amazing technology because it will show you, in one click, all the photos taken with a particular camera make and model, or a particular type of lens (Photoshop Lightroom gathers all this info automatically from the built-in EXIF data put there by your digital camera, with no input from you). In our case, we're going to use a very helpful piece of IPTC image data (data you add yourself here in Lightroom). In the Metadata Browser (found at the bottom of the left side Panels area), click on Location. A list of all the countries where your photos were taken appears (there's the Netherlands), and if you click on the flippy triangle, it breaks things down even further—by province (Utrecht and North Holland) and city (Amsterdam and Rotterdam). Here, I clicked on Netherlands, and most of the shots were taken in Amsterdam, but the two shown here were taken in Rotterdam. Low and behold, that first shot is the one you were looking for.

Step Eight:

If you were wondering where you enter that info for a photo, just go to the Metadata panel in the right side Panels area (not the browser, the panel on the opposite side), and scroll down to the IPTC Image fields (shown here). Click on a field, and type in the info. Once you've done one photo, select all the rest from that city, province, and country, and then click the Sync Metadata button at the bottom right. When the Synchronize Metadata dialog appears, turn on the checkbox for IPTC Image, and turn off the main checkboxes for everything else. So, that's our quick look at different ways to find the photo(s) you're looking for, fast. Find them (1) by name, (2) by date, (3) by keyword, or (4) by location.

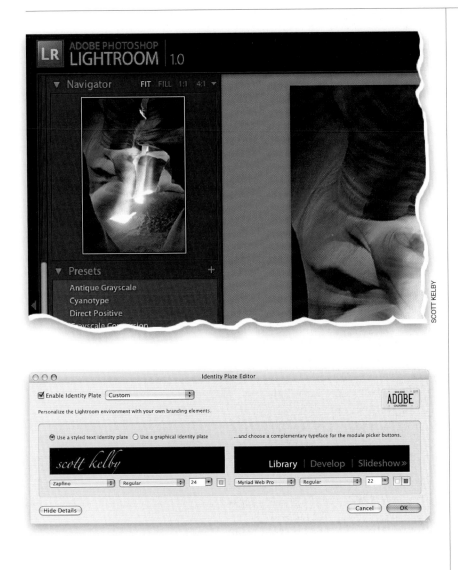

The first time I saw Photoshop Lightroom, one of the features that really struck me as different was the ability to replace the Adobe Photoshop Lightroom logo (that normally appears in the upper-left corner of Lightroom) with either the name of your studio or your studio's logo. I have to say, when you're doing client presentations, it does add a nice custom look to the program (as if Adobe designed Lightroom just for you), but beyond that, the ability to create an Identity Plate goes farther than just giving Lightroom a custom look (but we'll start here, with the custom look).

Adding Your Studio's Name and Logo for a Custom Look

Step One:
First, just so we have a frame of reference, here's a zoomed-in view of the top-left corner of Photoshop Lightroom's interface, so you clearly see the logo we're going to replace starting in Step Two. Now, you can either replace Photoshop Lightroom's logo using text (and you can even have the text for the Module Picker match), or you can replace the logo with a graphic of your logo.

Step Two:
To create your own custom Identity Plate, go under the Lightroom menu (the Edit menu on a PC), and choose Identity Plate Setup. This brings up the Identity Plate Editor (shown here). By default, the name you registered your software in shows up in the large black field in the middle left. To see your Identity Plate, turn on the checkbox at the top left for Enable Identity Plate. If you don't want your name as your Identity Plate, just highlight it and type in whatever you'd like (the name of your company, studio, etc.), then while the type is still highlighted, choose a font, font style (bold, italic, condensed, etc.), and font size from the pop-up menus (directly below the text field).

Continued

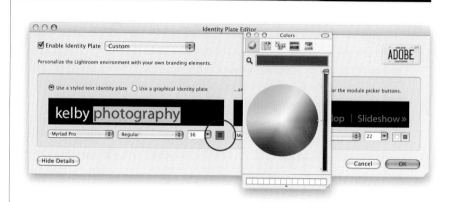

Step Three:

If you want to change part of your text (for example, if you wanted to change the font of one of the words, or the font size, or the color of a word), just highlight the word you want to adjust before making the change. To change the color, click on the little square color swatch to the right of the Font Size pop-up menu (it's shown circled here). This brings up the Colors panel (you're seeing the Macintosh Colors panel here; the Windows Color panel will look somewhat different, but don't let that freak you out. Aw, what the heck—go ahead and freak right out!). Just choose the color you want your selected text to be, then close the Colors panel.

Step Four:

If you like the way your custom Identity Plate looks, you definitely should save it, because creating an Identity Plate does more than just replace the current Adobe Photoshop Lightroom logo—you can add your new custom Identity Plate text (or logo) to any slide show, Web gallery, or final print by choosing it from the Identity Plate pop-up menu in all three modules (see, you were dismissing it when you just thought it was a task bar, feel good feature. Now it's more than just a task bar, feel good feature, baby—we get to feel pretty ego'd out in three more modules. Oh yeah!). To save your custom Identity Plate, click-and-hold on the Enable Identity Plate pop-up menu, then choose Save As (as shown here). Give your Identity Plate a descriptive name, click OK, and now it's saved. From here on out it will appear in a handy Identity Plate pop-up menu, where you can get that same custom text, font, and color in just one click.

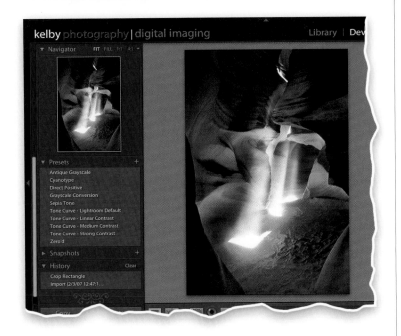

Step Five:

Once you click the OK button, your new Identity Plate text replaces the Adobe Photoshop Lightroom logo that was in the upper-left corner (as shown here). Okay, so what if you don't want to just type in some text and choose a font? What if you want to add your custom graphic? Well, that's what the next step is all about.

Step Six:

To add a graphic, you go to the same place (under the Lightroom menu on a Mac, and the Edit menu on a PC), and choose Identity Plate Setup, but when the dialog appears, click on the radio button for Use a Graphical Identity Plate (as shown here) instead of Use a Styled Text Identity Plate. Next, click on the Locate File button (found above the Hide Details button in the lower-left corner) and find your logo file (I put my logo on a black background with white text in Photoshop CS3), then click the Choose (PC: Open) button to make that graphic your Identity Plate. *Note:* When you click on Use a Graphical Identity Plate, a message appears where the text logo was that tells you not to make your graphic taller than 60 pixels deep. So, don't make your graphic taller than 60 pixels deep (pretty deep stuff, eh?).

Continued

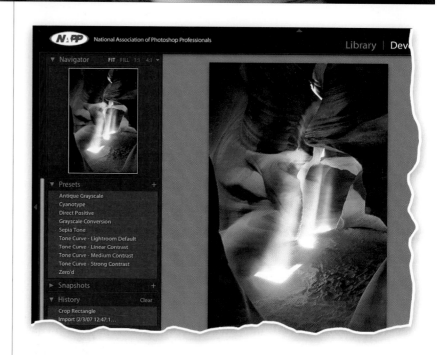

Step Seven:

When you click OK, the Lightroom logo (or your custom text—whichever was up there last) is replaced by the new graphic file of your logo (as shown here). *Note:* If you want your logo file to have a transparent background, create your logo and text on separate layers in Photoshop CS2/CS3. Then, delete the white background layer, which makes the background transparent. After you delete the white background layer, highlight your text and change the color to white (in Photoshop), then save the file in Photoshop (PSD) format to retain the transparency.

Step Eight:

If you like your new graphical logo file in Lightroom, don't forget to save this custom Identity Plate by choosing Save As from the Enable Identity Plate pop-up menu at the top of the dialog. Now you can choose a custom text logo or your graphic logo, and not just to appear in the interface, but for slide shows, building Web galleries, and for printing. If you decide at some point, that you'd like the original Adobe Photoshop Lightroom logo back instead, just go back to the Identity Plate Editor and turn off the Enable Identity Plate checkbox (as shown here). Remember, we'll do more with one of your new Identity Plates in three later modules.

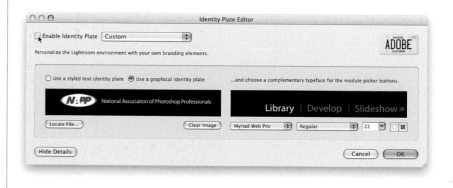

The filmstrip is more than just a running photo picker that's available in every module—well, I guess, that's exactly what it is. But, besides picking photos and filtering them down with ratings, flags, and color labels (all of which are on the top-right side of the filmstrip), the filmstrip has features to keep you from having to jump to the Library module every time you need to simply switch back to an earlier collection, or to results from a search (but if you do have to jump back, it can even help you with that).

The Hidden Power of the Filmstrip

SCOTT KELBY

Step One:
The top-left corner of the filmstrip is really an information center, and tells you a lot about the set of images or individual photo you're working on. For example, a quick glance down there shows you the name of the collection or folder you're currently working in, how many photos are in that collection or folder, and how many photos you have selected out of that group (very handy when you can't see all the photos in the filmstrip at once). Also, if you click on a photo, it shows the photo's filename (super handy if you are working in the Compact Cell view where the filename would be hidden).

SCOTT KELBY

Step Two:
If that weren't enough, the filmstrip is really helpful when you're in the Develop module, because if you click just about anywhere in that info bar (as long as you don't click in the Filters section on the right) a pop-up menu appears with the 12 most recent collections, folders, or results of a search you've used. To bring up those photos, just choose them from the list. You can also choose all three of your Library panel choices from here as well (you can use the Forward and Back Arrow buttons at the far left to toggle through these 12 recent groups of photos). Lastly, if you do need to jump to the Grid view, just click the four-square Grid icon on the far left.

Renaming Photos Already on Your Computer

So, you've already learned how to rename photos as they're imported from your camera's memory card, but if the photos are already on your computer (where your File Handling choice would be Import Photos at Their Current Location) there is no file naming section, or pop-up menu, or anything—it leaves the current filenames on the photos untouched. However, once they're in Photoshop Lightroom, you can (and should) rename them. Here's how:

Step One:
Go to a folder or collection of photos that you imported into Photoshop Lightroom that were already on your computer (in other words, you didn't just import them from a memory card straight into Lightroom). In our example, these photos are in a collection, and if you look at their names you'll see the generic names assigned by the digital camera, which are really no help at all (they're named _DSC0038.NEF, _DSC0039.NEF, and so on). Besides the fact they're not terribly descriptive names, before long you're going to have lots of photos with these same exact names, because digital cameras only have a limited number of naming options. So, press Command-A (PC: Ctrl-A) to select all of the photos in this collection.

Step Two:
To rename these photos, go under the Library menu and choose Rename Photos, as shown here, or press F2 on your keyboard.

Rename 10 Photos

File Naming: Year, Month, Type in Name, Auto Nbr

Custom Text: SantaFe   Start Number: 32

Example: 0607_SantaFe_032   Cancel   OK

Step Three:

When the Rename Photos dialog appears (shown here), you can choose one of the built-in naming presets from the File Naming pop-up menu. For example, there's one called Custom Name – Sequence which lets you type in any name you want, then it automatically adds a sequential number after that name. If you created your own custom File Naming preset (you can find out how to do that in Chapter 1), you can choose that preset from the pop-up menu instead. In our example, I chose the preset I created back in that Chapter 1 tutorial, which starts with the last two digits of the year the photo was taken, then the month, then the name you type in the Custom Text field (in this case, SantaFe), and a sequential number (in this case, I want it to start numbering at 32).

Step Four:

Now just click OK, and almost instantly all your photos are renamed with your new names that make sense. For example, now instead of the first photo shown here being named "_DSC0040.NEF," it's named "0607_SantaFe_035." The new name tells me at a glance the photo was taken in 2006 (06), in the month of July (07), the photos are of Santa Fe, and this photo is the 35th photo of that shoot. This whole process takes just seconds, but makes a big difference when you're searching for photos—not only here in Lightroom, but especially outside of Lightroom, in folders, in emails, etc., plus it's easier for clients to find photos you've sent them for approval.

Moving Photos and How to Use Folders

If you quit Photoshop Lightroom and looked inside the Pictures folder on your computer (or My Pictures folder on a PC), you'd see all the folders containing your photos, right? Well, you don't have to quit Lightroom, because there's a Folders panel right in the Library module which shows the hierarchical structure of your Pictures folder (actually, in it you only see the folders of photos you imported into Lightroom). This is really handy because not only are you one click away from these photos, you can move photos from folder to folder, rename folders, and even create new ones.

Step One:
Go to the Library module, and go to the Folders panel found in the left side Panels area (shown here). What you're seeing here are all the folders of photos that Photoshop Lightroom is managing (in other words, these are the folders you imported from memory cards or photos that were already on your computer). Anytime you see one of those "flippy triangles" you can click directly on it to reveal the subfolders inside. (*Note:* These are officially called "disclosure triangles," but the only people who actually use that term are…well…let's just say they probably didn't have a date for the prom.)

Step Two:
One of the things this Folders panel is very handy for is moving photos from one folder to another. When you move a photo in this panel, you're physically taking the photo from one folder on your computer, and moving it to another folder (just as if you were moving files between two folders on your computer outside of Lightroom). Here's how it's done: First, click on a folder to display the photos in that folder. Then, click-and-drag any photo and drop it on the folder where you now want it to appear (as shown here, where I'm dragging a photo from my Round 1 folder into my High Res Images folder).

Moving a Photo on Disk

This will cause the photo file(s) to be moved. If you are moving from one volume/partition to another, this may take a while. If you proceed, neither this move nor any change you've made prior to this can be undone.

☐ Don't show again   (Cancel)   (Move)

Step Three:

Because you're actually moving the real file here, you get a "Hey, you're about to move the real file" warning from Lightroom. The warning sounds scarier than it is—especially the "neither this move nor any change you've made prior to this can be undone" part. What that means is, if you move this file from the Round 1 folder to the High Res Images folder, you can't just press Command-Z (PC: Ctrl-Z) to instantly Undo it if you change your mind. That's true, but saying it *can't* be undone isn't. You can undo the move by simply clicking on the High Res Images folder, finding the photo you just moved, and dragging it right back to the Round 1 folder. So, I guess what I'm saying is it's okay to click the Move button (as shown here).

Step Four:

Once the big move has been made, if you click on the High Res Images folder to see what's inside, you'll see the photo you just moved over there in the Grid view (as shown here). So, it's pretty much just moving a file from one folder on your computer to another. In fact, it's exactly like moving a file from one folder to another—but at least here in the Folders panel, it displays how many photos are in a folder over to the right of the folder's name. For example, it originally showed four photos in my High Res Images folder, but once I dragged this other photo in there, it immediately updated to show that it now had five photos, so at least I know I dragged it into the right folder.

SCOTT KELBY

Continued

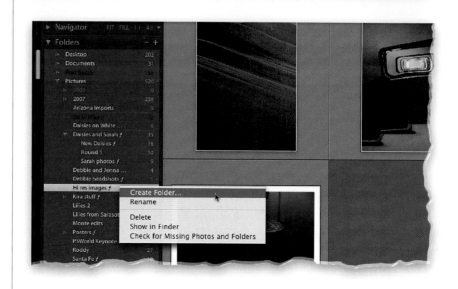

Step Five:

If you Control-click (PC: Right-click) on a folder, a contextual menu appears which lets you create a new subfolder inside that folder (just like you could outside of Lightroom), and lets you rename the folder. This menu also contains a Delete command, but this is where the Folders panel differs from your computer's operating system. On your computer, if you delete a folder, it goes straight into the Trash (PC: Recycle Bin). But in Lightroom, choosing Delete means this folder (and the photos inside it) will no longer be managed by Lightroom, and the folder will be removed from the Folders panel. However, this folder (and the photos inside it) will still be there in your Pictures (PC: My Pictures) folder (when you choose Delete, you'll get a warning dialog telling you just that).

Step Six:

Here's a close-up of my Folders panel. Starting at the top: I've imported 202 photos that were on my Desktop, 31 photos from my Documents folder, and 133 photos from an external hard drive named Free Space, but the majority of my photos managed by Lightroom are in my Pictures folder, and since the flippy triangle is expanded, you can see all the subfolders of photos inside my Pictures folder. However, you'll notice in this panel that my Free Space folder appears in red, as does a folder called Calla Lilies. That's Lightroom's way of letting me know that it can't find the original photos in these two folders. You can choose Check for Missing Photos and Folders from the contextual menu mentioned in Step Five, which basically refreshes your Folders list, and if it finds missing photos, it relinks them for you.

Note: The file structure you see here stinks. The right way is to have everything inside one main folder (the Pictures or My Pictures folder), and ideally inside of that you'd have subfolders for the shoots from each year. There should be no photos referenced directly to the Desktop or Documents folder (like you see here). So, how did mine get this way? I'm lame. Actually, it's more involved than that (meaning: I'm really lame). What you're seeing here is Lightroom running on my laptop computer—the one I use when I'm writing books, which has never been, nor sadly will ever be, very organized. For my photography work, I have a separate dedicated desktop system (no email, no writing stuff—it's just strictly for photography). On that machine, I started from scratch with Lightroom and set up the file structure properly from the start, and managing thousands of photos there is infinitely easier than managing just a few hundred here on my laptop, where chaos clearly reigns!

SCOTT KELBY

Step Seven:

The reason the Free Space folder appears in red is because Free Space is an external hard drive. When this disk isn't connected to my laptop, Lightroom can't find the original photos, but if I connect this external hard drive to my laptop, then click on the Free Space folder, it instantly reconnects the photos, and once they're found, it no longer appears in red (as shown here). Now, the Calla Lilies folder is a different situation. I actually did delete that folder from my laptop's Pictures folder (not from within Lightroom), so although those photos are actually no longer on my computer, Lightroom doesn't know that (so I would need to manually delete this folder).

Step Eight:

One more thing: Remember those daisies on a white background I imported in Chapter 1? Well, there were six of them. If I go onto my computer and drag five new photos into that same folder (not in Lightroom—right on my computer straight into that folder), Lightroom doesn't automatically detect that I added new photos to that folder. If you want Lightroom to manage these new photos, you'll need to click Import and re-import the whole folder of photos. It won't overwrite or alter the photos in that folder that are already being managed by Lightroom, it will just add the new ones in. Now, if you move files within the Folders panel, those get updated immediately—it's just when you add photos to a folder outside of Lightroom that you need to re-import like this. Also, once your photos are in Lightroom, you're better off only moving them within Lightroom's Folders panel, not outside.

Working with Multiple Libraries

When you launch Photoshop Lightroom for the very first time, it creates a main library for you (a database that keeps track of all the photos you import into Lightroom), and by default it stores this library in your Pictures folder on a Mac or My Pictures folder on a PC. But besides that one library, you can actually create additional libraries, and then choose which one you want to work on. For example, if you wanted to have one library for your family photos, and another library for your client projects—no problem, and switching between them is a breeze.

Step One:
Here in the Library module, I'm working with my main library (which is the one Photoshop Lightroom created when I first installed it), and it's the library I use for of all my work-related photography. If I want to create a new library (in this case, a separate library for my family photos), the first step is to quit Lightroom (press Command-Q on a Mac or Ctrl-Q on a PC).

Step Two:
Now press-and-hold the Option (PC: Ctrl) key, then launch Lightroom again. Holding the Option key during launch brings up the Adobe Photoshop Lightroom – Select Database dialog (shown here). The pop-up menu shows you the current database (library) you've been using. To create a second library, click on the Create New Database button (as shown here).

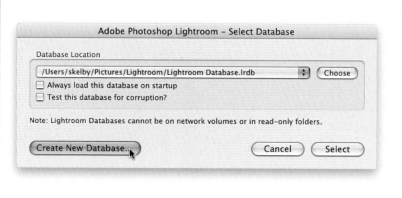

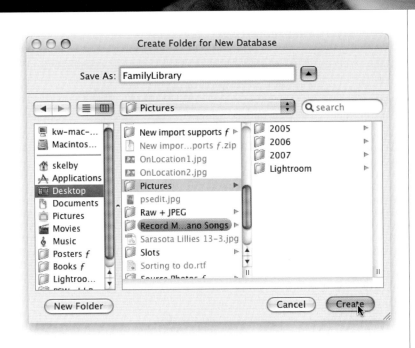

Step Three:
This brings up a Save As (PC: Browse for Folder) dialog, asking where you want to store this new library (it automatically creates a folder at this new location, because a new library consists of more than just a single database file—there are some other support folders and documents that must be created as well, so this folder keeps them all together). When you find the location for your second library, give it a name (I named mine "FamilyLibrary"), then click the Create (PC: OK) button (as shown here).

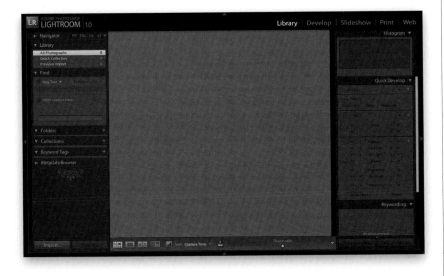

Step Four:
A brand-new, totally empty Lightroom library appears, and there are no photos in this new library whatsoever (as seen here). So, to populate your new library, click on the Import button in the lower-left corner and find some photos you want to import.

Continued

Step Five:

Here's my family library after just a few minutes of importing photos. Here's a tip that will help you instantly know which library you're working with: create a custom Identity Plate to replace the Adobe Photoshop Lightroom logo in the top-left corner and change the font for the Module Picker to match. That way you'll have a visual cue so you'll know instantly which database you're working with.
To do this, go under the Lightroom menu (PC: Edit menu) and choose Identity Plate Setup. When the Identity Plate Editor appears (shown here in the inset), highlight the text, type in your own text, and choose a font (I chose Bickham Script Pro, which comes with the Adobe Creative Suite package), and I chose the same font and size for the Module Picker text as well.

SCOTT KELBY AND KALEBRA KELBY

Step Six:

Lastly, turn on the checkbox for Enable Identity Plate (at the top left of the Identity Plate Editor), and then click OK. Now you'll see your new Identity Plate has replaced the standard Adobe Photoshop Lightroom logo, and the Module Picker fonts now match, as well. (*Note:* Identity Plates are unique to each library, so any Identity Plates you create while this library is open will be saved only with this library.)

Adobe Photoshop Lightroom – Select Database

Database Location

✓ /Users/skelby/Desktop/Pictures/FamilyLibrary/Lightroom Database.lrdb   Choose
  /Users/skelby/Pictures/Lightroom/Lightroom Database.lrdb

☐ Test this database for corruption?

Note: Lightroom Databases cannot be on network volumes or in read-only folders.

Create New Database...   Cancel   Select

Step Seven:
Now, go ahead and quit Lightroom, then hold the Option (PC: Ctrl) key and relaunch Lightroom. This brings up the Adobe Photoshop Lightroom – Select Database dialog again, but now in the Database Location pop-up menu, both of your libraries are listed (as shown here). Choose your original database (mine is my work database), and then click the Select button. (*Note:* Although we're only working with two library databases here, you can have as many libraries as you have drive space.)

TIP: When you launch Lightroom, if you'd like to always choose which library database to work with for that session, go to Lightroom's General Preferences, and in the Default Library section choose Prompt Me When Starting Lightroom from the first pop-up menu.

Step Eight:
Here's my work library, and now to make it visually obvious which Library database I'm working with, I added a custom Identity Plate here as well—this time with the logo of my association.

Note: If you want to open a Library database you created, but it doesn't appear in the Database Location pop-up menu (seen in Step Seven), then you can click the Choose button that appears to the right of that pop-up menu, and locate the database using the standard Open dialog.

DAVE MOSER

How to Automatically Back Up Your Database

Photoshop Lightroom's database tracks all the metadata you've embedded into your photos, plus all your tonal edits, and your keywords, and collections, and well... just about everything but the pixels themselves. That's part of the secret behind Lightroom's ability to do non-destructive editing—the edits aren't really applied to your actual photos, they're stored in a sophisticated database, and your edits are only actually applied to your photo when you export it outside of Lightroom. That's why backing up this database regularly is an absolute must.

Step One:

Start by opening Photoshop Lightroom's Preferences by going under the Lightroom menu (the Edit menu on a PC), and choosing Preferences (as shown here).

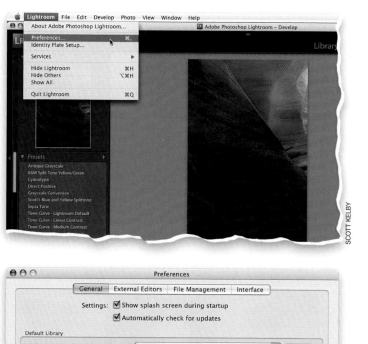

SCOTT KELBY

Step Two:

When the Preferences dialog appears, click on the General tab up top (shown highlighted here), and at the bottom of the Default Library section, you'll see the Automatically Back Up Library pop-up menu. To turn on this automatic feature, choose how often you want to have Lightroom perform a backup of the library database from the pop-up menu. If you use Lightroom daily, you might want to back up Lightroom's database once a day (as shown here), so if for some reason the database should become corrupt, you'd only lose a maximum of one day's editing.

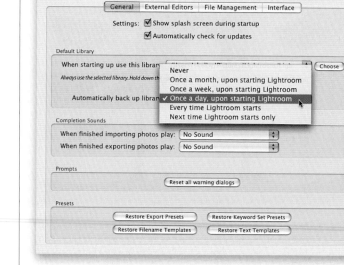

Step Three:

The next time you launch Lightroom, a reminder dialog will appear asking if you want to back up your library database (my answer would be yes, so I would click the Backup button, as shown here). By default, these database backups are stored in subfolders inside a Backups folder, which lives inside your Lightroom folder, which by default resides in your Pictures folder (on a Mac) or My Pictures folder (on a PC). However, I recommend saving your backups to a safer location, like an external hard drive, because having both your working database and its backup on the same hard drive is just too risky (everybody knows someone who's had a fatal hard drive crash). But if your backups are stored on an external drive, and your computer's hard drive crashes and burns, you have a safe, untouched backup copy to get you back up and running. So, go ahead and click on the Choose button, then select a folder to back up to on an external drive.

Step Four:

When you click the Backup button, if you had the Test This Database for Corruption checkbox turned on, it will ask you basically, "Are you sure you want to do this?" That's because the testing can take quite a while, and that's why I do this test very, very rarely. The actual backing up of your database happens very quickly, and you can find your backup files in the Backups folder (which hopefully is on an external drive). Should your working database become corrupted one day (or if your computer is lost, stolen, or the hard drive dies), you can quickly restore the database using your latest backup (the backup subfolders are named by date and time, making it easy to find the latest backup).

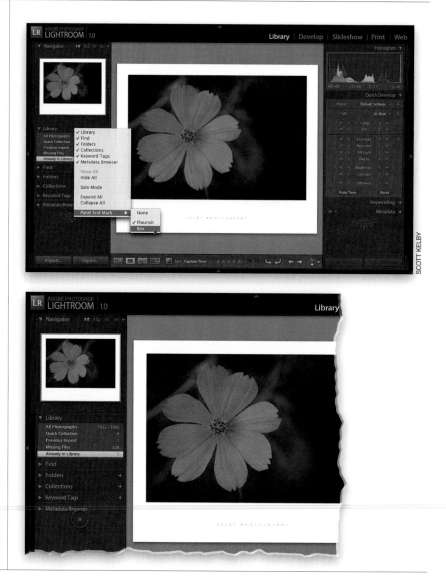

Changing Those Ornaments Below the Last Panel

Okay, technically they're not called ornaments, they're called panel end marks, and they're there to give you the visual cue that you've reached the bottom panel on that side (sort of a visual way of saying "Hey, this is the last panel!"). So, they added that ornamental looking thingy, that to me feels totally out of place in Photoshop Lightroom's high-tech black interface. The first time I saw that ornament, I said "Please tell me there's some way to change that!" Luckily, there is—you can use the other panel end mark (hey, it's actually better) or download some from the Web. Here's how:

Step One:
To change the panel end marks (if you change one, they all change), you scroll down until you actually see the Flourish end mark (that's its official name. Now seriously, how could something with the name Flourish end up in a high-tech black interface? I'll bet once you've quit Photoshop Lightroom for the day, the panels tease him unmercifully). Then you Control-click (PC: Right-click) directly on the Flourish and at the bottom of the contextual menu that appears, there's a submenu for Panel End Mark, and you can choose None (my favorite) for no end marks, Flourish (for the default antique ornament), or Box (shown selected here).

Step Two:
You can imagine what the None option looks like, you've seen the Flourish option, so here's what the Box end mark looks like (remember, when you change one—it changes them all). If you're not crazy about these choices, then visit Lightroom-Extra.com, click on their Download link at the top, and you'll find more than 30 free end marks you can download. Once downloaded, it's as easy as putting them in a folder and restarting Lightroom (the site has instructions on which folder they go in, for both Macs and Windows PCs).

Quick Develop
making minor adjustments

I know we'd like to think that every shot we take is worthy of the same level of careful color correction and individual selective sharpening, but the sad reality is some of our photos just don't require it. Not every photo we take is destined to hang in some famous gallery. Some photos, like those taken for insurance claim purposes after a fender bender in your car, will only wind up being shown in some of the smaller galleries, fetching only a few hundred dollars—perhaps a thousand on rare occasion—but they have little chance of competing with your more serious pieces. It's those instances where you have to decide, "Do I really need to go into the Develop module and process the living daylights out of this puppy or can I just click a few buttons here in the Library module's

Quick Develop panel and be done with it?" It's an age-old question, but you can make the decision easier if you take the time to ask yourself a few questions beforehand. First, ask yourself this, "When this shot of my dented fender is displayed, will it be exposed to high ultraviolet light content, and will that affect its overall sale price?" If the answer is "No," then you can safely correct this photo using the Library module's Quick Develop panel. However, if the answer is "Yes," then in order to maintain consistent color rendition you need to give careful consideration to the spill and angle of the fill lights in the gallery and whether using an undimmed, low-voltage 20W dichroic lamp will minimize any potential fluctuation in the color temperature. By the way, I have no idea what any of that means.

Doing Quick Fixes to Photos Right within the Library Module

Photoshop Lightroom has two places where you can adjust the exposure, brightness, white balance, etc.—in the Library module using the Quick Develop panel, and in the Develop module using the Basic panel and a whole bunch of other panels. However, Quick Develop is for more than just quick fixes, as it has all but one of the features of Develop's most important panel: the Basic panel. So what's the big difference between the two? Develop's panel uses sliders and Quick Develop's uses buttons, so the controls aren't as precise, but they're still very powerful (as you're about to see).

Step One:

I imported some studio shots of model Susan Hill, which I took for another one of my books called *The iPod Book* (from Peachpit Press). I double-clicked on one of the photos so I could see it larger (and all by itself) in the Loupe view. I also hid the left side Panels area and the filmstrip at the bottom, so I would have more space to view my photo with fewer distractions around it (as shown here). I'm going to make some simple edits to the photo using the Quick Develop panel, which appears in the right side Panels area of the Library module, right below the Histogram panel.

Step Two:

Here's a quick look at the Quick Develop panel: The top section (1) lets you choose any of the built-in presets for various adjustments (later in the book, you'll see how to create and add your own presets to this list). The next section down (2) gives you some control over how any cropping you use will be applied, and it's also where you choose to work in color or grayscale (black and white). The next section (3) is where you'll do your essential adjustments to the white balance (which is the color temperature of your photo), and then the bottom section (4) is for your main exposure controls and color saturation. If you don't see all the choices shown here, click on the down-facing double arrows along the right side of the Quick Develop panel to expand each section.

Step Three:

If you're squeamish about making your own adjustments, there is an Auto Tone button (shown circled here in red), which when clicked applies an automatic adjustment to just the Exposure, Brightness, Contrast, and Blacks settings (not the white balance, or any of the other tonal controls). Now, I have to be honest—I'm not a big fan of Auto Tone. To me, the changes either seem too subtle (like in the photo shown here) or too extreme (in many cases, it seems to overexpose the photo in my opinion), but go ahead and open a few images, click the Auto Tone button, and see what you think. If you don't like it, you can press Command-Z (PC: Ctrl-Z) to Undo your Auto Toning.

TIP: Never be afraid to try an adjustment in Quick Develop, because you can always undo all the changes you made in any one control by just double-clicking directly on the adjustment's name.

Continued

Step Four:

When editing photos, I always start by fixing the problem that bothers me the most. In this case, since I took the shot, I know that the background is supposed to be light gray, but it looks real bluish to me, and that's because the white balance wasn't set properly in my camera. Luckily, fixing it is easy. First, there's a WB pop-up menu at the top of the Quick Develop panel with white balance settings that correspond with the white balance settings in your camera. So, if you should have set the white balance to Flash, you can do it now (so…do it now—choose Flash from the WB pop-up menu, as shown here). Look how much warmer the photo looks—the background isn't nearly as blue (in fact, it's almost gray), and her skin tone is much warmer. However, it might be a little too warm, so try some of the other white balance presets.

Step Five:

When it comes to using those white balance presets, here's something that might help. There are basically two types of presets: ones that make your photo's color temperature warmer, and ones that make it cooler. For example, Daylight generally makes things warmer. Cloudy, even warmer, and Shade is the warmest of all. Tungsten (which is what you'd choose in your camera if you were shooting in regular indoor lighting) makes things cooler (bluer), and Fluorescent (for shooting under typical office lighting) makes things cooler (and bluer) yet. Now, we tried Flash, but it was a bit too warm. So, try the Auto WB preset. For this particular photo, it seems to work best (as shown here).

Step Six:

Now, if you're happy with the white balance of your photo, you're set and you can move on to the next set of adjustments. However, if you're not thrilled with any of the presets, then just use them as a starting place. For example, I think for this photo the Auto setting was the best choice of the presets, but it makes her skin a little bit cooler. So, for this photo, use the Auto WB preset as a starting place, and then go to the Temp adjustment, and click the right single arrow button once to warm up the white balance just a little bit. Each time you click the right single arrow button, it warms the white balance (color temperature) of your photo some more. Each click of the left single arrow button will cool it more. So, what are the double arrow buttons for? They just make the adjustments in larger increments, so if you need a photo much warmer, click the right double arrow button to get there faster.

Step Seven:

Before we go on, if you totally mess up in this panel and want to start over from scratch, just click the Reset button at the bottom-right corner of the Quick Develop panel (it's circled in red here). Now, the other tonal controls in this panel work the same way, (meaning you click the right single arrow buttons to increase their effects, left single arrow buttons to decrease, and the double arrows to move each way in larger increments). Perhaps the most essential of these adjustments is Exposure, which controls the brightness of your photo (it's kind of like the highlight slider in Adobe Photoshop's Levels dialog). To make your overall photo brighter, click the right arrow(s), or to darken the exposure, use the left arrow(s). In our example, I clicked the right single arrow button twice to brighten the overall photo.

Continued

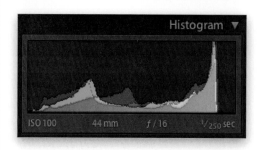

Step Eight:

Now, how did I determine that I should increase the exposure? Well, the photo looked a little dark to me (my first clue), and a quick look up at the Histogram panel (at the top of the right side Panels area) confirmed that. See that gap on the right, where the graph just stops before it reaches the right side? This gap tells me that I can increase the highlights in the photo (which I control by increasing my Exposure setting) a little bit more without losing detail in the highlights of my photo. Ideally, your graph would extend from end to end, with no large gaps. That way, you get the maximum range from your photo. You don't want the graph stacked up against the right side or you'll be losing detail in the highlights, or stacked up on the left side either, where you'll lose detail in the shadow areas.

Step Nine:

When I increased that Exposure setting back in Step Seven, I might have gone a bit too far (look at the histogram back there—it's a little stacked up on the right side, which means we're probably losing some highlight details in the brightest parts of our photo). Now, your first inclination might be to lower the Exposure setting, right? Well, what's bad about that is it affects the overall brightness—not just the brightest highlights. So now the photo's going to be too dark again, right? Well, that's why you're going to *love* the adjustment right under Exposure. It's called Recovery in the Quick Develop panel, but its full name is Highlight Recovery. Increasing the Recovery amount brings back (recovers) just those brightest of highlights, without having to lower the overall exposure. This rocks! So, click the right double arrow two or three times until the brightest highlights look good to you (as shown here).

Step Ten:

Let's now jump down to the Blacks control. This is really the shadows control, and increasing the Blacks amount increases the darkest areas of your photo, which tends to increase the contrast of your photo (which I like). Try clicking the Blacks right double arrow two times so the shadow areas look nice and rich. If you look at the histogram now, you'll see some of the colors are just beginning to stack up on the left, so that's about as far as we can go without losing some detail in the shadow areas of our photo. I don't mind losing a little detail in the dark shadows in her hair next to her left eye, and dark shadow areas that don't really have a lot of detail to begin with, but beyond that I start to get concerned.

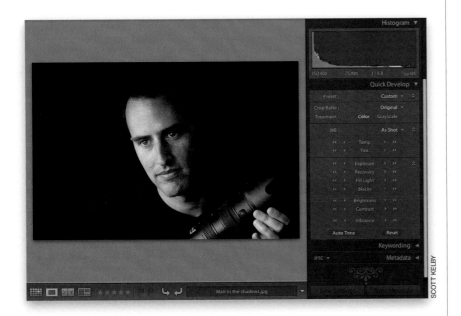

Step Eleven:

Another control here is the Fill Light control. Although you probably won't need this adjustment as much as the others (I almost always adjust the white balance [WB], Exposure, Recovery, and Blacks settings for every photo), you'd only use the Fill Light control to open up really dark shadow areas in your photo (somewhat similar to what the Shadows controls do in Photoshop's Shadow/Highlight adjustment). This photo we've been working on doesn't need this Fill Light fix, so I'm going to temporarily switch to this shot I took of my buddy (and *Adobe® Photoshop® TV* co-host) Matt Kloskowski. The shadows on his face and shirt, and part of the lens, are so dark that they're covering up lots of important detail. This is when I would leap for the Fill Light control (and I rarely leap).

SCOTT KELBY

Continued

Step Twelve:

So, simply go the Fill Light control and click a few times on the right double arrow. As you do, you'll see the shadow areas open right up, as if we had positioned a fill light (or at the very least, a reflector) on him to open up those shadows. I had to click four times on that right double arrow to get to the image you see here. I probably could have gone another click, but I didn't want to lose the drama of the light. Look at how the shadows on the right side of his face have opened up, how his blue shirt now has detail (and you can even tell it's blue!), and look at how the lens he's holding (a Nikon 70–200mm f/2.8, just in case you care) has detail as well. It's amazing what just a few clicks of this Fill Light control can do when you have a photo that needs it.

Step Thirteen:

Another control that's important in the right circumstance is Vibrance. I think of Vibrance as a smarter version of a standard Saturation control (most Saturation controls boost all the colors in your photo across the board). However, Vibrance kicks Saturation's butt because it boosts the less vibrant colors in your photo more than the colors that are already vibrant. Plus, it's especially sensitive to skin tones and does its best not to make them too red or yellow. This enables you to boost the saturation of your color without making your photo look like a cartoon. Each time you click the right arrow(s), it adds more color vibrance (and vice versa with the left arrow[s]). So, back to our photo of Susan. We'll click the Vibrance right double arrow twice to boost the colors a bit.

Step Fourteen:

The final two tonal controls in this section are Brightness (which controls the midtones in your photo, kind of like the midtones slider in Photoshop's Levels dialog) and Contrast. Increasing the Contrast setting does just that—it increases the contrast in your photo by making the shadows darker and the highlights brighter. Try it by clicking on the Contrast right double arrow twice (as shown here, where the photo looks way too contrasty. Well, for me anyway). I generally don't use this control all that much unless I'm making a black-and-white (grayscale) photo, because increasing the exposure and blacks usually adds enough contrast to color photos. The past two steps have kind of trashed this photo a bit, so I'm going to press Command-Z (PC: Ctrl-Z) a few times until I undo the contrast completely, and one of the vibrance adjustments (as seen in the next step).

TIP: Another way I use the Quick Develop panel is to select a bunch of questionable photos and quickly find out if they're worth keeping. If they're way underexposed, overexposed, dark, have a glaring color cast, etc., with just a couple of clicks in the Quick Develop panel, I can see whether I'll be able to save them later in the Develop module, or if I need to go ahead and delete them now.

Continued

Step Fifteen:

To recap: We used the white balance Auto preset to get our white balance "in the ballpark," then we warmed up the white balance by clicking the right Temp (color temperature) single arrow once. Next, we increased the exposure a bit, and then used Recovery to pull back the very brightest highlights. Lastly, we increased the blacks a decent amount to add more contrast, and we did it all with just a few clicks. Now, if you need more tonal editing power, you can switch to the Develop module and all the changes you made here would be applied to the Basic panel in the Develop module, which is very handy. There are still two things we haven't covered yet—one is cropping. You can have your photo automatically cropped to different preset ratios (full cropping capability is in the Develop module). You just choose a preset ratio from the Crop Ratio pop-up menu near the top of the Quick Develop panel (as shown here, where I chose 8x10). See how much tighter the full photo is now cropped?

Step Sixteen:

The last thing is the grayscale conversion. Matt makes a better black-and-white photo than Susan, so we'll use him. This is pretty much a no-brainer—click on the word Grayscale in the Treatment section at the top of the Quick Develop panel, and well...there ya have it. Now, I did make a minor tonal adjustment here, but it only took three clicks in all. I clicked once on the Exposure right single arrow to make the highlights brighter, and then I clicked twice on the Contrast right double arrow to increase the contrast (I like really contrasty black-and-white images). That's it. Luckily, there's a lot more on black and white in the Develop chapter, but for three clicks, that ain't too bad.

How to Apply that Same Fix to a Bunch of Other Photos

Okay, so we've now edited one photo using the Quick Develop panel. Since the other photos in this shoot were all shot in similar light, we can take the edits we just applied to that one photo, and apply them to the all the rest of these photos simultaneously. This automates our editing process, and speeds up our workflow big time. Plus, using this technique, we could even make some edits to a photo here, jump over to the Develop module to apply more detailed edits, then jump back here and instantly apply the changes we made in both modules to as many photos as we want. This just rocks!

SCOTT KELBY

Step One:

So, we want to take the same adjustments we just made to one photo and apply them to a bunch of similar photos. You start by making sure you've clicked on the photo you adjusted (as shown here). As you can see, the other photos are darker, and have the bluish background, rather than the gray background that should be there. Plus, the cropping is different as well (remember, we used that preset Crop Ratio in Quick Develop).

Step Two:

Now, select any other photos you want to have the same adjustments by Command-clicking (PC: Ctrl-clicking) on them. In our case here, I wanted to apply those changes to every photo in this folder, so after clicking on the adjusted photo, I pressed Command-A (PC: Ctrl-A) to Select All. (By the way, because I clicked on our adjusted photo first, it has a lighter highlight around it, letting us know that it is the "most selected" photo. In other words, that's the one the adjustments will be drawn from.) Now, click on the Sync Settings button at the bottom-left corner of the right side Panels area (it's circled here in red).

Continued

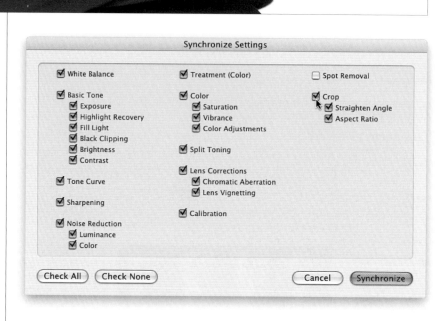

Step Three:

This brings up the Synchronize Settings dialog (shown here). This is where you get to choose which of the adjustments you applied to the first photo will get applied to your other selected photos. (*Note:* If some of the checkboxes here sound unfamiliar, it's because those live in the Develop module, instead of in the Library's Quick Develop panel. You can just ignore those here.) If you want to apply just some of the changes you made, first click the Check None button (so all the checkboxes are turned off), then only turn on the checkboxes for the adjustments you want applied. In our case, we can leave everything on, but the Crop Ratio adjustment we did is off by default, so you'll have to turn on the Crop checkbox.

Step Four:

Now you can click the Synchronize button in the bottom-right corner of the dialog, and all the changes you turned on the checkboxes for will be applied to your selected photos, as shown here where the photos are now color corrected and tightly cropped. (*Note:* The speed at which these changes are applied depends on how many photos you have and how large they are.) This method gives you total control over exactly which edits you applied to the first photo get transferred to the rest of the selected photos. However, if you know that you want the exact same edits you applied to the first photo applied to a bunch of other photos, there's a faster way: First, click on the photo you want to edit, then, in either the grid or filmstrip, select all the other photos you want to have the exact same edits. This puts you in Auto Sync mode, and now any changes you make to that first photo (the "most selected" photo) will automatically be applied to all your other selected photos. Sweet!

Saving Your "Quick Developed" Photos as JPEGs

Even though at this point you've just used the Quick Develop panel to apply some quick edits to your photos in the Library module, those quick edits might have been enough, and now you're ready to save your files as JPEGs (or TIFFs, or PSDs, etc.). Near the end of the next chapter (on the Develop module, where you go to do some serious editing), I've got an in-depth tutorial on exporting your photos in different formats, but for now I'm just going to give you a quick step-by-step on saving a JPEG. Again, for more on this topic, turn to the end of the next chapter.

SCOTT KELBY

Step One:

Okay, so here's a photo we've adjusted in Photoshop Lightroom using the Quick Develop panel, and now we just want to quickly save it as a JPEG—no fancy export stuff, you just want a simple JPEG saved to your desktop, so you can email it to a friend, relative, etc. (remember, the full tutorial on exporting photos appears at the end of the next chapter—this is the "quickie" version for now). You start by clicking on the Export button (as shown here), or you can use the keyboard short-cut Command-Shift-E (PC: Ctrl-Shift-E).

Continued

Step Two:

This brings up the Export dialog (seen here). For now, ignore the Preset pop-up menu at the top of the dialog, and instead go to the next section down, where you choose where to save your JPEG photo. In our case, choose your desktop by clicking on the Choose button (as shown here), and when the Save (PC: Browse for Folder) dialog appears choose your desktop as the destination. Below that is a File Naming section with a Template pop-up menu, but since we're just saving one photo we don't have to worry about that (it's so easy to rename one photo after the fact, once it's exported to your desktop, right?).

Step Three:

So, we ignore the file naming thing for now, but in the Image Settings section of the dialog, you should choose a color space for your photo from the pop-up menu. If you took the shots in JPEG or TIFF format, I recommend choosing the same color space as your digital camera. Most digital cameras are set to sRGB, so if you haven't changed your camera's color space, then choose sRGB. However, if you've read any of my books on Photoshop for digital photographers, you've probably changed your camera's (and Photoshop's) color space to Adobe RGB (1998), so for consistency, choose it. If you shot the photo in RAW format, then you can keep the photo in ProPhoto RGB (the default).

Step Four:
If you want to shrink the file's physical dimensions (so it's smaller for emailing), then turn on the Constrain Maximum Size checkbox and type in the size you want. Leave the resolution as is, and in the Post-Processing section, choose Do Nothing from the After Export pop-up menu (as shown here). Then click the Export button, and in a few moments, your JPEG photo will be waiting there on your desktop (as shown here). You can export multiple photos the same way: from the Library module's Grid view, just Command-click (PC: Ctrl-click) on the photos you want to export as JPEGs, then start back at Step One. *Note:* The choices you make in the Export dialog will apply to all your selected photos. You might want to put all these photos in a folder (so they're not scattered all over your desktop). If that's the case, turn on the Put in Subfolder checkbox, give your new folder a name, and your JPEGs will be saved in there.

Exposure: 1/8   Focal Length: 75mm   Aperture Value: ƒ/5.0

Editing Essentials
how to develop your photos

Everything we have done up to this point— every click of a button, every slide of a slider, every drag of a dragster, has all been leading up to this one single moment. The moment when you leave the relative safety and comfort of the Library module and venture into a wild, untamed territory that many seek but only few survive. This, my friends, is the Develop module—a scary and intimidating place with more complicated-looking buttons, checkboxes, and sliders than the Space Shuttle and a 747 combined. Now, if you're thinking that all this looks too technical and advanced for you, you're right. Nobody understands this module. I don't know what

it does. Adobe doesn't know. I think a lot of the sliders are just put there for looks, and moving them doesn't actually affect anything in the photo whatsoever. For example, try moving the Deflatulator slider all the way to the right. I'm not sure it really does anything, but it sure took the wind out of me. Okay, that was pretty lame, but wait—I have more. Open an image shot in RAW format, set your exposure and shadows, then try dragging the Cutlery Sharpening Amount to 75%. I'll bet your image still looks dull, and it just doesn't cut it. Are you getting any of these puns? I hope you are, because I swear, they're cracking me up.

Setting Your White Balance in the Develop Module

You take a photo into the Develop module when you've got some serious adjusting to do, so don't be fooled by the fact that the top panel in the right side Panels area is named "Basic." Those "Basic" controls are more advanced than the controls found in Adobe Photoshop CS2/CS3's acclaimed Camera Raw plug-in, so I vote that they be renamed "Essentials" or "Critical," because the term Basic is a bit misleading. We're going to start with perhaps the most essential Develop module setting: white balance.

Step One:

Before you dive into this chapter, make darn sure you read the previous chapter (Quick Develop), because many of the tools you're going to use here were explained in detail there. If you 100% for sure read that chapter, then charge ahead! Go to Photoshop Lightroom's Library module and click on a photo you want to do some serious adjusting to, then click on the word Develop at the top right of the interface, or better yet just press the letter D on your keyboard, to jump over into the Develop module. (By the way, the model shown here is Debbie Stephenson, NAPP's seminar tour team leader, and I took this shot live onstage during the Los Angeles leg of my Photoshop Power Tour seminar.)

Step Two:

Like the Quick Develop panel, the Basic panel lets you set the white balance using either the WB pop-up menu or by adjusting the Temp and Tint sliders, shown circled here. If you forget which way to drag to make a photo warmer or cooler, look at the color bar inside the slider itself for a visual clue. Both sliders show the color you'll get if you drag in either direction (if you wanted to warm the photo, you'd drag the Temp slider to the right toward yellow; to cool it, you'd drag left toward blue, as shown).

Step Three:

Just to see how it works, go ahead and drag the Temp slider to the right, and watch how the photo warms up. It works the same way in Quick Develop, but there if you forget which way to click, you're on your own. Now, let's reset the Temp slider to its original location by double-clicking directly on the slider control knob itself. By the way, this little "double-click to reset the slider" trick works for most of the adjustment sliders in the Develop module, so this is a really good tip to remember.

TIP: When you've got Auto Sync turned on in the Develop module, here's a way to give a bunch of selected photos in the Library module a custom white balance in just seconds. In the Library module, select the photo you want to edit, then select the others that need the same fix. Press W to take the first selected photo into the Develop module with the White Balance tool selected, so you can just click on a neutral gray area in your photo. Once you click, all the photos you selected will be updated with that custom white balance. Press G to return to the Library module's Grid view.

Step Four:

Okay, so the WB pop-up menu is used the same here as in Quick Develop, and the Temp and Tint sliders still adjust the color temperature, but the big advantage here in the Develop module is the White Balance Selector tool (it's that huge eyedropper that lives in the top-left corner of the Basic panel, as you can see in the previous step). To use it, you can just click on it and your cursor changes to that tool (as shown here).

TIP: You can also press the W key on your keyboard to instantly get the White Balance Selector tool.

Continued

Step Five:

As you move the White Balance Selector tool over your image, a pixel magnifier appears (as shown here) called the "Loupe" (named thus just to make things a little more confusing). This Loupe shows you a highly magnified view of the pixels your cursor is hovering over. It also displays the RGB readings of those pixels, measured from 0% (solid black) to 100% (solid white). So, to set your white balance with this tool, first you'd need to find a neutral area within your photo (ideally a light gray area). I usually try and find a light gray area where all three readouts (R, G, and B) are right around 60 to 65%. Chances are you won't be able to get all three readouts to be exactly the same number, but at least if they're close, you'll know you're in the ballpark.

Step Six:

Once you find a neutral light gray area, just click once (as shown here) and it sets an accurate white balance (more on this in a moment). Before we go on, in the toolbar below the center Preview area there are options for the White Balance Selector tool, but they only appear while you have the tool selected. First, you can change the level of magnification by clicking-and-dragging the Scale slider (shown circled here). Perhaps more importantly, you can make the Loupe (a.k.a. the annoying Loupe) go away by turning off a simple checkbox. Also, when you do click within your photo, it instantly returns the White Balance Selector tool to its home in the Basic panel. If you'd like the option of trying other neutral areas to see how they look without having to grab the tool again every single time, just turn off the Auto Dismiss checkbox. Then, when you're done, either return the tool to the Basic panel or click the Done button in the toolbar.

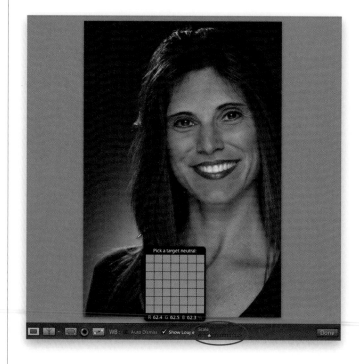

Step Seven:

Okay, now before you go clicking away, how would you like a live preview of how your white balance setting will affect your photo before you even click it? Well, get the White Balance Selector tool, move it over an area of your photo (here I'm hovering it over the left side of Debbie's hair), then take a look over at the Navigator panel at the top of the left side Panels area. You'll see a live white balance preview as you hover the tool over different parts of the image. That way, you can see if the area where you're thinking of clicking will actually make your photo look warmer or cooler. In the example shown here, you can see in the Navigator panel that the photo would look much cooler (bluer) if I were to click in her hair (which obviously isn't a light gray).

Step Eight:

Now, here's the thing about white balance: you can find a perfectly neutral light gray area, choose that to set your white balance, and you'll have an accurate white balance. But accurate doesn't necessarily look good. Your grays might be dead on, but your flesh tones might look dead awful. That's why many wedding and portrait photographers (who prefer that their subjects have a warm skin tone) use special lens accessories (like the ExpoDisc Digital White Balance Filter – Portrait) or intentionally warmer gray cards (called "warm cards") that leave your subject's skin with a warmer look. The bottom line is white balance is a creative decision made by you, the photographer, so if you use the White Balance Selector tool properly, and you think your subject looks too cool, then just drag the Temp slider slowly to the right a little bit until it looks right to you.

Continued

Step Nine:

When I'm setting the white balance using the White Balance Selector tool, I usually try clicking in a few different neutral areas just to see how they differ. Sometimes, clicking just a few pixels away from your first choice can give you a slightly cooler or warmer white balance. In the example shown here, I made three virtual copies of our photo, and clicked the White Balance Selector tool in slightly different places in each one, so I could compare the four versions side-by-side in Survey view and choose the one I like best. By the way, virtual copies are just that—they're not real copies of your photo (that would eat up too much hard drive space). Instead they're just virtual "metadata only" versions of your original photo, which are great for experimenting with different techniques (like different white balance settings) without ballooning the size of your photo library. If you like the adjustments you made to a virtual copy, you can choose to apply them to the real photo when you export it. Cool, eh?

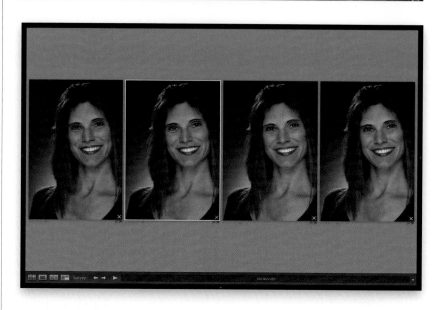

Step Ten:

To create a virtual copy of your real photo, just Control-click (PC: Right-click) on your photo, and choose Create Virtual Copy from the contextual menu that appears (as shown here). By the way, you can also do this in the Library's Grid view or in the filmstrip. Your virtual copy is automatically stacked with your real photo in the Library module's grid, so finding these virtual copies is easy. Plus, the Grid view and filmstrip thumbnails for virtual copies have a small curled page icon in the bottom-left corner (shown circled in red in the inset) to let you know you're not working on the real photo. You can create as many virtual copies as you'd like, because they don't add any file size to your photo library.

Step Eleven:

Don't ever hesitate to try different white balance settings, because you can always return to the original "as shot" white balance setting by either choosing As Shot from the WB pop-up menu (as shown here), or by double-clicking on the letters "WB" (shown circled here) which appear to the right of the White Balance Selector tool in the Basic panel. Of course, if you ever just want to start over, and return the photo to how it looked when you imported it, just click the Reset button at the bottom of the right side Panels area. By the way, this Reset button is always there while you're working in the Develop module, so anytime you want to start over just click on it and all your Develop module changes are undone.

Step Twelve:

The bottom line is this: white balance is a creative decision made by you, the photographer, so if you use the White Balance Selector tool and think your subject looks too cool, then just drag the Temp slider slowly to the right a little bit until it looks right to you. Okay, now let's set our white balance. Find a neutral gray area (I chose a light gray area of the background), and click once on that area. Although the photo looks "technically" accurate, in real life Debbie's skin is quite tan, so to match what she looks like in person, drag the Temp slider slowly to the right until the skin tone looks warmer (as shown). The most important thing is not that the white balance is accurate or that the RGB numbers add up. It's that your subject looks at least as good, if not better, in the final print as they do in person, and that's a call that only you can make. Now, on to the rest of the Basic panel (see, I told you the name "Basic" was misleading).

Making the Essential Adjustments

Now that your white balance is set, we can make some reasonable decisions about how the rest of the photo looks. We make these essential adjustments in the rest of the Basic panel (again, I think it should be named the Essentials panel. Don't get me started). Luckily, these adjustments are easy, they make sense, and Photoshop Lightroom even helps to keep you out of trouble while you're making these adjustments.

Step One:

Once you set the white balance (in the top section of the Basic panel, as you just learned in the previous tutorial), we move on to the middle section of the Basic panel, which controls the overall tonal range of your photo (that section is shown within a red rectangle here). Before we make any manual adjustments in this middle section, there is an automatic tonality adjustment feature (sometimes known as "the chicken's way out") that lets Photoshop Lightroom automatically adjust all the settings in this one section of the Basic panel to give you what it thinks is the best tonal correction (it sets the highlights, midtones, and shadows for you, but does not adjust the white balance). To use this feature, just click the Auto button (as I have done in the second capture here). Depending on the photo, this Auto button can work quite nicely. Other times it's…well…let's just say "less than optimal." My biggest problem with the Auto adjustment is that it generally increases the exposure to just below the point of losing detail in the highlights, which is good, but in a photo that is supposed to be dark and low key (like a dramatic portrait or a nighttime cityscape), it tends to make the photo way too bright. So, give the Auto button a try and if it works, great. If it doesn't, press Command-Z (PC: Ctrl-Z) to Undo it.

SCOTT KELBY

Step Two:

If you tried the Auto button method, go ahead and hit Reset (at the bottom of the right side Panels area), because now we're going on to my suggested method of adjusting the tonal range of your photo—using the tonal control sliders. The first slider in this section, Exposure (shown circled here), is probably the most important slider (maybe that's why it's first, eh?). Basically, it lets you set the white point for your image by controlling the highlights in your photo. Dragging the Exposure slider to the right increases the highlight exposure (as shown here, where the image is much brighter), and dragging to the left decreases the exposure. Again, you get a visual cue by looking at the sliders themselves—white is on the right side of the slider, which lets you know that dragging toward white makes this adjustment lighter, and black is on the left side, so dragging that way would make your exposure darker.

Step Three:

If you wanted to increase the overall brightness of your photo, you'd start by dragging the Exposure slider to the right. Easy enough. However, there is a concern, and that is "how far is too far?" In other words, at what point have you dragged to the right so far that you're actually losing detail in your highlights? Well, Lightroom gives you two types of visual warnings to keep you from blowing out your highlights (or "clipping" your highlights, as it's commonly called). If you press-and-hold the Option (PC: Alt) key before you start dragging the Exposure slider, your image preview turns black (as shown here).

Continued

Step Four:

Now, as you drag the Exposure slider to the right (increasing the exposure in the highlight areas), any colors that are blowing out (losing highlight detail) will start to appear onscreen. If red and yellow areas appear (as seen in this image), that lets you know that the reds and yellows in that area are blowing out (although the blues may still have some detail). If you start to see blue areas appear as you drag further, that lets you know that the blue in that area is now blowing out, too. If you see white areas (as shown here), that's pretty bad because all three colors are blown out in those areas, and if the Exposure slider is left at its current setting, those areas will have no detail whatsoever.

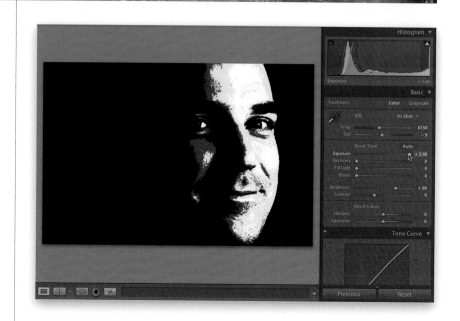

Step Five:

Well, before you cure the problem, you have to decide if losing detail in this area is actually a problem. To do that, look at the photo itself without the Option (PC: Alt) key held down. If this was a sunset photo and your blown-out area appears in the center of the sun, you can pretty much ignore it—the center of the sun isn't supposed to have detail. There are often lots of very bright things in photos that will have no detail—like a shiny reflection of the sun on a chrome bumper (these bright reflections are called "specular highlights"). So, before you cure the problem, first make sure the area that is blowing out is an area you care about, and one that should have detail. If you look at the photo and determine that it is an area where you do need to hold detail (like in our case, where those blown-out areas are in a critical area—our subject's face), then you'll have to fix this. But first...

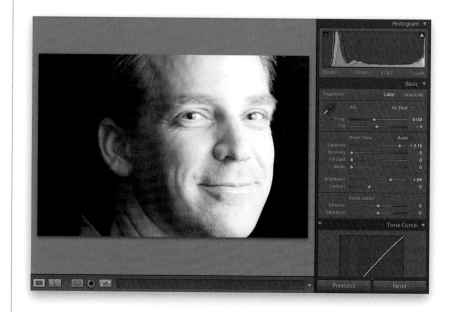

Step Six:

Before we look at the cure for blown-out highlights, I need to tell you about the other highlight clipping warning method. Some people prefer this method because it doesn't require holding down any keys—once you turn it on, it stays on, and it doesn't turn your preview black (you see your color photo the entire time). Instead, any blown-out areas appear in solid red. To turn this highlight clipping warning on, just press the letter J. When activated, you'll see two white boxes appear in the top corners of your histogram—the right one for highlights (shown circled here) and the left for shadows. (*Note:* These boxes also give visual cues. For example, if a tiny red, green, or blue triangle appears in that box, it means that color is getting clipped. If a white triangle appears, it means all the colors are getting clipped. You can also click on either box to toggle just that warning off/on.) Lastly, if you don't want to keep them on, you can get a temporary clipping preview anytime by just hovering your cursor over either one of the boxes. Okay, now it's time to learn the cure.

Step Seven:

So, if you see a highlight clipping warning (using either of the early warning methods outlined moments ago), you can lower the Exposure setting until the highlight warnings go away. You do that by dragging the Exposure slider to the left until those solid red warning areas disappear (as shown here). If you're using the Option-click [PC: Alt-click]-on-the-slider method instead, you still lower the exposure, but you do it until the preview turns solid black again. However, lowering the exposure like this isn't ideal, and it really only works in cases where you're getting just a tiny bit of highlight clipping (you'll see why in the next step).

Continued

Step Eight:

Here's the problem: let's say you dragged the Exposure slider to the right until the overall exposure looked much better to you, but some small areas began to blow out. You can drag the Exposure slider back to the left a little, and those blown-out areas will go away, right? As long as the overall exposure still looks pretty good, you're set. But what if you use the Exposure slider to set what looks to you like the ideal overall exposure, but there are a lot of blown-out areas? Your only recourse would be to drag it back to the left until those blown-out areas go away. Unfortunately, that might make the photo look under-exposed again (like the photo shown here). That's when you grab the Recovery slider—one of the most brilliant features in the Develop module.

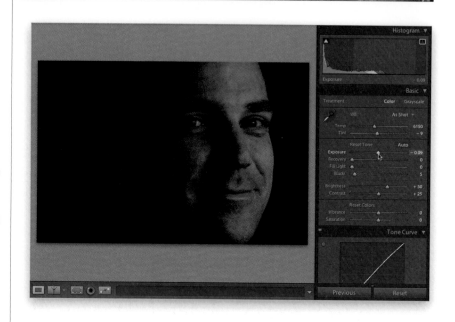

Step Nine:

The advantage of the Recovery slider is that as you drag it to the right, it pulls back only the very brightest highlights, so it doesn't lower your overall exposure—just the bright-est areas. This is incredibly useful, because now you can set the Exposure slider to what you feel is the ideal exposure, and if the highlights get a little blown out, you can recover them with the Recovery slider. So, I always start by adjusting the Exposure slider first, and then if I blow out a few of the highlights, I go to the Recovery slider and drag it to the right until my highlights come back into line. In this example, drag the Exposure slider to the right until some highlights start to blow out. Then, drag the Recovery slider to the right until those blown-out highlights go away. Nice. (Note: You can also press-and-hold the Option (PC: Alt) key to see the same highlight clip-ping warning you get with the Exposure slider. It's a great way to see when you've really recovered those clipped highlights).

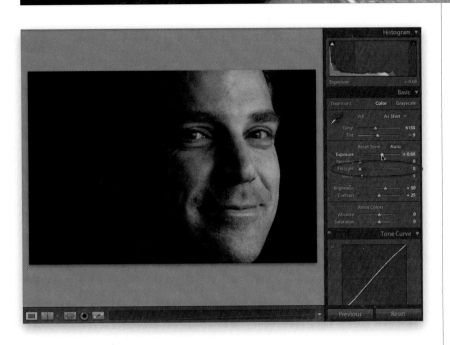

Step Ten:
That exposure still looks a little hot to me, so I'm going to pull it back to the left just a bit. Now, the next slider down in this tonal adjustment section is the Fill Light slider (shown circled in red here). Basically, this brightens just the shadow areas within your photo, and it does a very nice job of it at that. This can be incredibly handy because chances are, if you have a major lighting problem with a photo, it's in the shadow areas. Maybe you shot a portrait with the sun behind the subject, so the subject is mostly in shadows, or there are just areas of your photo where there's not enough detail in the shadows. Or in this case, you've got a photo where there's too much shadow on one side of the face.

Step Eleven:
The photo we've been working on is one I took of my buddy Scott Cowlin (Peachpit Press' Marketing Director) during a live Photoshop training session in the middle of a tradeshow floor. It was shot using a single Nikon SB-800 flash mounted on a Bogen/Manfrotto light stand (using a Bogen/Manfrotto model 175F spring clamp [called a "Justin" clamp] with a flash hotshoe). I diffused the harsh direct flash by shooting it through a Lastolite TriGrip 1-Stop Diffuser (mounted on another identical stand, with the same Justin clamp). I wanted a dramatic look, so I positioned the flash in front and to the right of the camera to create dark shadows on the left side of his face, but I felt they came out too dark. I should have used a reflector to bounce some of that light into the shadow side of his face, but since I didn't, now I need Lightroom's Fill Light slider. Just drag it to the right (as shown here) to open up those shadow areas and reveal detail.

Continued

Step Twelve:

The next slider down is Blacks, which adjusts the shadow areas in your photo. Dragging to the right increases the amount of black in the shadows; dragging to the left opens up the shadow areas. Just like with the highlights, you want to avoid losing detail in the shadows (clipping the shadows so they turn solid black). So, use one of the clipping warnings we used with highlights: (1) Press-and-hold the Option (PC: Alt) key while dragging the Blacks slider to the right, and the screen will turn solid white. Any shadow areas that are losing color detail will appear in red, green, or blue (you can see the red and yellow channels clipping here big time), or if all three colors are clipping, those areas appear as solid black (and you can see quite a bit of that here too—remember, if there's no clipping, the preview should be solid white).

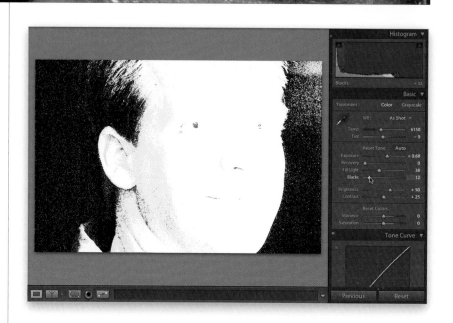

Step Thirteen:

You can try that, or (2) press J on your keyboard to turn on the shadow clipping warning, where any clipped areas will appear in blue on your photo (as shown here). Of course, when you see shadow areas being clipped, first let go of the Option (PC: Alt) key so you can look at the photo and see if those clipped areas are worth saving. For example, if those areas are supposed to be solid black (like the midnight sky, or the inside of a well), then you can ignore them. If they have detail you need to keep, then either press-and-hold the Option key again and drag the Blacks slider back to the left until the screen turns solid white, or you can try increasing the Fill Light amount to open up some of those shadows (be careful about dragging the Fill Light slider too far—it can magnify any noise in the photo).

Step Fourteen:

Okay, remember earlier how I mentioned that Lightroom would help you with your tonal editing chores? Well, more help is on the way, but this next part goes even beyond warning you about clipping the highlights or shadows. You see the Histogram panel at the top of the right side Panels area? It's very helpful because, by just looking at it, you can tell even before you make any adjustments if your highlights are blown out. For example, if you open a photo and the histogram shows a bunch of pixels stacked up against the far right-side wall (like the one shown here), it tells you right there that plenty of your highlights are clipped. If the opposite were shown—where a bunch of pixels are stacked right up against the left side, that would tell you that a load of the shadows are clipped off. Pretty standard stuff, right?

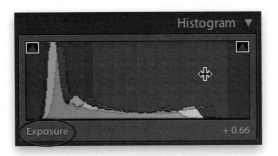

Step Fifteen:

The histogram in Lightroom looks pretty much like the histogram in Photoshop CS2/CS3, or even like the one on the back of your digital camera. But that's where the similarities end, because the one in Lightroom does two pretty darn amazing things: (1) it can show you exactly which slider adjusts exactly which part of the histogram, and (2) you can even click-and-drag right within the histogram itself to make adjustments to your image. Let's try the first one first. Move your cursor up over the histogram, and you'll notice that as soon as you do, the area in which your cursor is currently located gets lightened, and the name of the slider that controls that part of the histogram appears right there on the histogram (as shown).

Continued

Step Sixteen:

As you move your cursor to the left or right, hovering over different parts of the histogram, when you reach an area of the histogram controlled by a different tonal slider, that slider's name will appear (go ahead and give that a try. I don't mind waiting). Okay, now if showing you which slider controls which area isn't enough, take a look down at the sliders themselves. When your cursor is over the Fill Light area (for example), the Fill Light slider is highlighted for quick identification (you'll see that its name is highlighted, and the number field to the right of the Fill Light slider is also highlighted). Now you instantly know which slider controls which range of pixels in your photo (see, I told you Lightroom would help, but there's even more help to come. In fact, there's still more to this histogram, as you'll soon see).

Step Seventeen:

While you've got your cursor up there floating over the histogram, you might as well put it to work. Here's how: Let's say you're working on a photo, and you look up at the histogram and see that the right side of the histogram graph stopped well before any of it got anywhere near reaching the far right wall of the histogram, like the one shown here. In other words, there's a large flat area or gap where there would normally be some highlight data. That missing pixel data is the missing highlights in this photo. (*Note:* In portraits, ideally I like to have a very small gap between the right side of the histogram and the wall—that lets me know that the highlights in my skin tone areas aren't blowing out.) You can probably bring that missing highlight data back if you happen to know exactly which slider will bring it back, or…

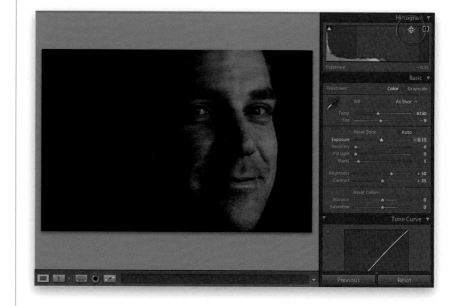

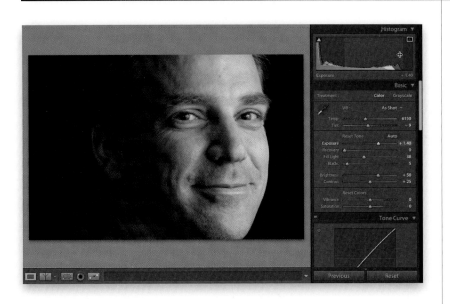

Step Eighteen:

Just move your cursor over the last bit of data on the far right side of the graph (right within the histogram itself), click your cursor on this data, and literally drag the histogram to the right. This expands the tonal range of your photo and brings back those lost highlights (of course, stop before you hit the right wall, as shown here, or you'll blow out some of your highlights). Now, whether you drag the histogram itself or use the sliders in the Basic panel, it makes no difference (use whichever you're most comfortable with), but I do recommend turning on the highlight and shadow clipping warnings to help you keep as much detail in your prints as possible.

Step Nineteen:

There are two more sliders in this middle section of the Basic panel. The first is the Brightness slider which kind of acts as a midtone slider. So if you wanted to open up the midtones a bit, you would drag this slider to the right (to darken the midtones, of course you'd drag to the left). This slider has a broad, coarse range so you have to be careful not to push it so far to the right that you start clipping highlights or so far to the left that you start clipping shadows. There is no press-and-hold-the-Option-key highlights or shadows clipping trick with it. You'll have to turn on the highlight and shadow clipping warnings (press J on your keyboard), so things don't get accidentally clipped. Now, I have to tell you, since I've been using the Recovery and Fill Light sliders, I find myself using the Brightness slider less and less. It seems just too broad in most cases, but give it a try for yourself and see what you think.

Continued

Step Twenty:

Below Brightness is the Contrast slider and it does just what you'd imagine—dragging to the right adds contrast by making the shadows darker and the highlights brighter. Here, I dragged the Contrast slider quite a bit to the right, and you can see the photo has gotten really contrasty (and I'm not sure contrasty is really even a word, but I'm counting on the book's editors not looking too closely at this step). Although this control is an easy way to add contrast, it's not the most effective because it's also too broad. When it comes to creating contrast, the Tone Curve controls (in the Tone Curve panel) do a much better job than this simple slider (we'll cover the Tone Curve panel later in this chapter).

Step Twenty-One:

In the bottom section of the Basic panel are two controls that affect the color saturation. The Vibrance slider totally rocks, and is much more usable than the Saturation slider (which appears right below it). Here's why: When you use the Saturation slider, it saturates all the colors in the photo—the shadows, midtones, and highlights—everything gets saturated at the same intensity (it's a very coarse adjustment). If you drag the Saturation slider to the right (as shown), your photo does get more colorful, but in a clownish, oversaturated, unrealistic kind of way (as seen here—though some of the oversaturation will have been lost in the book's CMYK conversion for printing). Go ahead and return the Saturation amount to 0 by double-clicking on the slider control knob. By the way, this works for all the sliders in the Develop module.

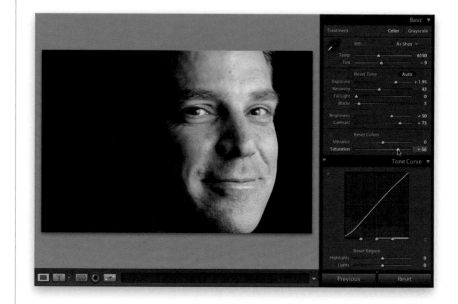

Step Twenty-Two:

However, the Vibrance slider has a bit of nuance, as it gives more of a color saturation boost to the least saturated colors and less to colors that are already somewhat saturated. This gives a much better result, with more realistic-looking saturation across the board, especially in skin tones (and that's by design), which makes this a more usable tool. Here's the same photo with the Vibrance slider set at a higher amount than the Saturation setting was in the previous step, yet look how much less clownish the colors look. His eyes are much bluer, but yet his skin tone isn't totally trashed (though it's a bit warmer than I'd probably choose). So, unless I'm desaturating an overly colorful photo, I pretty much avoid the Saturation slider altogether, and just use the Vibrance slider.

Step Twenty-Three:

Now you can reset the Vibrance and Contrast amounts to 0, and basically return the photo to how it looked before we messed with the bottom of the panel (as shown here, in the final edited photo). So, let's say you have corrected this photo, but now you've got another 15 to 20 photos of the same person in a similar pose, taken in the same light, that you have to process. The good news is you can apply all those edits to the other 15–20 photos all at once, and the step-by-step tutorial on how to do exactly that is on the next page. How convenient.

TIP: If you've made changes in the Tone or Colors sections of the Basic panel, and you want to undo just one of those (without resetting the entire photo), then press-and-hold the Option (PC: Alt) key and the words Tone and Colors change to Reset Tone and Reset Colors. Click on the one you want, and it resets just the sliders for that section.

Taking the Changes You Made to One Photo and Applying Them to Others

This is where your workflow starts to get some legs, because once you've edited one photo, you can apply those exact same edits to other photos. For example, let's say you did a portrait shoot in your studio, where you shot 260 photos and most of those were taken in a similar lighting situation (which is fairly common). Well, now you can make your adjustments (edits) to one of those photos, then apply those same adjustments to as many of the other photos as you'd like. Once you've selected which photos need those adjustments, the rest is pretty much automated.

Step One:

Okay, we're picking up right where we left off (with a portrait of Scott Cowlin), but now you've adjusted this one photo just the way you want it. Once you've done that, there are three basic ways to apply those changes to another photo. The first is to simply copy the settings from this photo and paste them onto another photo (or photos). If you're in the Library module, go under the Photo menu, under Develop Settings, and choose Copy Settings (as shown here), or just click on the photo and use the keyboard shortcut Command-Shift-C (PC: Ctrl-Shift-C). If you're in the Develop module, just click on the Copy button in the lower left Panels area.

SCOTT KELBY

Step Two:

Whichever way you choose, it brings up the Copy Settings dialog (shown here), which lets you choose which settings you want to copy from the photo you just edited. By default, it wants to copy every tonal attribute you can apply in the Develop module, but since at this point we've only adjusted the white balance and Basic panel Tone adjustments, start by clicking on the Check None button (as shown), then turn on the checkboxes for White Balance and Basic Tone, and click the Copy button.

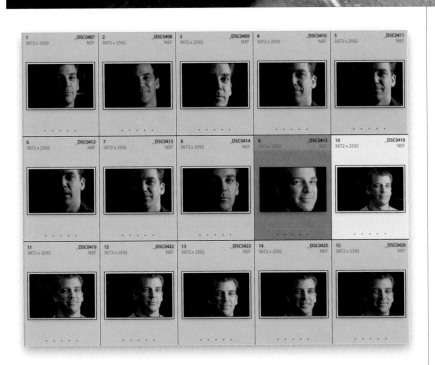

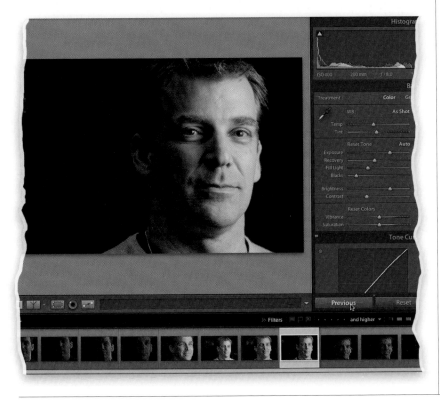

Step Three:

Now you simply click on one of the photos you want to apply those same edits to, then press Command-Shift-V (PC: Ctrl-Shift-V) to paste those copied settings onto this photo. Of course, rather than just selecting one photo the idea here is to click on the first photo, then Command-click (PC: Ctrl-click) on all the rest of the photos you want to have the same edit, and then do that pasting shortcut you just learned (as shown here, where all the photos have now been corrected by pasting). The second method is handy if you want to apply your edits to just one other photo. First, make your edits to a photo in the Develop module, then go to the filmstrip and click on the next photo you want to have those exact same edits.

Step Four:

While you're still in the Develop module, click the Previous button at the bottom of the right side Panels area (as shown here). This takes every editing attribute from the previous photo and applies it to the currently selected photo(s). If you're in the Library module, then use the keyboard shortcut Command-Option-V (PC: Ctrl-Alt-V). The third way works if you're in the Develop module. You can Command-click (PC: Ctrl-click) on any photo(s) in the filmstrip and apply all the edits you've made to the current photo by clicking the Sync button in the lower right side Panels area. This brings up the Synchronize Settings dialog, which looks identical to the Copy Settings dialog. So, what's the difference? None that I can tell. Now, which of these three ways is best? The one you feel is most convenient for you. There is no single right way, as all three pretty much do the same job.

The "No Risk" Way to Try Different Versions of Your Photo

Remember the portrait we edited earlier? Well, what if you wanted to see a version in black and white, and maybe a version with a color tint, and then a real contrasty version, and then maybe a version that was cropped differently? Well, what might keep you from doing that is having to duplicate a high-resolution file each time you wanted to try a different look, because it would eat up hard drive space like nobody's business. But luckily, there's a way to create versions you can experiment with that don't eat up your hard drive space.

Step One:

So, here's the scoop: if you want to experiment and create some different looks for your photo, rather than duplicating your RAW, TIFF, or JPEG file each time you want to save a new look, instead you're going to make a "virtual copy." (You create a virtual copy by going under the Photo menu in the Library module and choosing Create Virtual Copy, as shown here.) These virtual copies look and act the same as your original photo, and you can edit them just as you would your original photo, but here's the difference: it's not a real file, it's just a set of instructions, so it doesn't add any real file size. That way, you can have as many of these virtual copies as you want, and experiment to your heart's content without filling up your hard disk.

Step Two:

When you create a virtual copy, that copy appears right next to your original photo. You'll know which version is the copy because the virtual copies have a curled page icon in the lower-left corner of the image (circled in red here) in both the Grid view and in the filmstrip. (*Note:* To delete a virtual copy, just click on the virtual copy and press the Delete [PC: Backspace] key, and it's gone—no warning dialog, no nuthin'.)

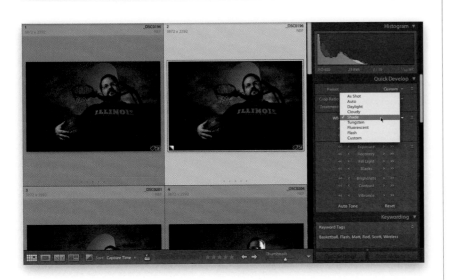

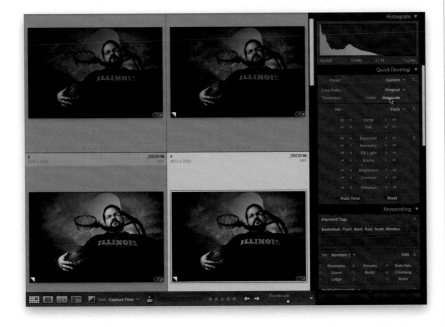

Step Three:

Now you can experiment away, with multiple virtual copies of your original photo at no risk to your photo or your hard drive space. So, pick one of your photos, make a virtual copy, then change the white balance setting of that copy (as shown here) just so you can see the difference. Here, the original photo is on the left and the virtual copy, with the white balance change, is on the right. At this point, if you want to try other looks for your photo, you can either: (a) go back to your original photo and make another virtual copy, or (b) make a copy of the virtual copy where you just changed the white balance (that's right—you can make copies of your virtual copy).

Step Four:

Click back on your original photo, and then choose Create Virtual Copy (from the Photo menu) two times in a row to create two more virtual copies. Click on the first copy, and increase the Exposure amount in the Quick Develop panel, so the photo looks lighter (as seen here, bottom left). Now click on the other virtual copy, and then click the Grayscale button (as shown) to see a version in black and white (seen at the bottom right). Now, let's say that you really like the edits you made to one of the virtual copies. Now what? Well, you can do one of two things: (1) you could copy the settings you used (using one of the techniques you learned in the previous tutorial) and paste them on the original photo, or (2) you can open the virtual copy in Photoshop (it creates a real copy of your original file and applies your editing instructions before it opens in Photoshop), or click to export the photo, where it creates a real copy with those settings that will be saved.

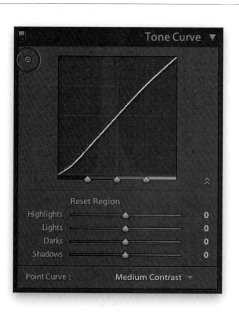

Using the Tone Curve to Add Contrast

Once we've made our edits in the Basic panel, next we head down to the Tone Curve panel to adjust the overall tonal range and contrast in our photos (I recommend doing your basic edits in the Basic panel, then using the tone curve to finish things off). Many people like the tone curve in Photoshop Lightroom better than the Curves control in Adobe Photoshop CS2/CS3 because: (1) the tone curve is designed to help keep you from blowing out your shadows or highlights, (2) it actually helps you see which areas to adjust, and (3) it lets you adjust the curve interactively.

Step One:

If you scroll down from the Basic panel, you'll find the Tone Curve panel (shown here), which is my preferred control for adding overall contrast and brightness (rather than the Contrast and Brightness sliders from the Basic panel, which seem too broad in most cases). The tone (contrast) curve you see here is controlled by the four sliders under it—Highlights, Lights, Darks, and Shadows—which all correspond to areas along the tone curve. Luckily, you don't have to intuitively know how this works, because Photoshop Lightroom will help you learn and use the tool if you start by clicking on that little round target icon in the upper-left corner of the panel (shown circled here).

Step Two:

When you click on that little icon, your cursor changes to the cursor you see here—a precise crosshair cursor to the top left of a little target icon with arrows on the top and bottom. This tool lets you interactively adjust the tone curve by clicking-and-dragging it right within your photo. The crosshair part is actually where the tool is located—the target with the arrows is there just to remind you which way to drag the tool, which (as you can see from the arrows) is up and down.

SCOTT KELBY

Step Three:

So, let's give it a shot. Take that tool, leave the Tone Curve panel, and move it out over your photo. As you hover this tool over different areas in your photo, take a look over at the tone curve. You'll see a point added to the curve which represents where the tones you're hovering over are located on the curve (also look at the bottom center of the curve grid—it says "Darks" to let you know that you're over a part of the curve that is controlled by using the Darks slider, which appears below the tone curve). As you move around the photo, your curve point moves as well. If you were to pause over an area that needs fixing, then click-and-drag upward, it would lighten that area. In our example, this photo badly needs the shadow areas boosted, so instead you would drag downward.

Step Four:

So, while your cursor is over the dark area of the barn, click-and-drag downward, and as you do, the curve point moves downward, darkening the dark tones in your photo (as shown here) and increasing the contrast (the steeper your curve, the more contrast it creates). Did you also notice that as you dragged downward, not only did the curve point move downward, but the Darks slider (in the section below the tone curve) moved to the left quite a bit? That's because dragging the cursor up/down while you're in the Darks section of the curve, moves the Darks slider. If you drag upward, it lightens the Darks setting, which is the same as moving the Darks slider to the right. In this case, you dragged downward, which gives the same effect as dragging the Darks slider to the left. (If you don't like dragging your cursor up and down in your photo, you can use the Arrow keys on your keyboard.)

Continued

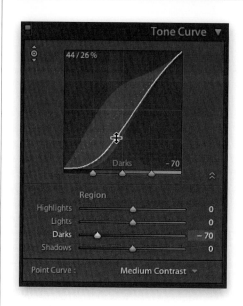

Step Five:

You can also move the curve point up or down by using the Up and Down Arrow keys on your keyboard, so go ahead and try that now. When you're moving the curve point using these Arrow keys, the point moves in small 5-point increments. To move in larger 20-point increments, just press-and-hold the Shift key while you use the Up and Down Arrow keys. For really precise adjustments to the curve point, you can move in 1-point increments by pressing-and-holding the Option (PC: Alt) key, while you use the Arrow keys. Besides clicking-and-dragging in your photo, and using the Arrow keys on your keyboard, you can also move your cursor back over the tone curve itself where you can click directly on the point and drag it up or down manually, as shown here (this is my least favorite way, because to me this feels a bit sluggish and clunky).

Step Six:

The final method of adjusting the curve is to simply drag the tone curve sliders, and as you do it adjusts the shape of the curve. This is probably the method I use the most, because once you use the click-and-drag method for even just a short time, you start to get a feel for which slider moves which part of the curve. Here, I dragged the Highlights slider to the right toward white (as shown), and I darkened the deepest shadows by moving the Shadows slider to the left toward black. By the way, when you start to adjust a curve point (no matter which method you choose), a gray shaded area appears around the point (as shown here). This area shows you the range of that slider (in other words: exactly how far, in either direction, you'll be able to move that curve point without trashing your photo).

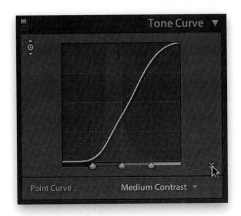

Step Seven:

So, that's the scoop. To adjust the tone curve, you're going to either: (a) move the sliders manually, (b) move your cursor over your photo and click-and-drag up/down to adjust the area your cursor is over, (c) adjust the area your cursor is over by using the Up and Down Arrow keys on your keyboard, or (d) you can just grab the curve point yourself and drag up or down. *Note:* If you find that you're not using the sliders, you can hide them from view by clicking the double upward-facing arrows just outside the bottom-right corner of the tone curve. If you decide you want them back one day, click those same arrows (as shown here).

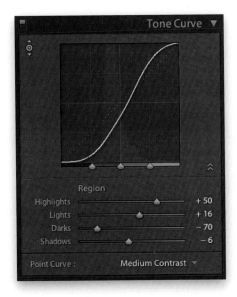

Step Eight:

So you're thinking, "Okay, I understand the controls now, but how do I use them to create more contrast?" Your curve starts flat (well, as a flat diagonal line). As you steepen the curve, the contrast in your photo increases. For example, if you raised the Highlights and Lights areas on the curve (moving the points upward), and lowered the Shadows and Darks points downward (where the three-quarter-tone shadow areas of the curve start to steepen, and the shadow areas are pushed closer to black), the curve becomes steeper (as shown here). What you're basically doing is creating the classic S-curve, which creates contrast. The steeper this curve becomes, the more extreme the contrast in your photo.

TIP: Want to reset the tone curve without resetting the Point Curve preset? Or, do you want to reset just the Region sliders under the curve (the Splits)? Just Control-click (PC: Right-click) within the curve itself, and a contextual menu will appear with a list of things you can reset individually or all at once, including flattening the curve.

Continued

Step Nine:

This brings us to the three slider control knobs that appear along the bottom of the tone curve grid. (You knew I was eventually going to get to those, right?) Those are called Range sliders and essentially they let you choose where the black, white, and midpoint ranges are that the tone curve will adjust (you determine what's a shadow, what's a midtone, and what's a highlight by where you place them). For example, the Range slider on the left (shown circled here in red) represents the shadow areas, and the area that appears to the left of that knob will be affected by the Shadows slider. If you want to expand the range of what the Shadows slider controls, click-and-drag the left Range slider to the right (as shown here). Now your Shadows slider adjustments affect a larger range of your photo.

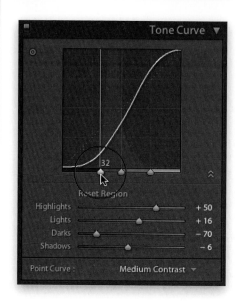

Step Ten:

The middle Range slider between the shadows and highlights Range sliders (shown circled here) covers the midtones. Dragging that midtone Range slider to the right decreases the space between the midtone and highlight areas, so your Lights slider now controls less of a range, and your Darks slider controls more of a range. To reset any of these Range sliders to their default settings, just double-click directly on the one you want to reset. Besides creating your own custom tone curves (using the sliders, dragging in the image, or moving points with your Left and Right Arrow keys), Lightroom also comes with three built-in preset contrast curves to make getting additional contrast easy.

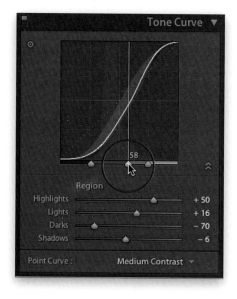

Step Eleven:

These tone curve presets are found in a pop-up menu at the bottom of the Tone Curve panel, next to the words "Point Curve." If you choose Medium Contrast, you get a slightly steep curve, whereas choosing Strong Contrast (as shown here) gives you a much steeper curve, with much stronger contrast. By the way—if you want to see the effects of this tone curve preset, you can toggle it on/off by using the On/Off button at the top left of the Tone Curve panel's header. On is with the button in the up position, and to turn it off just click on it and it toggles to off. So, now you're just seeing any adjustments you made previously in the Basic panel. (Remember: Changes in the Tone Curve panel are *added* to the changes you made in the Basic panel.)

Step Twelve:

To finish this photo off, let's make it look like it was taken in the fall (it actually was taken in Vermont during the first week of October). Go back up to the white balance section and drag the Temp slider to the right a little to make the photo warmer, and then to add the red in, drag the Tint slider below to the right a little bit, too (to give you the image you see here). Now, go ahead and click the Reset button, so you can see a before/after view of your photo (it's come a long way since we first saw it in Step Three, eh?). Speaking of before/after views, seeing them side-by-side can be really helpful, and in the next tutorial you'll learn how to do just that. But before you go to the next page, to return the current photo to its edited version, press Command-Z (PC: Ctrl-Z), which undoes your Reset command.

Seeing Before/After Versions While You Edit

Sometimes, seeing the before/after views can be a big help when you're making your edits in Photoshop Lightroom, and seeing them side-by-side as you edit can even be more helpful. Photoshop Lightroom gives you a number of different options of how to do this, depending on your personal preferences and the physical orientation of the photo you're editing. Here's how to make the most of the before/after views:

Step One:

When you're working on a photo in the Develop module and want to quickly see what the original, unedited version of your photo looked like (the "before" photo), just press the Backslash key (\) to toggle between the before and after views (the word "Before" appears in the bottom-right corner of the Preview area—it's circled here in red. Also, since this photo is in the landscape orientation, I hid the left side panels so the preview would be larger). If you'd like to see both the before and after versions onscreen at the same time, then you'll love the next step.

Step Two:

To see your photo in a split-screen view (where the left half is the Before view and right half shows the After view, as shown here), just click the Before/After view button at the bottom-left corner of the Preview area (shown circled here). Each time you click this button, it toggles you through one of the four different before/after views (going from horizontal side-by-side to split screen, and then vertical side-by-side to split screen). Of course, there are keyboard shortcuts for these views as well: pressing Shift-Y will toggle you between the horizontal side-by-side before/after view and the horizontal split-screen before/after view seen here.

Step Three:

You can also choose different views by clicking on the little down-facing arrow to the right of the Before/After view button, and a pop-up menu will appear (shown here), with a list of Before/After view choices. Here I chose Before/After Top/Bottom. To get the biggest preview possible, I also pressed Shift-Tab to hide the right side panels and the filmstrip as well. By the way, when you're in one of these Before/After views, zooming in and moving around one photo affects both photos at the same time. So if you zoom in on the After photo and start scrolling around, the Before photo zooms and moves right along with it (as shown here, where I zoomed in on the After photo, then moved around the image by clicking-and-dragging. As you can see, the two zoom views and the zoom locations are identical).

Step Four:

There are two other buttons that appear to the right of the Before/After view button, but these only appear once you're in a Before/After view. These two buttons (shown circled here) let you either copy the Before image's settings to the After image (the left button) or copy the After image's settings to the Before image (the right button). I have to be honest with you—I haven't come up with a scenario yet that I've wanted or needed to use these two buttons, but if they're in Photoshop Lightroom, somebody must have wanted them, and if that somebody was you, well there they are. Lastly, to return to the regular view (where you're back to seeing only the photo you're currently editing), just press the letter D on your keyboard.

Saving Your Favorite Settings as Presets

If you really want to leverage the power of Photoshop Lightroom to keep your workflow moving along, then you'll want to learn how to use and create presets. That way, you can apply your favorite settings (like your favorite black-and-white conversion, or a set of edits that fix overexposed photos) with just one click. Once you start creating your own presets, you'll wonder how you lived without them. Here's how to start making your own:

Step One:

The best time to create a preset is right after you've applied a set of changes that (a) you really like, and (b) you think you'll be able to use again on a set of different photos. If you shoot in a studio (where the lighting situation is controlled), then this is a no-brainer. You may only need to make a few presets. If you're a wedding photographer, maybe a few more, and if you're an outdoor or event photographer, you'll be making these puppies all the time. To get you rolling, let's open a photo, create a duotone look, and then save that as a preset so you can apply it to different photos on another day. Once the photo's open, go to the Develop module (as shown here).

Step Two:

First, so we get to see a bigger preview of our photo, hide the left side panels. Then, go to the Basic panel and at the bottom of the panel, lower the Saturation amount to –100 (as shown here) to remove all the color from the photo (don't worry— better ways to convert to black and white are coming in Chapter 6, but for this example on presets, this method is quick and easy).

Step Three:

Without going into a big explanation about what split toning is (that explanation is also coming in Chapter 6), scroll down to the Split Toning panel. Increase the Highlights Hue to 43, and Highlights Saturation to 50. Then go to the Split Toning Shadows controls, drag the Shadows Hue to 43, and the Shadows Saturation to 50 (as shown). This gives a brownish duotone tint to our black-and-white photo (seen here).

Step Four:

To add some additional contrast (making the highlights brighter and the shadows darker), go to the Tone Curve panel, and from the Point Curve pop-up menu choose Strong Contrast (as shown here). Okay, we're on our way, but we're not quite there yet—let's make a few more edits here in the Develop module.

TIP: Want to jump right to a panel without scrolling or clicking? Press Command-1 to jump to the Basic panel, Command-2 for the Tone Curve panel, Command-3 for the HSL/Color/Grayscale panel, and so on (on a PC, you'd use Ctrl-1, etc.).

Continued

Step Five:

Now head back up to the Basic panel, and let's really give this baby some juice—increase the Blacks quite a bit, then bring up the Recovery amount (as shown here) until it looks good to you, then finally bring up the Fill Light a little to open up some of those shadows. (Honestly, for this example, it doesn't really matter which Basic sliders you change, or how much you change them, because I just want you to see—in the end—how many slider moves you can save by creating one simple preset. So... knock yourself out. Tweak that pup until it looks good to you, which is, of course, the bottom line.)

Step Six:

Once you're done tweaking things in the Basic panel, make the left side panels visible again, then go to the Presets panel. Click once directly on the + (plus sign) that appears on the top right side of the Presets panel itself (it's circled here in red). This brings up the New Develop Preset dialog (shown here). Give your new preset a name (I named mine "My Duotone." I know—pretty clever). Now click the Create button (as shown) to save every change you just made (from removing color, to tinting, to the tone curve, to all your slider tweaking in the Basic panel) as your own custom preset, which will be now added alphabetically to the list of presets.

TIP: Want to copy-and-paste some settings, but you don't want to have to mess with the Copy Settings dialog? Then don't just click Copy, Option-click (PC: Alt-click) Copy and it will copy all the settings for that photo.

Step Seven:

Open a different photo, and then hover your cursor over your new preset (I'm hovering over the preset I named "My Duotone" in the example shown here). Now, look up above the Presets panel (at the Navigator panel), where you'll see an instant preview of the preset you're hovering over (as shown here, where you're seeing what your current color photo would look like if you applied your custom duotone preset). Seeing this preview before you actually commit to it is a huge time-saver, because you'll know in a split second whether your photo will look good with the preset applied or not, before you actually apply it. So, for now, go ahead and click on the duotone preset, and watch how quickly all those adjustments are applied to your photo. Ahhh, now you see why this is so cool. (If you want to delete a preset, just click on it, then click the – [minus sign] that appears to the left of the + [plus sign] that creates new presets.)

Step Eight:

By the way, presets are cumulative, so if you click on a preset, it applies those edits. Then, if you click on another, it applies its edits on top of the changes the first preset made (it other words, it doesn't replace what the first preset you clicked on did—it adds to those changes). Another nice thing about creating your own presets is that you now have access to them while you're in the Library module's Quick Develop panel. Just click on the Preset pop-up menu and a list of all the Develop module presets appears, including the one you just created (as shown here). Nice. And unlike copying-and-pasting settings, presets are permanent and will still be there the next time you launch Lightroom.

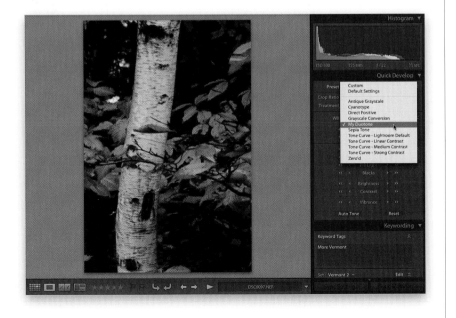

Boosting (or Reducing) Individual Colors

Since Photoshop Lightroom doesn't have selection tools (like Adobe Photoshop has), how do you tweak or change just one individual color? You do it using the HSL/Color/Grayscale panel, which lets you adjust individual colors within your image. This is great for removing obvious color casts, repairing skin tone problems, or just changing the color of an object within your photo. Don't let all the sliders throw you off—this is much easier than it looks.

Step One:

When you want to adjust an area of color (for example, let's say we didn't like the color of the bouquet the bride is holding in the photo shown here), the HSL/Color/Grayscale panel (shown here, in the right side Panels area) is the place to go. By the way, those words in the panel header (HSL/Color/Grayscale) aren't just a description, they're clickable. So, to adjust the Hue, Saturation, and Luminance of your photo, click once directly on HSL to display the HSL section of the panel. In that section, the four words that appear across the top of the panel are clickable as well. So, if you want to adjust the Hue of your photo, click the Hue link and Hue controls appear (as seen here).

Step Two:

There are two other sections that are hidden (Saturation and Luminance), and if you click on their names, their sections replace the Hue section that's currently visible. If you click on All (as shown here), it displays all three sections—one on top of the other (as seen here). If this sounds complicated, don't worry, it really isn't—especially if you're familiar with Adobe Photoshop's standard Hue/Saturation dialog (as you'll soon see).

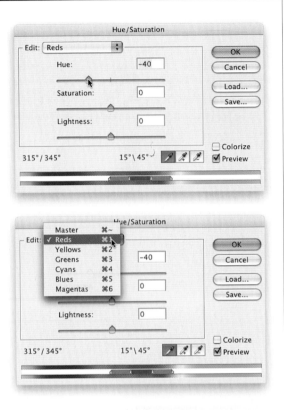

Step Three:

The Adobe Photoshop CS3 Hue/Saturation dialog is shown here. You'll notice that you can adjust the Hue, Saturation, and Lightness settings using these three sliders, and you can do that for six different colors by choosing which colors you want to edit from a pop-up menu. So, if it weren't for the pop-up menu, which lets you choose individual colors (seen in the bottom capture here), you'd have 18 individual sliders, right? (Each of the six colors would have one slider for Hue, one for Saturation, and one for Lightness, which totals 18 sliders.) Well, that's what you've got in Photoshop Lightroom—pretty much the same functionality as Photoshop's Hue/Saturation dialog, but with three minor differences. They are: (1) Lightroom calls it Luminance, not Lightness, (2) Lightroom calls cyan "Aqua," and (3) instead of just being able to edit six colors, Lightroom adds two more—purple and orange.

Step Four:

So, that's what those sliders all do—the same thing that Photoshop's Hue/Saturation adjustment does, but Lightroom gives you two more colors (which is nice). For example, look at the Hue sliders. Without having to choose from a pop-up menu, you can instantly adjust the reds, oranges, yellows, greens, aquas, blues, purples, and magentas. If you want to adjust how intense and vibrant these colors are, use the Saturation sliders (if you look at the color bars inside the sliders themselves, you'll see that dragging these to the right will make the colors that slider controls more vibrant and colorful). The bottom set of sliders, Luminance, acts like Photoshop's Hue/Saturation Lightness slider—they control the overall lightness or darkness of the colors you're adjusting.

Continued

Step Five:

Okay, so let's start tweaking the color of the bouquet. If you wanted to change the color of the flowers in the bouquet, which section would do that? It would be the Hue section—because that's where you change colors. You wouldn't choose the Saturation section, because that only controls how vivid (or pale) each color will be. And the Luminance section only controls the overall brightness of each color. So, try dragging the Orange Hue slider to the left (as shown here) to see how that affects the flowers. They are more orange for sure, but so are her flesh tones, too. That's because when you drag a slider, it affects all the orange in the photo—not just in the flowers. Since that looks bad, click the Reset button at the bottom of the right side panels.

Step Six:

Rather than just dragging sliders and hoping for the best, instead click on the little target icon in the top-left corner of the Hue section (when you roll over it with your cursor, two arrows pointing up and down will show. It's circled in red here, and its official name is the Targeted Adjustment tool). This tool lets you interactively adjust color areas in your photo by clicking-and-dragging. So, once you have the tool, go over to the bouquet, click directly on the flowers (as shown here), and drag downward. As you drag, the sliders that affect the colors your cursor is over will start moving. If you drag downward, the Red and Orange Hue sliders move toward being more red and more orange. If you drag upward, it drags away from those colors and more toward yellow (give it a try and you'll see what I mean).

Step Seven:

Get the flowers where they look good to you, and then we're going to bring out the greens in the leaves of the bouquet. Click with the crosshair directly on the leaves (the target and arrows icon simply shows you which directions you can drag) and drag upward to make the leaves greener and richer. Now, how did I know to drag upward this time, rather than down? By looking at the color bars under the sliders. As soon as you start dragging in either direction, you'll see which sliders move (in this case, it was the Yellow and Green Hue sliders), and the color bars show that if you move the sliders to the right, those colors will become darker and more green. So, initially I dragged downward, but one glance at the color bars within the sliders showed me I was dragging in the wrong direction. That's the trick. So give it a try—click on the green leaves and drag upward until the leaves look greener, but as always, keep an eye on the rest of the photo so the bride doesn't turn green.

Step Eight:

Greening up the leaves did make the ribbon on the bouquet a bit greenish, so to adjust just that area, move your cursor over the ribbon (as shown here) and drag downward, which moves just the Yellow Hue slider back to the left, away from the greenish end of the slider. That's all it takes to get the ribbon looking right again, and if you look at the leaves, they still look nice and green. Now, click on the word Saturation at the top of the HSL/Color/Grayscale panel to reveal just the Saturation sliders.

Continued

Step Nine:

Now that you're in the Saturation section (remember, this controls how vivid the colors will appear), we can make her skin tone warmer (without changing the Hue), by clicking on her arm (as shown here) and dragging upward. This moves the Orange and Yellow Saturation sliders to the right (as shown here), increasing the saturation of those two colors. Now, click on the word Luminance at the top of the panel to bring up that section. (*Note:* When you're working with the Targeted Adjustment tool, you can also change sections using a special pop-up menu to the right of Target Group in the toolbar.)

Step Ten:

The Luminance section controls the brightness of the colors, and in this case, we want to bring back some of the highlights in her face. So click on a highlight area of her face (as shown here) and drag upward. As you do, you'll see those areas become significantly lighter (don't drag too far or you could wind up blowing out some highlights, so as always, keep an eye on the photo as you use this tool). That gives you a pretty good overview of what the three sections of the HSL part of the panel do, and how to use the all-important Targeted Adjustment tool (by the way, since Adobe added this tool to Lightroom, I pretty much use it exclusively for adjusting the hue, saturation, or luminance of colors in my photos, because it helps you target just the area of color you want to adjust). Dragging the sliders is just too much of a guessing game, unless it's really obvious where the color you want to adjust is (i.e., you want to make a blue sky bluer, so you can pretty much figure that you'd use the Aqua and Blue sliders).

Step Eleven:

If you're from the old school and prefer Photoshop's way of adjusting Hue/ Saturation (using the Hue, Saturation, and Lightness sliders grouped together for each color), then in the HSL/Color/ Grayscale panel's header, click on the word Color. This brings up the panel you see here, which is more like Photoshop's Hue/Saturation control. At the top, you click on the color swatch you want to adjust and a Hue, Saturation, and Luminance slider appears for that color, just like in Photoshop (as shown here).

Step Twelve:

If you click the All button at the end of the row of swatches (as shown here), it displays each individual color and the three sliders (Hue, Saturation, and Luminance) for each of the colors. This makes for quite a long scrolling list of sliders, and it's probably rare that you'd need to adjust nearly each and every color, so I think it's easier just to click on the swatch for the color you want to adjust. Of course, I prefer the HSL panel over this Color panel all the way around, but I did want to show you this just in case you feel it fits your workflow better. (*Note:* If you totally mess up with the sliders in any of these sections [Hue, Saturation, or Luminance], just press-and-hold the Option [PC: Alt] key and the section's name changes to a Reset button [i.e., Reset Saturation].) Lastly, in the HSL/ Color/Grayscale panel's header, you can also click on Grayscale. We'll cover that in the chapter on converting to black and white, because…well…that's where it belongs.

Using Auto Sync to Fix Lots of Photos at Once

When you're in the Library module, by default it's in Auto Sync mode, which means if you select a number of photos (let's say 45), any changes you make to the first photo you selected (the "most selected" photo) are automatically applied to the other 44 photos. However, since the Develop module doesn't have a grid, it doesn't work that way by default. But luckily, you can turn this feature on for the Develop module, and I actually find I use Develop's Auto Sync more than I do the Auto Sync in the Library module. Here's how it's done:

Step One:

In the Develop module, click on the photo you want to work on, then go down to the filmstrip and Command-click (PC: Ctrl-click) on all the other photos you want to have the same adjustments as the first one (as shown here, where I've selected four photos that all need a white balance adjustment because they're too blue). The preview onscreen is of the first photo I selected (the "most selected" photo). Now, press-and-hold the Command (PC: Ctrl) key and you'll notice that the Sync button at the bottom of the right side Panels area has changed to Auto Sync. Click once on that button to turn Auto Sync on.

Step Two:

Get the White Balance Selector tool and click on something in your photo that is supposed to be a neutral gray (in the example here, I clicked on a light gray area of stone, which gave me a much warmer white balance). More importantly, look at the selected photos in the filmstrip—they all got the exact same white balance adjustment without any copying-and-pasting or Synchronize Settings dialogs to deal with. This Auto Sync feature will stay on until you go and turn it off (which, for me, is hardly ever) by Command-clicking (PC: Ctrl-clicking) on the button again.

The ability to create your own Develop module presets is a huge time-saver, but if you don't even have time for that—don't worry—there are already websites popping up with lots of free pre-designed Develop module presets (some of them are created by well-known photographers, instructors, and even Adobe engineers), and all you have to do is download 'em and install 'em (by the way, a great resource for these is the UK-based site Inside Lightroom [http://inside-lightroom.co.uk/]).

Importing Develop Module Presets from Someone Else

SCOTT KELBY

Step One:

If you download a Develop module preset from the Web (or a friend emails you a preset she created), getting it into Photoshop Lightroom is easy, you just have to know where to look (and no big surprise here—it's buried deep within folder after folder). That's why the quickest way to get to the right spot is to go to the Presets panel and simply Control-click (PC: Right-click) on any one of the existing Develop module presets, which brings up a contextual menu (shown here). Choose Show in Finder (PC: Show in Explorer), and the Develop Presets folder where Lightroom's presets are stored will appear (as seen below).

Step Two:

Drag-and-drop your downloaded preset(s) into this Develop Presets folder, then all you have to do to complete the installation is: (a) quit Lightroom, then (b) relaunch it. When you look at the Presets panel now, your new preset will appear in the list (as shown in the inset at right, where my custom preset, Scott's B&W w/Shadow Tint, now appears in the list). That's all there is to it.

When to Jump to Adobe Photoshop, and How and When to Jump Back

While Photoshop Lightroom is great for organizing your photos, processing your images, making slide shows, and printing, it's not Adobe Photoshop. Photoshop Lightroom doesn't do special effects, or photo retouching, or pro-level sharpening or one of the bazillion (yes, bazillion) things that Photoshop does. So, there will be numerous times during your workflow where you'll need to jump over to Photoshop to do some "Photoshop stuff" and then jump back to Photoshop Lightroom for printing or presenting. Luckily, these two applications were born to work together.

Step One:

Once you've made all the tonal changes you want in Photoshop Lightroom, if you want to do things Lightroom just can't do (for example, in this photo I'd like to remove the white line on the right side, plus I want to hide some distracting little things on the car itself, plus I'd like to add a zoom effect, and sharpen the photo significantly), it's time to jump over to Photoshop CS2 (or CS3, if you have it). Go under the Photo menu and choose Edit in Adobe Photoshop CS2/CS3 (as shown here), or use the keyboard shortcut Command-E (PC: Ctrl-E).

Step Two:

This brings up a dialog where you choose exactly how your photo goes over to Photoshop for further editing. The first two choices, Edit Original and Edit a Copy (only available when your photo is a JPEG, TIFF, or PSD), ignore all the changes you've made in Lightroom and send either an untouched original or a copy over to Photoshop. However, the third choice—Edit a Copy with Lightroom Adjustments—creates a copy of your photo with all the edits you made in Lightroom already applied, and sends that copy over to Photoshop. *Note:* If you're working on a RAW photo, this third choice is your only available choice.

Step Three:

If you have either Photoshop or Photoshop Elements (the consumer version of Photoshop) installed on your computer, Lightroom chooses it as your default external editor, but there are some options for how your files are sent over to Photoshop (or Elements). Press Command-, (comma; PC: Ctrl-,) to go to Lightroom's Preferences, and click on the External Editors tab (as shown here). At the top, you'll see options for choosing the file format of photos sent to Photoshop (I use TIFF, which also lets you choose a compression method so the files aren't so large), along with your choice of color space and bit depth. You'll see right in the dialog that Adobe recommends ProPhoto RGB as your color space at a bit depth of 16 bits for the best results. If you shoot in RAW, that's good advice because thus far no color profile has been embedded in your photo. However, if you're working with JPEGs or TIFFs from your camera, your camera already embedded a color profile in them (like sRGB, or hopefully Adobe RGB [1998]), so from the Color Space pop-up menu, choose that same color space to keep everything consistent.

Step Four:

If you don't have Photoshop or Photoshop Elements installed, then you can choose an Additional External Editor in the lower portion of the dialog. Just click the Choose button (as shown here) and choose a pixel-based editor (here, I chose Apple's iPhoto, which came pre-installed on my computer). You can choose the options for how files are sent there as well.

Continued

Step Five:

Once you close Lightroom's Preferences dialog, your External Editor choices are saved, and if you go under Lightroom's Photo menu (shown here), you'll see your default choice (in this case, mine is Photoshop CS3), and the shortcut to jump over to Photoshop, which is Command-E on a Mac or Ctrl-E on a PC. Right under your default choice will be your Additional External Editor choice (remember, I chose Apple's iPhoto). Now, Edit in iPhoto appears in the menu as well, and to jump to this additional external editor, you'd press Command-Option-E on a Mac, or Ctrl-Alt-E on a PC).

Step Six:

When you send a photo for editing to an external editor, by default Lightroom automatically embeds the ProPhoto RGB color space into your photo (ProPhoto RGB is Lightroom's native color space. It has a very wide color gamut, and in many ways it's an ideal color space for today's digital photographers). However, as soon as your photo arrives in Photoshop, unless you already have Photoshop's working color space set to ProPhoto RGB, the Embedded Profile Mismatch dialog (shown here) will appear. So, ideally you'd change Photoshop's color space to ProPhoto RGB (in Photoshop's Color Settings preferences) before your photo leaves Lightroom, or you can convert the file to your working color space (hopefully Adobe RGB [1998] and not sRGB) by choosing Convert Document's Colors to the Working Space in the Embedded Profile Mismatch dialog when it appears, shown here.

Step Seven:

Now that our photo is in Photoshop, the first thing we want to do is remove that distracting white line in the lower-right corner. Get the Clone Stamp tool (S), Option-click (PC: Alt-click) to the left of the white line, and begin cloning over the line (as shown here).

TIP: Lightroom is fully compatible with Adobe Bridge, Photoshop CS3, and even CS2 if you go to Adobe's website and download the latest update to Adobe Camera Raw (ACR; it's free, and you need version 3.7 or higher). Then, you can drag-and-drop directly from the Lightroom's filmstrip or grid onto the Photoshop or Bridge icon on the Mac Dock or PC Taskbar. If you're working with RAW images and want to maintain the changes you've made in Lightroom, go to the Metadata menu, under XMP, and choose Export XMP Metadata to File. That way, your changes will move with the RAW file, which will open in ACR.

Step Eight:

Now switch to the Spot Healing Brush tool (J), and click once directly on any spots or other distracting things on the ground around the car, so the track looks clean and clear (if you look closely at the photo in Step Seven, you'll see lots of spots and specks in the foreground and to the left of the car, by the back tire. Of course, we could have removed the white line back there as well. If you're up for it, switch back to the Clone Stamp tool, and clone over it. You might be wondering why I didn't get rid of those spots using the Remove Spots tool in Lightroom. I could have removed them in Lightroom, but Photoshop's Spot Healing Brush is much faster and easier to use, and since I was coming over to Photoshop anyway, it saved time and trouble to do it here.

Continued

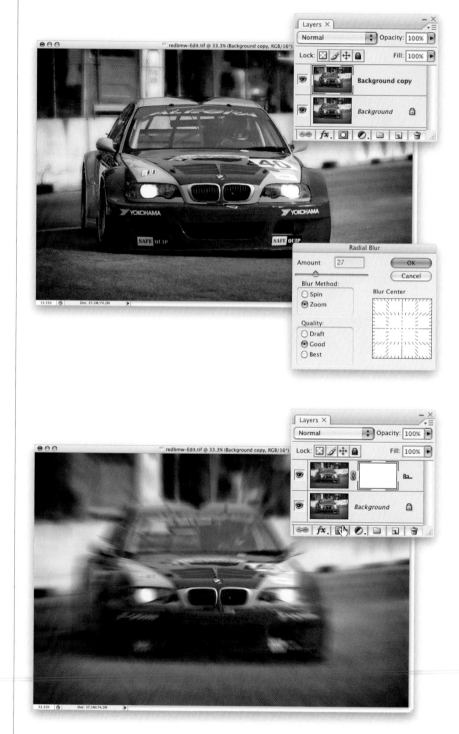

Step Nine:

Now, to add the zoom effect, start by duplicating the Background layer by dragging it onto the Create a New Layer icon at the bottom of the Layers palette. Then go under Photoshop's Filter menu, under Blur, and choose Radial Blur. When the filter's dialog appears, for the Blur Method choose Zoom, increase the Amount to 27 (as shown here), and click OK.

Step Ten:

When you click OK, the zoom radial blur is applied to the layer, and although the center of the zoom is somewhat clear, the effect is too overwhelming, and covers too much of the detail on the car. So, we're going to add a layer mask, which will let us basically paint away any area of the zoom effect we want (that's why we duplicated the layer—so we'd be able to add a layer mask later to edit where the filter was applied without destroying the photo). To add a layer mask, go to the bottom of the Layers palette and click on the Add Layer Mask icon (as shown here). This adds a white layer mask to your layer (you can see it added to the right of the layer's thumbnail in the Layers palette).

Step Eleven:

Now that your layer mask has been added, get the Brush tool (B), press X to set your Foreground color to black, and choose a very large, soft-edged brush. Now, take that brush and paint over the front of the car (as shown here) and a little bit of the sides, but don't paint all the way to the back of the car because it looks good with a little bit of that zoom effect still visible back there. If you make a mistake, just press X again to switch your Foreground color to white and paint over the area you didn't mean to paint, and the zoom blur will reappear in the area you're painting (that's the power of layer masks—you can always go back and fix or change your edits). Okay, that's enough effect—let's sharpen this puppy and head back to Lightroom.

Step Twelve:

Flatten the layers by choosing Flatten Image from the Layers palette's flyout menu (found in the top-right corner of the palette itself). Now, to sharpen the photo, go under the Filter menu, under Sharpen, and choose Unsharp Mask. When the dialog appears, for Amount enter 120%, for Radius enter 1, and for Threshold enter 3, then click OK (as shown here). This gives a nice punchy amount of sharpening, and when your subject has a lot of well-defined edges like a car, it can take a lot of sharpening like this without damaging the photo (whereas, if this were a portrait, that would probably be too much sharpening and the photo would have little halos around the edges and would look notice-ably oversharpened).

Continued

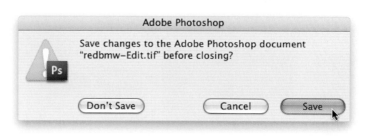

Step Thirteen:

So, you've hidden lines, removed spots, added a zoom filter effect, and majorly sharpened the photo. Now it's time to save the photo and return to Lightroom. You can either go under the File menu and choose Save (don't choose Save As because you don't want to change the name of this file, and it won't go back to Lightroom automatically, thus it will hose your workflow) or simply close the image. If you close the image, the dialog shown here will appear, asking if you want to save the changes you just made in Photoshop. (Notice how the name of your photo has "-Edit" added to the end of it? Lightroom automatically added that to let you know that this is a copy of your original created for editing outside of Lightroom.) If you click Don't Save, the photo closes and goes back to Lightroom, but without any of the changes you just applied in Photoshop. Instead, click the Save button (as shown here) to save the changes you just made and send the photo back to Lightroom with those Photoshop edits intact.

Step Fourteen:

When you switch back to Lightroom, it takes you right back to where you last were (in our case, the Develop module), and your Photoshop-edited photo, with all the edits applied, now appears within Lightroom (you can see the zoom blur and sharpening in the image shown here).

TIP: While you can drag-and-drop thumbnails directly from Lightroom onto the Photoshop or Adobe Bridge icon to open those photos in those programs, you cannot drag virtual copies to either (virtual copies only live inside Lightroom). If you want a virtual copy to open in Photoshop or Bridge, you have to export it as a JPEG, TIFF, PSD, or DNG.

Step Fifteen:

If you press G on your keyboard, you'll return to the Library module's Grid view, and there you'll see your newly edited copy appearing right alongside your original photo (as shown here). By the way, if you'd like to compare these two photos side-by-side, just Command-click (PC: Ctrl-click) on both photos to select them, then press C to enter Compare view where you'll see them side-by-side. When you're done, to return to the Grid view, just press G again. Now, see that little number 2 on top of the upper-left corner of your original photo? That's letting you know that your edited copy is stacked with the original photo for housekeeping purposes.

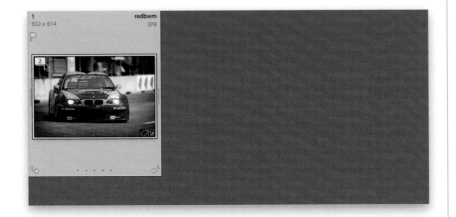

Step Sixteen:

If you click directly on that little number 2, the edited copy tucks right under the original, creating a little stack with the original on top (as shown here). If you want to see the edited version, then just click on that little 2 again and it will pop right back out, just like it looked in Step Fifteen. This works not only here in the grid, but in the filmstrip as well. This helps you from becoming confused when you've got multiple copies of the same photo. *Note:* The only reason we have two thumbnails of our file is because we chose to work on a copy in the Edit Photo dialog that appeared back in Step Two. If you have a JPEG or TIFF file and choose to work on the original, then you're doing just that—working on the original in Photoshop, and when you return to Lightroom, you'll see just one photo because you've edited your original photo.

Saving Your Photos as JPEGs, TIFFs, PSDs, or DNGs

Once you're done editing, tweaking, and otherwise processing your photos in Photoshop Lightroom (and/or Photoshop), how in the world do you get them out of Photoshop Lightroom as a TIFF, JPEG, a Photoshop PSD file, or an Adobe DNG? It's easier than you'd think.

Step One:
You start by selecting which photo(s) you want to save as a JPEG, TIFF, PSD, or DNG. You can either do this in the Library module by Command-clicking (PC: Ctrl-clicking) on all the photos you want to save (as shown here), or you can do this in the filmstrip while you're in any of the modules (you select the photos in the filmstrip the exact same way).

TIP: If you're wondering why I'm not talking about the specifics of processing RAW files that much, it's because Lightroom treats RAW, JPEG, TIFF, and PSD files almost the same. In fact, the only real differences occur in the presets available in the Develop module's White Balance pop-up menu, and when you go to the Edit in Photoshop command, as discussed in the previous tutorial.

Step Two:
Next, if you're in the Library module, click on the Export button at the bottom of the left side Panels area (circled here in red). If you're in a different module and using the filmstrip to select your photos, then use the keyboard shortcut Command-Shift-E (PC: Ctrl-Shift-E). Whichever method you choose, it brings up the Export dialog (shown in the next step).

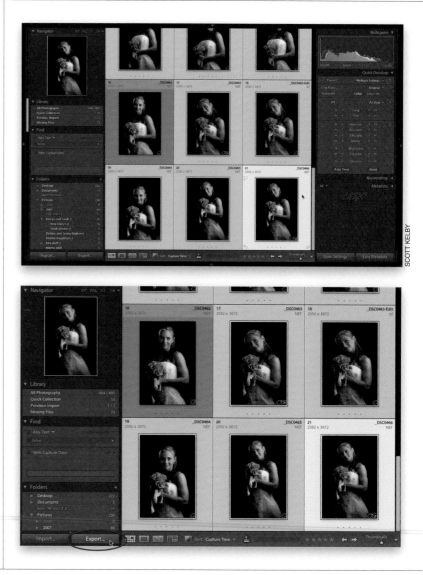

SCOTT KELBY

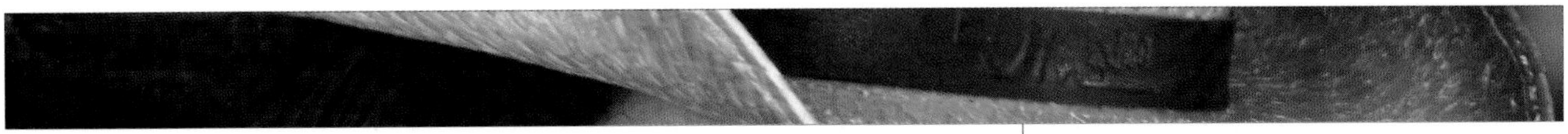

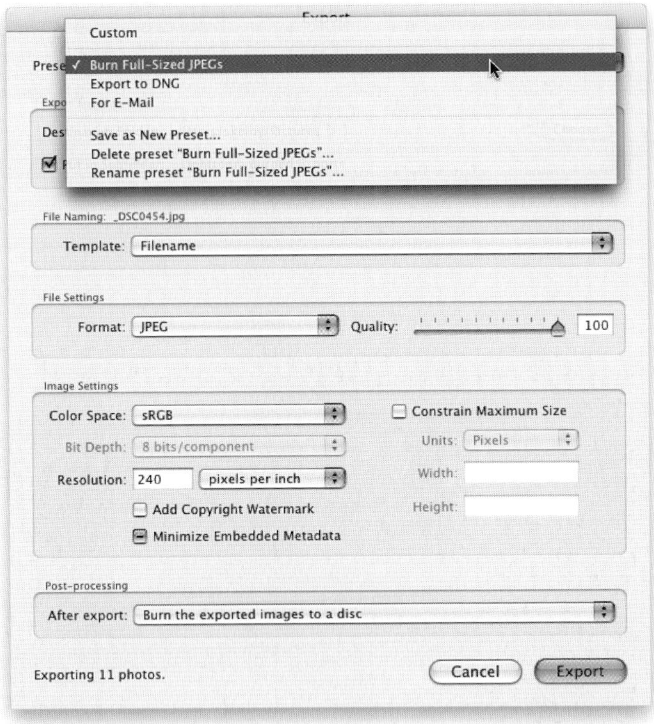

Step Three:

At the top of the Export dialog is a Preset pop-up menu with a list of built-in presets, like the one shown here that burns (saves) your photos as full-size images in JPEG format at the maximum quality setting. If you have a RAW photo and want to export it as an Adobe DNG file (see the importing tutorial in Chapter 1 for more on DNG), then choose the Export to DNG preset and it fills in all the appropriate settings for you. If you want Photoshop Lightroom to prepare these photos for easy email-ing, choose the For E-Mail preset and it will enter the proper settings to lower the photo's file size, resolution, and physical dimensions so they're ideal for emailing. If you don't want to use these presets, then ignore this menu and enter your own settings. However, once you enter your own settings, if you think you'll be using these settings often, you should save them as a preset by going to the Preset pop-up menu and choos-ing Save as New Preset. When the New Preset dialog appears, give your preset a name and click Create. From now on, your preferred settings will appear as an Export preset in that pop-up menu.

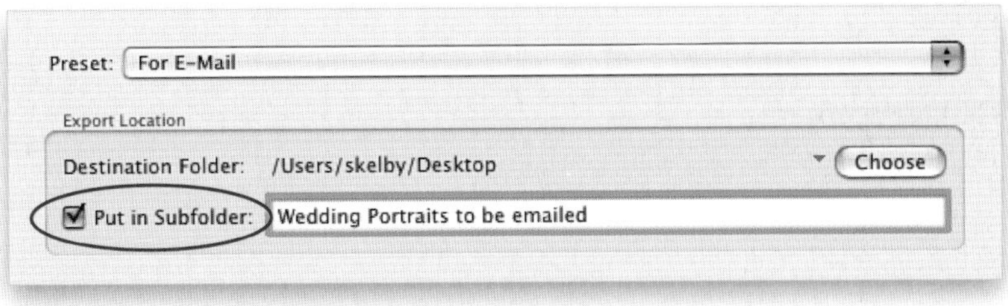

Step Four:

We'll assume for now that you want to enter your own custom settings. Start by choosing the folder you'd like your pho-tos exported into by clicking the Choose button (at the top right) and then navi-gating to the folder where you want your photos saved. If you want your photos put in a subfolder within that folder, turn on the Put in Subfolder checkbox (shown circled here) and give that subfolder a name in the field that appears to the right of the checkbox.

Continued

Step Five:

If you'd like, you can leave the filenames as they currently are, or you can have them automatically renamed as you export them (it's totally up to you). There are built-in naming templates, and the one I personally like best (because it's just so simple) is Custom Name – Sequence. This template lets you type in any file-name you'd like, and then it automatically adds a number to the end of your new name, starting at whichever number you tell it to by typing it in the Start Number field to the right of the Custom Text field (as seen here). Here, I simply named these shots "Bridal Shots" and Lightroom will add the numbers after, so the photos will wind up being named Bridal Shots-1, Bridal Shots-2, and so on.

Step Six:

Next you choose which file format to save your photos in. Under File Settings, there's a Format pop-up menu (shown here) where you can choose to save your photo as a JPEG, Photoshop PSD, TIFF, or an Adobe DNG (digital negative). If you choose JPEG (as I did here), a Quality slider appears on the right (as seen here). The higher the quality, the larger the file size. I generally choose a Quality setting of 80, which I think is a good tradeoff between quality and file size, giving you a photo that looks nearly identical to a 100 quality setting, but with only a fraction of the file size. PSD and DNG have no extra options, but if you choose TIFF, a pop-up menu will appear (where the JPEG Quality slider once was), where you can choose whether you want to compress your TIFFs as they're saved.

File Naming: Bridal Shots–1.jpg

Template: Custom Name – Sequence

Custom Text: Bridal Shots   Start Number: 1

File Naming: Bridal Shots–1.jpg

Template: Custom Name – Sequence

Custom Text: Bridal Shots   Start Number: 1

File Settings

Format: ✓ JPEG
PSD
TIFF
DNG

Quality: 80

Image Settings

Color Space: sRGB

Bit Depth: 8 bits/component

Resolution: 72   pixels per inch

☐ Add Copyright Watermark

☐ Minimize Embedded Metadata

☐ Constrain Maximum Size

Units: Pixels

Width:

Height:

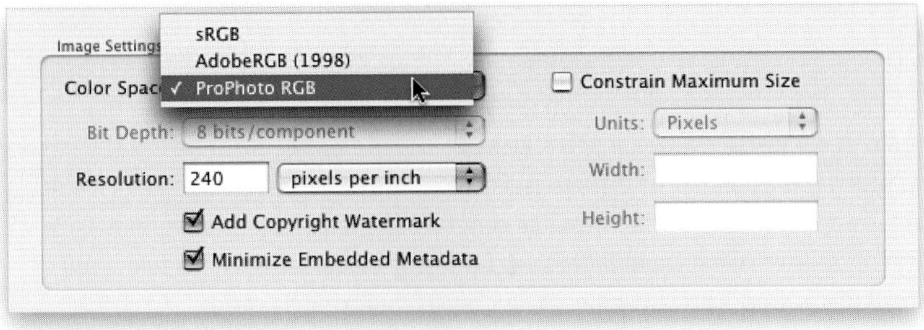

Step Seven:
Near the bottom of the Export dialog, in the Image Settings section, you can choose to embed the color space of your choice from the Color Space pop-up menu (choose sRGB for photos that are destined to appear on a webpage. Choose Adobe RGB [1998] or the wider-gamut ProPhoto RGB [Lightroom's native color space] if you'll be printing these or editing them again in Photoshop). Under that, you can enter the resolution you want your exported files to be. You can also choose to constrain them to a particular size (handy for the Web and/or video production). Below that are checkboxes for having your copyright info added as a visible watermark and for having much of the EXIF metadata automatically stripped out of your photo (handy because your clients don't need to know the background info on your camera, lens, etc., especially if you're selling these as stock photography).

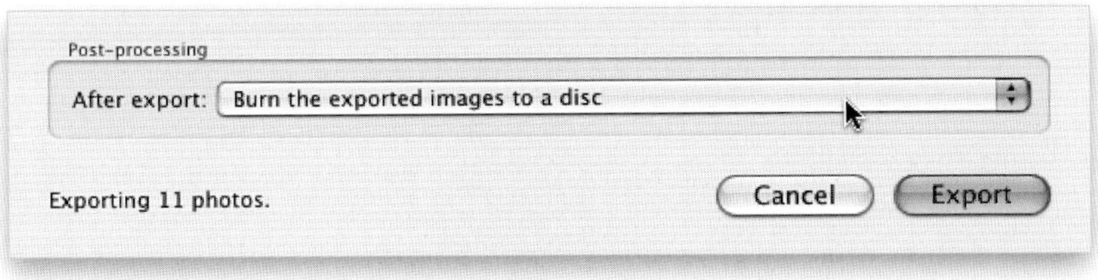

Step Eight:
At the bottom of the dialog is a Post-Processing section, where you can choose to have a simple task take place immediately after your export. For example, if you'd like your exported photos to be automatically backed up to a CD or DVD, choose Burn the Exported Images to a Disc from the After Export pop-up menu (as shown here) and after they're exported, it will launch your CD-burning application, and burn those same exported photos to a blank CD or DVD for safe backup of your final images (it will even ask you to insert a blank disc). Now, click the Export button and Lightroom will take it from here, placing the processed, saved files in the folder you choose in this Export dialog. Not bad, eh?

How to Email Photos From Photoshop Lightroom

Photoshop Lightroom does have an export to email function, but all that does is process your photos as small-sized JPEGs so they're easier for emailing, and it sticks them in a folder. However, if you take just a minute to tweak this feature, it can do so much more—in fact, it can process the photos for emailing, then launch your email application, and attach your photos to the email—all automatically. Then you're really emailing from Photoshop Lightroom, not just getting a folder full of small JPEGs. Here's how to set it up (luckily, it's surprisingly easy):

Step One:

The key to getting the full automation I just mentioned in the introduction to this tutorial is to create what's called an Export Action, which is basically telling Photoshop Lightroom what to do after it exports the photos as small JPEGs. In our case, we're going to ask Photoshop Lightroom to launch our default email application and attach our photos. You set this up in two places: (1) in the Export dialog, and (2) on your computer itself (don't worry—it's easy). Start by going to the File menu and choosing Export (as shown here).

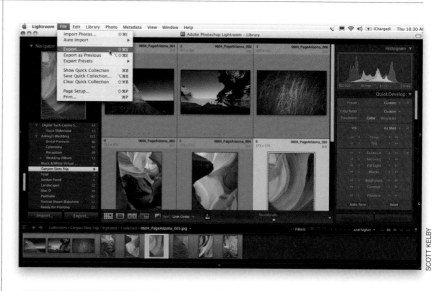

Step Two:

When the Export dialog appears, go to the bottom of the dialog to the Post-processing section, and from the After Export pop-up menu choose Go to Export Actions Folder Now (as shown here).

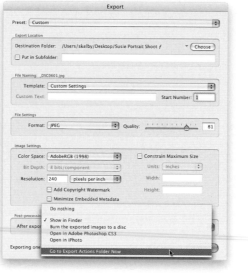

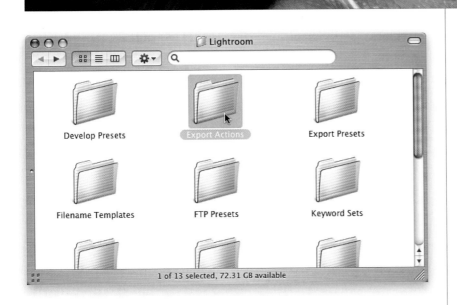

Step Three:
This brings up the folder on your computer where Lightroom's Export actions are stored (as shown here).

Step Four:
Leave that window with your Export Actions folder open, but then go to the folder on your computer where your applications are stored (on a Mac, it's your Applications folder; on a PC, it's your Program Files folder). Find your email application, and what you're going to do next is create an alias (on a Mac) or a shortcut (on a PC) to that application (basically, these are pointer icons that point to the real application). To create an alias on a Mac, you'd Control-click on your email application icon, and from the contextual menu that appears, choose Make Alias. Your alias icon would appear right beside your real email application's icon and it would have the word "alias" added to the name. On a PC, to create a shortcut, you'd Right-click on your email application icon and choose Create Shortcut from the contextual menu. Your shortcut would appear in the same folder.

Continued

Step Five:

Now, click-and-drag that alias (or shortcut) into Lightroom's Export Actions folder. If you open that folder, you should see your alias (or shortcut) in that folder (as shown here). Go ahead and click Cancel to close the Export dialog. Next you're going to create an Export preset that processes your photos as small JPEGs, then launches your email program, and attaches these smaller JPEG photos automatically (it's easier than it sounds, especially since you've done all the hard parts of this process already).

Step Six:

Go under the File menu, and choose Export to bring up the Export dialog again. From the Preset pop-up menu at the top, choose For E-Mail (as shown here). This loads settings that work well for emailing photos (it chooses the right quality setting, color space, resolution, size, etc., for emailing photos), however you can override any of these if you like (if you want a higher quality, just drag the slider to the right. Personally, I turn on the checkbox for Minimize Embedded Metadata, so it just includes my copyright and contact info in the metadata, and not all the info on my camera and settings). Next, go to the Post-processing section at the bottom, and from the After Export pop-up menu choose Mail Alias (on a Mac) or Shortcut to Outlook (on a PC), as shown here. Lastly, you want to save all this as a preset, so go up to the Preset pop-up menu, and choose Save as New Preset. When the New Preset dialog appears, give your new preset a name (I chose "Send in email") and click the Create button. Now, click Cancel in the Export dialog (it's okay, because we only came here to create a preset, and it's saved).

Step Seven:
Command-click (PC: Ctrl-click) on the photos you want to send in an email to select them. Once they're selected, go under the File menu, under Export Presets, and choose Send in Email as shown here (that's the Export preset you created in the previous step).

TIP: There are some differences for PC users: (1) when using Microsoft Outlook, you can only attach one photo at a time, and (2) this does not work on a standard installation of Outlook Express or Vista's Windows Mail at this time, although some users have been able to add a script to make this work for both.

Step Eight:
Lightroom takes it from there, and the next thing you'll see onscreen is your email application with a new email window open, with all your selected photos resized and attached to the email. All you have to do now is enter the email address of the person you want to send this to, add a Subject line, and hit Send. Since you've created this Export preset, the whole process will be just Steps Seven and Eight—select the photos and choose Send in Email. See, it was worth that little extra effort this one time to set up such an effortless emailing system.

Exposure: 1/25   Focal Length: 12mm   Aperture Value: ƒ/11

Problem Photos
correcting digital camera dilemmas

It's hard to believe that with the technology packed into today's digital cameras, that you could even take a messed-up photo. Seriously, you can buy point-and-shoot cameras that use high-tech satellites circling miles above the earth in a geosynchronous orbit to pinpoint the exact longitude and latitude of your camera's position at the moment a photograph is taken, but they still haven't come up with a solid solution for red eye. I can't believe we still have to deal with red eye, but we always have—probably always will. In the future, long after we're all gone, and people travel around with jet backpacks and flying cars, and they've cured everything from spontaneous baldness to bacterial meningitis, you'll find these photographers of the future hovering on some sort of floating platform, looking at an intricate lifelike 3D holographic photo, and you'll hear one of them say, "Oh no—it's got red eye. Didn't you turn on the pre-flash?" What's sad is that many digital camera manufacturers already have the technology to forever rid us of red eye, but the Red Eye Coalition and its high-powered Washington-based lobbying group have such a powerful grip over the Senate's Pop-up Flash Committee that I doubt we'll ever see the day when we take a photo using built-in flash and it doesn't look like our subjects are totally possessed. I'm just sorry I had to be the one to tell you this.

How to Undo Any Change at Any Time

Photoshop Lightroom keeps track of every edit you make to your photo in the Develop module, and it displays your edits as a running list in the History panel (in the order they were applied). So if you want to go back and undo any step, and return your photo to how it looked at any stage during your editing session, you can do that with just one click. Now, unfortunately, you can't just pull out one single step and leave the rest, but you can jump back in time to undo any mistake, and then pick up from that point with new changes. Here's how it's done:

Step One:
To see the history of your edits in the Develop module, click on the History panel header in the left side Panels area to expand it. This displays a list of all the changes you've made to your currently selected photo in this editing session, with the most recent changes at the top (as shown here). If you see a scroll bar along the left side, it means that there's more history in the list, and you can click on the scroll bar and drag downward to reveal the additional history states.

Step Two:
If you move your cursor over one of the history states, the small Navigator panel preview (which appears above the History panel) shows what your photo looked like at that point in history (as shown here, where a few steps back I had briefly converted this photo to grayscale. You can see the grayscale version in the Navigator panel's preview window).

SCOTT KELBY

Step Three:

If you actually want to jump back to what your photo looked like at a particular stage, then instead of hovering over the state, you'd click once on it and your photo reverts to that state. By the way, to undo steps, you don't have to use the History panel—you can also press Command-Z (PC: Ctrl-Z) on your keyboard. Each time you do, it undoes the previous edit. To move forward (adding back in your edits one by one), press Command-Shift-Z (PC: Ctrl-Y). When you use these keyboard shortcuts, the specifics of the history undo are displayed in very large letters near the bottom of your photo (as shown here). This is handy because you can instantly see which edits and settings you're undoing without having to keep the History panel open all the time.

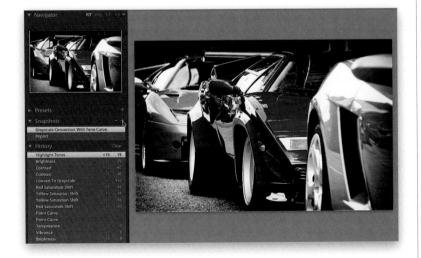

Step Four:

During your editing process, if you come to a point where you really like what you see, you can save that particular moment in time as a snapshot by clicking on the + (plus sign) button at the top right of the Snapshots panel (as shown here). That moment in time is saved to the Snapshots panel, and it appears with its name field highlighted so you can give it a name that makes sense to you (I named mine "Grayscale Conversion With Tone Curve" so I'd know that if I clicked on that snapshot, that's what I'd get—a black-and-white photo with the extra contrast I added using the Tone Curve panel. You can see my snapshot highlighted in the Snapshots panel shown here).

Continued

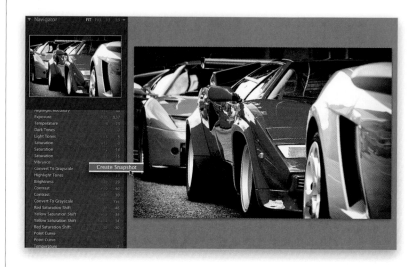

Step Five:

After you've created a snapshot, go ahead and continue editing this photo, then at some point go back and click on that snapshot to see Photoshop Lightroom instantly return your photo to how it looked at that moment in time. Two quick tips: (1) If you jump to a snapshot, the History panel lists that jump, too. So, if you jump to a snapshot, then change your mind, just go back and click on the state before your snapshot. And, (2) you don't have to actually click on a previous History state to save that state as a snapshot. Instead, you can just Control-click (PC: Right-click) on any state and choose Create Snapshot from the contextual menu that appears (as shown here). Lightroom will add that state as a snapshot without you having to actually change to that moment in time. Pretty handy.

Step Six:

Here's another important thing to know: let's say you do decide to jump back to a snapshot you've taken (here, I've jumped back to that Grayscale Conversion With Tone Curve snapshot I took earlier), and then you wind up improving on the look you had there (I went and increased the brightness a bit, and I like it better). Well, you can update your snapshot with your new, better settings—just Control-click (PC: Right-click) on your snapshot (in the Snapshots panel), and choose Update with Current Settings from the contextual menu that appears (as shown here).

Step Seven:

Okay, ready to start leveraging some more power? Great—check this out. So let's say you have created a snapshot and when you jump back to it, you really like the way your photo looks and think you might like to apply these same exact settings to other photos (for example, I kind of like the black-and-white conversion I've got going on in my Grayscale Conversion With Tone Curve snapshot). You can now save all those settings that got you to that look as a preset. That's right: first click on your snapshot, then go to the Presets panel and click on the + (plus sign) to add these settings as a preset. When the New Develop Preset dialog appears, give your preset a name and click Create (as shown here).

Step Eight:

Later, when you open a different photo, you can apply that same black-and-white conversion to this photo by going to the Presets panel and clicking on your new preset (you're only seeing a preview of the conversion in the Navigator panel up top, because I didn't click on the preset—I'm just hovering my cursor over it so I can see a preview before I commit). How cool is that?

TIP: A separate history is kept for each individual photo, so if you change to a different photo, it gets its own separate list of history states. If you return to the previous photo, that photo's history states will still be intact in the History panel.

Sharpening and Reducing Noise

Photoshop Lightroom gives you some simple controls for sharpening your photos and removing noise. I say simple because there's not much to them, and they honestly don't do a really kick-butt job of either task. I recommend doing all your sharpening in Photoshop CS2 or CS3, and I would do any noise reduction strategies (or use Photoshop plug-ins) there too, as opposed to using the basic controls found here in Lightroom. However, if you don't have Photoshop, you can use these basic tools (but I would make Photoshop CS3 my very next purchase).

Step One:

In the Develop module's right side Panels area, scroll down to the Detail panel, and you'll see a Sharpening Amount slider (shown circled here). That's pretty much it—one slider that controls the amount of sharpening applied to the photo. The default setting is 25%, but the sharpening is pretty subtle, so to see a change you'll have to really pour it on. Now, before you do that, I recommend two things: (1) to be able to see the effects of the sharpening, go to the Navigator panel (at the top of the left side Panels area) and click on the 1:1 zoom view; and (2) click on the Before/After view button in the toolbar so you can see how the sharpening looks alongside the original (as shown here).

Step Two:

To add sharpening to your image, just drag the Sharpening Amount slider to the right (in the example shown here, I dragged it all the way to 100%, and you can see the effects of the sharpening in the After version of the photo seen here). Again, I personally don't do any sharpening here in Photoshop Lightroom—I do all my sharpening in Photoshop CS2 or CS3, as the last thing I do before saving the file, because (as I mentioned in the intro above) it provides more control and better sharpening overall. But hey, that's just me.

Step Three:

If you're shooting using a high ISO or are taking photos in low light, chances are your photo has some noise in it (a visible graininess or those annoying red, green, and blue spots—or both). Just below the Sharpening slider (in the Detail panel), you'll find two Noise Reduction sliders (shown circled here in red). How effective are these sliders? Let's just say, "they ain't great" and leave it at that. Again, I'd try to reduce the noise in Photoshop CS2 or CS3, but if you want to give it a shot here in Lightroom, this is the place to try. Start by zooming to a 1:1 view, so you can see if the noise is really being reduced (at any less magnification, it's really hard to see the effect). The photo shown here, of my buddy Matt Kloskowski teaching in Tokyo, is packed with both types of noise.

Step Four:

Before we work on reducing the noise, this is another place the split-screen Before/After view really helps, so I'd bring that up now. To reduce the graininess, drag the Luminance slider to the right (as shown here) until the noise is reduced, or ideally is no longer visible. If you've got the red, green, and blue spots instead (or in addition, like we do here), then try dragging the Color slider to the right. In this case, to reduce the noise enough so it wasn't visible, I had to really drag those sliders over quite a bit (as shown here). There are two things to keep an eye out for when reducing noise using these sliders: (1) while they do reduce the noise in many cases, at the same time they can blur the details in the photo, so watch out for that, and (2) they can also desaturate the colors some-what, so again—just keep that in mind.

Fixing Chromatic Aberrations (a.k.a. That Annoying Color Fringe)

Sooner or later you're going to run into a situation where some of the more contrasty edges around your subject have either a red, green, or more likely a purple color halo or fringe around them (these are known as "chromatic aberrations"). You'll find these sooner (probably later today, in fact) if you have a really cheap digital camera (or a nice camera with a really cheap wide-angle lens), but even good cameras (and good lenses) can fall prey to this problem now and again. Luckily, it's easy enough to fix in Photoshop Lightroom.

Step One:

Here's a photo taken with an inexpensive point-and-shoot camera. If you look closely, it appears as though the roof of the white building has a color fringe or halo around it. This sometimes happens with very contrasty edges like this, where the white roof on the building meets the green trees and grass behind it. If you see something like this, go straight to the Lens Corrections panel in the right side Panels area of the Develop module (as shown here).

Step Two:

Click on the photo to zoom in tight on the white roof. By zooming in (you're seeing a 1:1 view here), it's much easier to determine the color of the edge fringe, which is the first step to reducing the problem (you'll need to know the fringe color for the next step). Now that you're zoomed in on that roof, you can see there is a red line running right along the edge of it, almost as if someone had traced along the roof with a thin red magic marker. That red line is a chromatic aberration.

Step Three:

Once you've identified which color the fringe is (it's red, in this case), go to the Chromatic Aberration section of the Lens Corrections panel and you'll see two sliders: one named Red/Cyan and one named Blue/Yellow. In our case, since our problem is red, drag the Red/Cyan slider to the left, toward red (as shown here). As you can see in the zoomed-in photo here, it greatly reduced the red border around our roofline. Of course, if the fringe you found in your photo was blue or yellow, you'd use the next slider down and drag toward the problem color. That's all there is to reducing chromatic aberrations.

Step Four:

Here, we returned to the zoomed-out Fit view, and you can see how much better the roof now looks, since we were able to reduce the red fringe quite a bit.

TIP: This tip really has nothing to do with fixing chromatic aberrations, but since there's some empty space here, it's as good a place as any. Another way to get finer control of the sliders in the Develop module panels is to make the panels wider—then the sliders are longer and the controls are not as broad when you drag them. To make the panels wider, click directly on the inside edge of the Panels area and drag in toward the Preview area to make the panels much wider. Now try dragging any of the Develop sliders and you'll see what I mean.

Removing (or Adding) Edge Vignetting

Vignetting is a lens problem that causes the edges of your photo to appear darker than the rest of the photo. This problem is usually more pronounced when you're using a wide-angle lens, but can be caused by a whole host of other issues, including the angle of the sun and not using the proper lens shade for your particular lens to name just a few. Now, a little darkness in the edges is considered a problem, but many photographers (myself included) like to exaggerate this edge darkening and employ it as a lighting effect in portraits. Here's how to fix it, and to add it:

Step One:

We'll start by removing the edge vignetting in a photo (in the photo shown here, you can see how the corner areas look darkened and shadowed). Scroll down to the Lens Corrections panel, and you'll see a section for Lens Vignetting. There are two vignetting sliders here: the first controls the amount of brightening in the edge areas, and the second slider lets you adjust how far in toward the center of your photo the corners will be brightened.

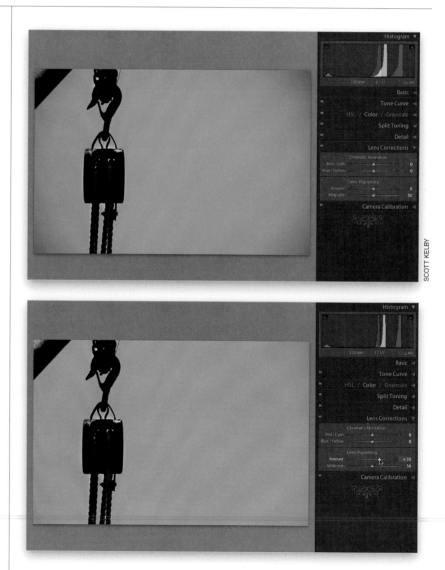

Step Two:

In this photo, the edge vignetting is fairly small (it's pretty much contained in the corners, and doesn't spread too far into the center of the photo). So, start to slowly drag the Amount slider to the right and as you do, keep an eye on the corners of your image. As you drag, the corners get brighter, and your job is to stop when the brightness of the corners matches the rest of the photo (as shown here). If the vignetting had extended further into the center of the photo, then you'd drag the Midpoint slider to the left to make your brightening cover a larger area. That's how easy removing this problem is.

Step Three:
Although the Lens Vignetting sliders are generally used for removing edge vignetting problems, they can also be used for adding a darkened edges effect to make your photo look like a soft spotlight has been aimed at the center of your photo. For years, I've been adding this effect to my photos manually in Photoshop (in the Camera Raw plug-in or in the Lens Correction filter in CS2 and CS3), but that same feature is also in Photoshop Lightroom, so now I do it here. The photo shown here has no vignetting applied yet, but by darkening the edges all the way around, it will put more focus on the riders and the heads of the horses.

Step Four:
Start by dragging the Lens Vignetting Amount slider nearly all the way to the left (as shown here), so the edges get pretty dark (the farther to the left you drag, the darker the edge areas of your photo will appear). However, if you only move this one slider, your photo now looks like it actually does have a vignetting problem, and that's not what you want. You're looking for a soft-edged spotlight effect, and to get that you'll need to now drag the Midpoint slider quite a bit to the left as well (as shown here). This both softens the effect and extends it much farther into the center of the photo, giving you the darkened outside edges and soft lighting effect you see here.

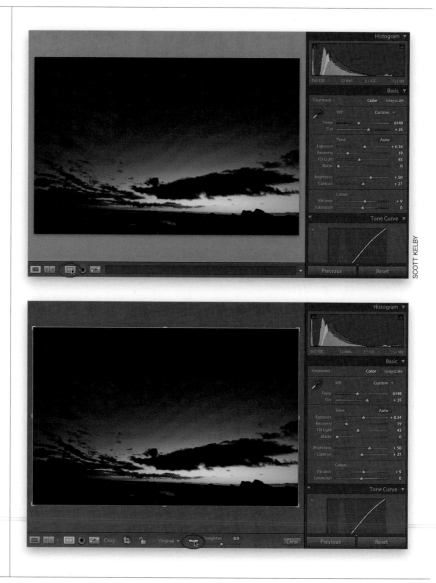

Cropping and Straightening

Photoshop Lightroom can both crop and straighten photos, and the straightening control in Photoshop Lightroom is among the best I've ever seen in any program. Cropping is a different story. If you're used to cropping in a program like Adobe Photoshop CS2 or CS3, then this might throw you for a loop, because it uses an entirely different way of cropping, and you might find you like it better. Hey, I said, "you *might* find you like it better," so I have a pretty big out if you don't like it, because it's way crazy different. It works. It's non-destructive. But it's different.

Step One:
The photo shown here has a huge problem—the horizon line isn't straight. In fact, it's so bad, we'd better fix this first (by the way, despite the fact that this shot was taken during the time frame that might be considered by some as "Happy Hour," I just want to say for the record, I was not the least bit hammered when I took this crooked shot—it takes more than the six or seven drinks I had before I shoot that crooked. Okay, you know I'm kidding here, right? Good). To be able to straighten your photo, you have to start by clicking on the Crop Overlay button, found on the left side of the toolbar below the Preview area (it's shown circled here), or pressing R.

Step Two:
When you click that button, a Crop Overlay border appears around your photo and if you look in the toolbar, the options for cropping and straightening are now visible. There are three different ways to straighten your photo, and once I show you all three, you can pick the one that's most comfortable for the way you work. We'll start with my favorite method, because I think it's the fastest and most accurate. Click on the Straighten tool (shown circled here) and it releases from the toolbar.

Step Three:

Now you simply take the Straighten tool, and click-and-drag it left to right along the horizon line, as shown here. (See why I like straightening like this? There's no guesswork or trial and error, but the catch is for this to work, you have to have something in the photo that's supposed to be straight—like a horizon, or a wall, or a window frame, etc.)

Step Four:

When you drag that tool, it shrinks and rotates the cropping border to the exact angle you'd need to straighten the photo (without leaving any white gaps in the corners). The exact angle of your correction is displayed in the toolbar (it's shown circled here in red). Now all you have to do is double-click anywhere inside that cropping border to lock in your straightening. If you decide you don't like your first attempt at straightening, just click the Clear button on the far right side of the toolbar, and it clears your straighten line, and returns the Straighten tool to the toolbar. So, to try again, grab the tool and start dragging. Here's the photo after being straightened using the Straighten tool.

Continued

Step Five:

The second method starts the same way—you click on the Crop Overlay button, but then you use the Straighten slider, dragging to the left to rotate your photo counterclockwise or to the right to rotate clockwise. As soon as you start moving the slider, a small grid with horizontal and vertical lines appears within the cropping border to help you align your photo (as shown here). This is pretty much a hit or miss proposition, and I only use this method if I can't get the Straighten tool to work.

Step Six:

The third method also starts the same way (click the Crop Overlay button), but then you move your cursor outside the cropping border—out into the gray area that surrounds your photo—and your cursor turns into a two-headed curved arrow. Now, you just click-and-drag your cursor straight up to rotate your photo counterclockwise or straight down to rotate clockwise. You'll see the Straighten slider move as you drag. Okay, here's my problem with this method (which is the same as my problem with the slider method): you're "eyeing" it. Sometimes, you have no choice but to eye it, and in those cases either method two or three will work, but if I can get away with using the Straighten tool, I'll always try it first. When you're done, you can click on the Crop Overlay button again to go back to your regular preview. So that's straightening, now on to cropping.

Step Seven:

To crop your photo, you have two choices: You can (1) click on the Crop Overlay button in the toolbar, and then resize that border to reflect the cropping you want for the photo. Now, since we straightened the photo first, you'll see that the photo itself has been rotated, but your cropping border is straight. Don't let this throw you—just focus on the straight cropping border and try to ignore the rotated photo, 'cause you've got work to do.

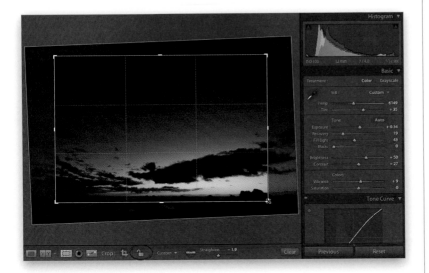

Step Eight:

To adjust the crop area, just grab one of the corners (or the sides, or anywhere on the border for that matter) and drag inward. As you drag, you'll notice that a grid appears dividing your cropped area into thirds, giving you a "rule of thirds" overlay (how sweet is that?!). By default, this crop area resizes proportionally (using the same aspect ratio as your photo). If you'd like a vertical cropping border (rather than the horizontal one shown here), just click on the bottom-right corner and drag up and to the left at a 45° angle, and it will flip over to being vertical. If you'd like a non-constrained freeform cropping border, just click on the lock icon in the toolbar to unlock the proportional constraint (shown circled in red here). Now you can move any side, the top, or bottom without it being constrained. When it looks good to you, just press the letter R on your keyboard to lock in your crop and hide the cropping border.

Continued

Step Nine:

The other way to crop is to click on the Crop Overlay button, then click on the Crop Frame tool (shown circled here in red) to release it from its home in the toolbar next to the word "Crop." Now you can just click-and-drag out a cropping border in the size and position you'd like it (by the way, you can reposition the photo within the cropping border any time by clicking within the border and dragging). If at any time you want to cancel your cropping, just click on the Clear button on the far right side of the toolbar.

Step Ten:

When your cropping border is right where you want it, just press the letter R on your keyboard to lock in your crop. Here's the crop I made using the Crop Frame tool in the previous step, with the constraint lock turned off, so I could create the panorama-like crop seen here.

Step Eleven:
Go ahead and press G on your keyboard to return to the Library module's Grid view. When you look at your thumbnail in the grid, you'll see it updated to show your new cropped version, and a new badge icon is added to the bottom-right corner of the thumbnail (shown circled here—it's the center icon). That icon is to let you know that the photo has been cropped. If you click directly on that icon, it returns you to the Develop module with the cropping border visible again, to show you the entire photo and where you positioned your crop. If you double-click on that icon, it will return you to the Develop module with the cropping border off.

TIP: You know how when you crop a photo by clicking-and-dragging the border that "rule of thirds" grid appears? Well, you can choose to have a grid appear within your cropping border at any time (or you can choose to have no grid at all, as it is by default) by just pressing the letter O. Each time you press it, it toggles through the different grid views.

Step Twelve:
Now, because of the non-destructive nature of Lightroom, any crop you apply can always be removed, and your original photo brought back unscathed. You do that by first clicking on the Crop Overlay button, and then clicking on the Clear button on the right side of the toolbar (as shown here). As you can see here, the original photo is now back—crooked horizon and all. If you just want to change your crop (rather than remove it altogether), then click on the Crop Overlay button, and your cropping border returns over your photo for easy editing. When you're done editing your crop, press R.

The Ultimate Way To Crop

When you crop a photo using the Crop Overlay tool in the Develop module, the area that will get cropped away is automatically dimmed to give you a better idea of how your photo is going to look when you apply the final crop. That's not bad, but it's not this either: if you want the ultimate cropping experience, where you really see what your cropped photo is going to look like, then do your cropping in Lights Out mode. You'll never crop outside it again—here's how it's done (and why it's so cool):

Step One:

To really appreciate this technique, first you have to do a regular crop, so click on a photo, go to the Develop module, press F5 and F6 to hide the task bar and the filmstrip, get the Crop Overlay tool (R) and crop an image (the photo shown here needs some serious cropping—the stem kind of goes off at an angle, and it was just badly composed to begin with. I'm pretty sure I was drinking heavily at the time. You know I'm totally kidding, right? About the drinking—not the bad composition). Anyway, you see the dimmed area that will be cropped away. Okay, click the Clear button on the right end of the toolbar to reset the cropping border (and undo your crop).

Step Two:

Press the letter L twice to enter Lights Out mode, where everything is hidden, your photo's centered on a black background, but your cropping border is still live. Now try cropping in with the Crop Overlay tool and watch the difference—you really see what you're going to get as you're dragging the cropping border. It's the ultimate way to crop (you can't tell from the static graphic here—you have to try this one for yourself, and you'll never go "dim" again! Well, you might have some dim moments, but…aw forget it).

Basic Camera Calibration in Photoshop Lightroom

Some cameras seem to put their own color signature on your photos, and if yours is one of those, you might notice that all your photos seem a little red, or have slight green tint in the shadows, etc. Even if your camera produces accurate color, you still might want to tweak how Photoshop Lightroom interprets the color. The process for doing a full, accurate camera calibration is kinda complex and well beyond the scope of this book, but I did want to show you what the Camera Calibration panel is used for, and give you a good resource to take things to the next level.

Step One:
Before we start, I don't want you to think that camera calibration is something everybody must do. In fact, I imagine most people will never even try a basic calibration, because they don't notice a big enough consistent color problem to worry about it (and that's a good thing. However, in every crowd there's always one, right?). So, here's a quick tutorial on the very basics of how the Camera Calibration panel works: Open a photo, then go to the Develop module's Camera Calibration panel, found at the very bottom of the right side Panels area, as shown here (see, if Adobe thought you'd use this a lot, it would be near the top, right?).

Step Two:
The topmost slider is for adjusting any tint that your camera might be adding to the shadow areas of your photos. If it did add a tint, it's normally green or magenta—look at the color bar that appears inside the Tint slider itself. By looking at the color bar, you'll know which way to drag (for example, here I'm dragging the Tint slider away from green, toward magenta to reduce any greenish color cast in the shadow areas).

Continued

Step Three:

If your color problems don't seem to be in the shadows, then you'll use the Red, Green, and Blue Primary sliders to adjust the Hue and Saturation (the sliders that appear below each color). Let's say your camera produces photos that have a bit of a red cast to them. You'd drag the Red Primary Hue slider away from red (as shown here), and if you needed to reduce the overall saturation of red in your photo, you'd drag the Red Primary Saturation slider to the left until the color looks neutral (by neutral, I mean the grays should look really gray, not reddish gray).

Step Four:

When you're happy with your changes, press Command-Shift-N (PC: Ctrl-Shift-N) to bring up the New Develop Preset dialog. Name your preset, click the Check None button (as shown here), then turn on only the Calibration checkbox, and click Create. Now, not only can you apply this preset in the Develop module and Quick Develop panel, you can have it applied to all the photos you import from that camera by choosing it from the Develop Settings pop-up menu in the Import Photos dialog (also shown here).

Note: If you want to tackle the full camera calibration process, I recommend this online article by Eric Chan (http://people .csail.mit.edu/ericchan/dp/acr/). Although this article is for calibration with Adobe Camera Raw (ACR), not only are the Lightroom controls the same, but many users are recommending that you do your camera calibration in ACR (because you can download a free script that will do it for you), then copy those settings into Lightroom's Camera Calibration panel.

SCOTT KELBY

Great Trick for "Dust Spotting" Your Photos

This trick barely made it into this book (in fact, it got in the book the same day it went to press), but it comes straight from the horse's mouth (so to speak). I read about it in an interview with Adobe's Mark Hamburg, known as the Father of Lightroom, where he told about an undocumented feature that helps you ensure that when you're checking an image to remove specks and dust, you actually inspect every inch of your image (that's harder than you'd think—especially with a large high-res photo), but now it's nearly automatic—thanks to Mark.

Step One:

The time-honored way to make sure you properly "spot" your image is to use the scroll bars or a combination of the Page Up and Page Down and Arrow keys to try and make sure you've inspected every inch of your photo. It's tedious, and even a little tricky, but it's really the only way to be sure (until now). Start by pressing Z to zoom in to a 1:1 view. Go to the Navigator panel (at the top of the left side Panels area), and drag the little rectangle inside the Navigator panel preview so you're just seeing the top-left corner of your photo (as shown here).

Step Two:

Now use the Remove Spots tool (N) and start dust spotting. Once you've "spotted" the area shown onscreen, press the Page Down key on your keyboard to move straight down by exactly one section and continue spotting. Previously, when you hit the bottom of your image window it would stop, so you'd manually try to position your photo back up at the top, but over one column so you didn't miss any areas (basically, you'd eye it). But now when you hit the bottom, just press the Page Down key again, and it wraps back up to the top of the photo, exactly one column over. If you keep doing this until you reach the bottom-right corner, you're guaranteed to see every inch.

Removing Spots and Other Nasty Junk

Although the Remove Spots tool in Photoshop Lightroom is certainly no match for Photoshop CS2/CS3's Healing Brush, or Spot Healing Brush, or Patch tool, or Clone Stamp tool, or… (seriously, stop me any time), it does a fairly decent job, and once you get used to using it (it's not the most intuitive tool), you'll be surprised how many times you actually do use it. Now, I have to say that if I know at some point I'm going to take this photo over to Photoshop CS3, I'll wait and use the tools there to do the job, but if I'm not going there, I'll do it here.

Step One:

If you find a photo that has visible dust, spots, or other nasty junk (we generally refer to all this unwanted stuff as "artifacts" because it makes us feel really smart), then head to the Develop module, because there's a tool there that can help. In the photo shown here, there are a number of different spots visible in the sky, and they're caused by dust appearing on our digital camera's sensor. The bad thing is if they're on this photo, chances are those spots are in the same place on every photo from this shoot (but we'll deal with that later—for now, let's fix this one photo).

Step Two:

The first step in getting rid of these artifacts is to zoom in tight, so you can really see what you're working on (and so you don't create a new problem—really obvious retouching—while you're trying to fix an existing problem). To zoom in, either click within your photo or press Command-+ (PC: Ctrl-+) to zoom in. (By the way, Command-- [minus sign] zooms you back out. It's Ctrl-- on a PC.)

Step Three:

Once you've zoomed in on the specks, dust, or spots you want to remove, click on the Remove Spots tool in the toolbar at the bottom of the Preview area, or just press the letter N to switch to that tool. Once you get the tool, the toolbar immediately displays the options for the tool, which are Clone (where it copies a nearby part of the photo over the spot) or Heal (where it samples the lighting, texture, and tone of a nearby area). Personally, I think the healing does a lot better job than the cloning option (meaning the repair is less noticeable in most cases), so click on the Heal option (circled here in red). There's also a size slider in the toolbar, which controls the size of the area to be healed.

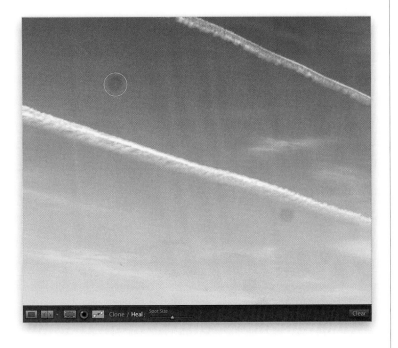

Step Four:

Now take the Remove Spots tool and move it over the spot you want to remove. The circle that appears shows the size of the area that will be affected by your healing, and you want that circle to be just a little bigger than the spot you want to remove (as shown here). You could use the Spot Size slider in the toolbar to change the size, but it's faster to use the Left and Right Bracket keys on your keyboard (they're to the immediate right of the letter P). Each time you press the Right Bracket (]) key it makes the circle larger; the Left Bracket ([) key makes it smaller. So, quickly "size it up."

Continued

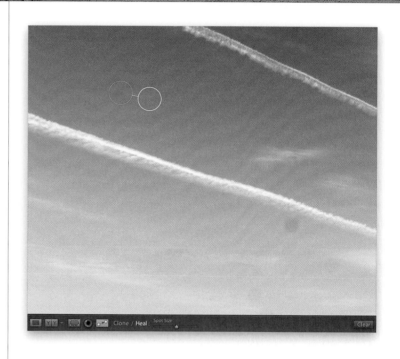

Step Five:

You don't paint with this tool, you just click once. If you click once, you'll see two circles appear: (1) the pink circle shows the area that is being fixed, and (2) the green circle shows where the texture, lighting, and tone are being drawn from if you're using the Heal option, or it shows where you're cloning from if you chose the Clone option. If you click, Photoshop Lightroom chooses a spot for you (it usually picks a very nearby area in about the 4 o'clock position, as seen here). If the background is pretty simple, like the one shown here, this one-click-and-you're-done method works pretty well, because Lightroom could hardly pick a bad area to sample from—it's a big blue sky with a few clouds. However, you'll want to know about a second method if the spot shows up in a trickier place.

Step Six:

Instead of just clicking once, click over the spot, hold, and drag your cursor to the area you'd like to have Lightroom sample from for its cloning or healing. When you first start dragging, a thin line connects both circles, but as you move further away, an arrow appears that points back to the area you're repairing (as seen here. I'll bet you thought I added that little white arrow to help illustrate what's going on, but believe it or not, that arrow is generated by Lightroom automatically as you drag further away. You gotta love that!). As soon as you let go of the mouse button, it fixes that area (here the Remove Spots tool, set to Heal mode, did a nice job of removing the left spot from this high-resolution photo in just seconds).

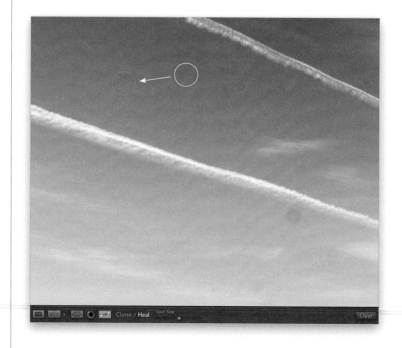

Step Seven:

To remove more spots, just move the tool over the spot, click, hold, and drag out your sampler (as shown here), and when you release the mouse button, the fix is in!

Step Eight:

Each time you use this tool, both the pink and green circles stay in place until you click somewhere else, leaving a single circle around your original spot. So if you've got a lot of spots, it won't be long before you've got a lot of circles onscreen. That's why it's helpful to take a quick look at the Before view, so you can really see if the tool is doing the job without being obvious. To see the Before view, just press the Backslash key (\) on your keyboard. The word "Before" will appear in the bottom right-hand corner of the screen (as shown here), and the spots you removed will reappear. To see the After view, just click once on the Remove Spots tool in the toolbar, and you'll see what your retouch looks like without the circles (and without the nasty spots), or just press the Backslash key again.

Continued

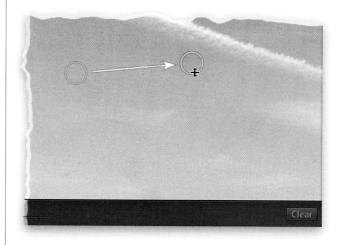

Step Nine:

If you've clicked the tool over a spot and the circle that determines the area to be fixed isn't large enough, you can move your cursor right to the edge of the circle, and it will change into a two-headed arrow (seen here). Now just click-and-drag outward to make both circles bigger, or click-and-drag inward to make them smaller. By the way, any-time you want to start over and forget the spot healing ever happened, just click the Clear button on the right side of the toolbar.

Step Ten:

There's another method of choosing the size of the area you're going to clone/heal from, and that is to press-and-hold the Command (PC: Ctrl) key and click-and-drag out a selection around your spot. I usually start by clicking just to the upper left of the spot, and drag across the spot at a 45° angle. As I do, it lays down a starting point, and then my circle drags right over the spot (as shown here, where my circle is a little too large. Since I'm using this "drag out a circle" technique, I can just drag back inward and resize the circle down a bit so it's a better fit).

Step Eleven:

Also, if you want quick access to the tool-bar options (this is especially handy if you don't like to have the toolbar visible, so you can have larger previews), just Control-click (PC: Right-click) within one of your two circles, and a contextual menu will appear. At the top of the menu (shown here) are the options for choosing to clone, heal, or reset the Spot Removal tool, so you can start over. Not too shabby!

Step Twelve:

Now, in the first step I mentioned that the dust on my camera's sensor created these annoying spots in the exact same position in every shot from that shoot. If that's the case (and with spots like this, it often is), then once you've removed all the spots, click the Copy button at the bottom of the left side Panels area. This brings up the Copy Settings dialog shown here. First, click the Check None button, so everything it would copy from your photo is unchecked. Then, turn on just the checkbox for Spot Removal (as shown here). Now, go to the filmstrip (or the Library Grid view) and select all the photos from that shoot that you suspect have those same sensor spots in the exact same location. Then click on any of the selected photos, and press the Paste button at the bottom of the left side Panels area. Now, all the same spots in all those photos are removed. Of course, take a quick look at the results, as it's possible that, depending on the background in your other shots, the fixes could look more obvious than on the photo you just fixed. If you see a problem, press Command-Z (PC: Ctrl-Z) to Undo the paste, then get the Remove Spots tool and redo that one shot manually.

Removing Red Eye

If you wind up with red eye in your photos (hey, it can happen. Especially if you have to grab a point-and-shoot camera to shoot your kid's birthday party at Chuck E. Cheese's—they're notorious as "red-eye generators" thanks to that flash being mounted so close to the lens), Photoshop Lightroom can get rid of it. This is really handy because it saves you from having to jump over to Photoshop CS2/CS3 just to remove red eye from a photo of your neighbor's six-year-old crawling through a giant hamster tube. Here's how it works:

Step One:

The Remove Red Eye tool is only available in the Develop module, so once you find a photo with red eye in the Library module, click on it, then press the letter D to take it over to the Develop module (shown here). The Remove Red Eye tool is located on the toolbar, right below the center Preview area (it looks like an eye).

KLEBER STEPHENSON

Step Two:

To make the tool active, click directly on it, and it'll turn red to let you know it's active (as you can see in the capture shown here). Take the tool and click-and-drag out a selection around one of the red eyes (I used the term "selection," but it's not really a selection in the Photoshop sense—it's more a box with a solid line). As soon as you drag it out, it removes the red eye. If it doesn't fully remove all the red, you can expand how far out it removes red by dragging the Pupil Size slider to the right (shown circled in red here).

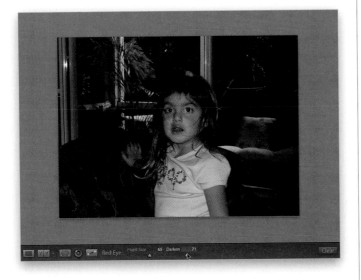

Step Three:

Once that eye looks good, go ahead and put a selection around the other eye (the corrected eye still stays selected, but it's "less selected" than your new eye selection—if that makes any sense at all, and I'm not sure it does). As soon as you click-and-drag out the selection, this eye is fixed too. If the repair makes the eye look too gray, you can make the eye look darker by dragging the Darken slider to the right (as shown here). The nice thing is that these sliders (Pupil Size and Darken) are live, so as you drag, you see the results right there onscreen—you don't have to drag a slider and then reapply the tool to see how it looks. If you make a mistake and want to start over, just click the Clear button on the far right side of the toolbar.

Step Four:

When you've completed your red eye repair, click your cursor back on the Remove Red Eye tool icon in the toolbar (as shown here), and it removes your selections so you can see the final results seen here. That's pretty much all there is to it.

Adding Photoshop Automation to Your Lightroom Workflow

With all the marvelous things Photoshop Lightroom does, one thing it really doesn't do is professional-level image sharpening. That's something we still have to jump over to Adobe Photoshop for. However, if you don't mind spending just a few minutes in Photoshop now, you can make this process almost fully automated from here on out, which will save loads of time in your daily workflow. We're going to do this by creating a sharpening action in Photoshop, saving it as a droplet, then using that droplet in Lightroom as an export action. Sound interesting? It is, and it's easy.

Step One:

We start this process in Adobe Photoshop, so go ahead and open a photo in Photoshop that could use some sharpening. What we're going to do here in Photoshop is create an action. Photoshop's Actions feature is basically a step recorder that records your steps as you do a particular task. Then it lets you apply that recording (those same steps) to a different photo automatically, and much faster, which is why they're ideal for repetitive tasks like sharpening.

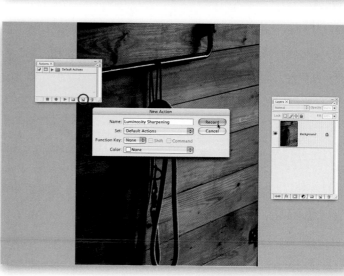

Step Two:

To create an action, go to the Window menu and choose Actions to make the Actions palette visible. Click on the Create New Action icon at the bottom of the palette (it looks just like the Create a New Layer icon and is circled here). This brings up the New Action dialog (shown here). Go ahead and give your action a name (I named mine "Luminosity Sharpening") and click the Record button, as shown here (notice the button doesn't say OK or Save, it says Record because it's now recording your steps).

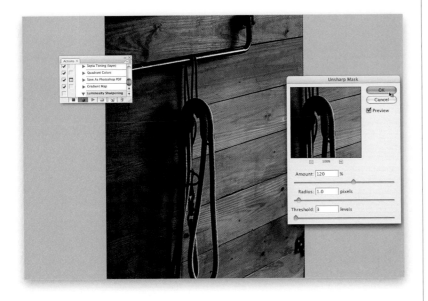

Step Three:
Now that you're recording, go under the Filter menu, under Sharpen, and choose Unsharp Mask. When the Unsharp Mask dialog appears, for Amount enter 120%, for Radius enter 1.0, and for Threshold enter 3 levels (as shown here), then click OK. This adds a nice snappy amount of sharpening to your photo.

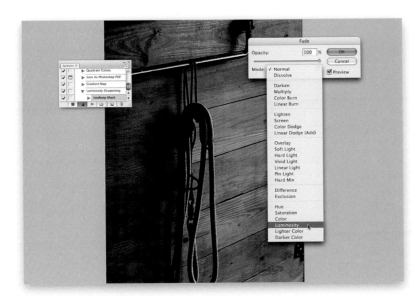

Step Four:
Now we're going to go under the Edit menu and choose Fade Unsharp Mask. This brings up the Fade dialog you see here. From the Mode pop-up menu, choose Luminosity (as shown here). We're doing this so our sharpening is only applied to the luminosity of the photo (the detail areas) and not the color in the image. By avoiding sharpening the color in our photo, it helps us avoid some of the color halos and color artifacts (annoying little color specks) that sometimes appear when you sharpen the full-color image. The result is that we generally apply more sharpening without damaging our photo, so this is a good extra step. (*Note:* Another way to do this is to convert to Lab Color mode, go to the Channels palette, click on the Lightness channel, and just apply your sharpening to that one channel. Then, switch back to RGB Color mode. It's totally up to you, but they basically do the same thing).

Continued

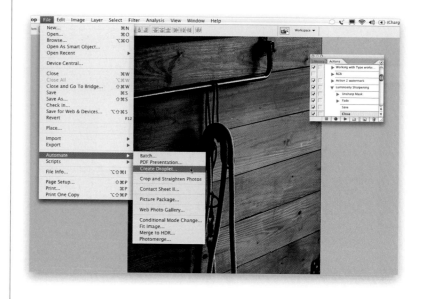

Step Five:

Now you can press Command-S (PC: Ctrl-S) to save your photo, then press Command-W (PC: Ctrl-W) to close your photo. Since it's been saved and closed, go back to the Actions palette and click the square Stop Recording button at the bottom left of the palette. That's it— you've created your action. Now, we're going to turn your action into a droplet by going under the File menu, under Automate, and choosing Create Droplet (as shown here).

Step Six:

So you're probably thinking, "What's a droplet?" I'll explain that in the next step (it's easier to explain then), so for now just follow along with me in the Create Droplet dialog (shown here). At the top of the dialog, click the Choose button, choose your Desktop as the destination for saving your droplet, and go ahead and name this saved droplet "Unsharp Mask." Then, under the Play section of this dialog, make sure to choose Luminosity Sharpening (that's what we named our action earlier) from the Action pop-up menu (as shown here). That's it—you can ignore the rest of the dialog, and just click OK.

Step Seven:

If you look on your Desktop, you'll see an icon with a large arrow on it, and the arrow is aiming at the name of the droplet. So, here's what a droplet does: If you drag-and-drop a photo that's on your Desktop, or in a folder on your computer, right onto this droplet (like a JPEG, TIFF, PSD, etc.), the droplet automatically launches Photoshop, opens that photo, and applies that Luminosity Sharpening action to the photo you dropped on there. Then it saves and closes that sharpened photo automatically (because you recorded that as part of the action). You can also create what are called batch actions, where you can drag-and-drop an entire folder of photos on there and it will process each one automatically. Pretty cool stuff.

Step Eight:

So, now that we've built our Unsharp Mask droplet in Photoshop, we're going to add that to our Lightroom workflow. Go back to Lightroom and go under the File menu and choose Export. When the Export dialog appears, go down to the Post-processing section, and from the After Export pop-up menu, choose Go to Export Actions Folder Now (as shown here). (*Note:* What this pop-up menu here does is, it lets you choose what happens to your exported photos once they leave Lightroom. We're going to add something to this list in the next step, but to do that we have to get to the folder on your computer where Lightroom stores all this stuff, and the quickest way to get there is to have Lightroom bring up the folder for us, which is what we're doing here).

Continued

Step Nine:

When you choose that menu item, it brings up the main folder with all of Lightroom's extras (like the Export Actions folder). What you need to do is take that Unsharp Mask droplet you created (the one on your Desktop) and click-and-drag it into the Export Actions folder (if you look inside that folder, you'll see the droplet you just dragged in there, as shown here). In our example, you also see the alias (shortcut) I added to the Export Actions folder from my "How to Email Photos from Right Within Lightroom" tutorial in Chapter 4. Okay, so that's the deal—drag your droplet into the Export Actions folder. Now you can head back to Lightroom and close the Export dialog.

Step Ten:

In Lightroom, choose a photo that you want to export from Lightroom as a JPEG, and that you want sharpened in Photoshop before you send it to a client, or burn it to CD, etc. Go under the File menu and choose Export. When the Export dialog appears, choose Burn Full-Sized JPEGs from the Preset menu at the top as a good starting place. Choose the destination folder for your saved JPEGs in the Export Location section, give your photo a name, and choose your JPEG quality setting. Then, in the Post-processing section at the bottom, from the After Export pop-up menu choose Unsharp Mask (your droplet), as shown here. When you click Export, your photo will be saved as a JPEG, then Photoshop will automatically launch, it will open your photo, apply your luminosity sharpening, then save and close the photo, so it's fully sharpened and now ready to send to your client. Pretty slick stuff!

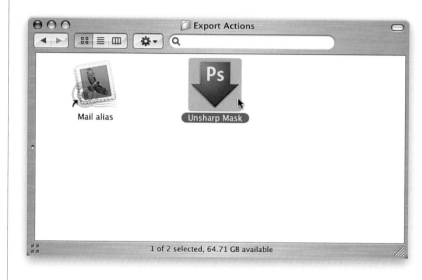

Exposure: 1/60 | Focal Length: 70mm | Aperture Value: ƒ/5.6

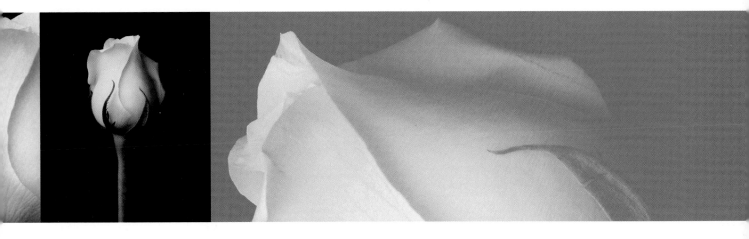

Gorgeous B&W
converting from color to black and white

I don't know many photographers who don't just love black and white. Well, actually the color black. You see, once you become a serious photographer, you want to sell your prints. Of course, once that happens once or twice, you're no longer satisfied with what you sold your first prints for, so now you have to find a way to charge more. But here's the catch: you can't just sell the same prints and charge more, right? You'd have to shoot new stuff, better stuff, in fact better stuff than you can actually shoot, which is tough because in reality you can only shoot as good as you can shoot. So, what's going to make up for your lack of talent and vision? Black clothing. You need a black shirt, pants, socks, coat, shoes, etc. Black clothing on a photographer is like magic because that tells the world you're not just a photographer,

you're an artist and obviously mourning something deep inside your soul. Perhaps an emotional loss, but you're so tortured by it that you can't talk about it. The only way to express your inner angst is through your "art" which is now worth a whole lot more because you're no longer some schmuck with a camera trying to make a buck; you're a deep, mysterious artist they could never understand. This makes your work irresistible to people who love buying the work of tortured artists (which is just about everybody). So now you're living in a luxury apartment on the Upper East Side and you've decorated it all in just one color—white. Why white? Because you needed to make a personal statement about monochromaticity, corporate plundering, and man's inhumanity to man. That, and you're really sick of black.

Basic Black and White (The One-Click Solution Using Quick Develop)

In this chapter, we're going to look at a lot of different methods for converting your color photos into black and white, because there are a lot of different ways to do it in Photoshop Lightroom, depending on how serious you are about your black and white. The first method is pretty much a "one-click wonder" because it converts from color to black and white, and it does a pretty decent job of it. But after we do that, we're going to look at another way to put this to use to help us with other black-and-white techniques.

Step One:
You can convert any photo to black and white right within the Library module (there are a couple of different ways to do it, but we'll start with the easiest first). Then, I've got a tip to help you with the hardest part of creating good black-and-white photos: finding which ones look great in black and white (it's more of an art than you'd think). Start by clicking on a color photo in the Library module to select it, then press E to enter the larger Loupe view.

Step Two:
Now go to the Quick Develop panel (in the right side Panels area) and click on the Grayscale button, shown circled here in red (if you don't see it, click on the double arrow at the top right to expand that section). I know that grayscale is not normally a term we use for a black-and-white photo. Black-and-white photos are just that—black and white. Grayscale is more of a term used by graphic designers, and I pointed that out to friends on Photoshop Lightroom's development team during Beta testing. You can see the impact I had, as it's still called grayscale. Don't get me started. Anyway, that's it—you click the button, it's done, but it usually produces kind of a flat-looking grayscale image (as seen here). In this case, to me it's also a little dark.

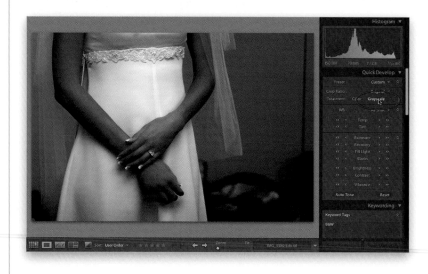

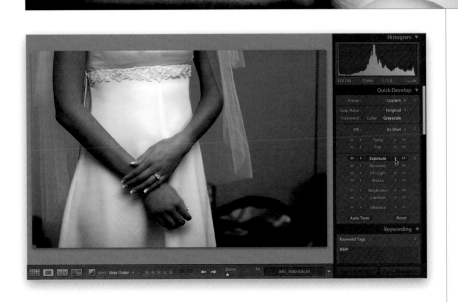

Step Three:

If you think the default conversion is a little dark, that's easy enough to fix, because you're already working in the Quick Develop panel. Go to the Exposure control and click once on the single right arrow to increase the exposure by 1/3-stop (as shown here). This looks a little better, but if you think it's still too dark, click it again. Just keep an eye on the Histogram panel up top. If your graph hits the right side wall, you're going to be losing detail in her white wedding dress, and she'll probably be really ticked (I wouldn't be surprised if she said something to you like, "Hey, you're clipping the highlights in my dress. Don't you ever check your histogram?").

Step Four:

If you'd like to start with a brighter, better black-and-white photo, then take advantage of the built-in presets. Even though they're technically in the Develop module, you can access them here in the Library module, at the top-right corner of the Quick Develop panel. Just click on the Presets pop-up menu and choose Grayscale Conversion (as shown here), and you'll usually get a better result (or at the very least, a much brighter result). Of course, after you choose this preset, you can always tweak the Exposure, Shadows, Fill Light, etc., settings right here in the Quick Develop panel. If you think it looks too bright, try clicking the Exposure control's single left arrow to back off the exposure by 1/3-stop. Either way, both of these are decent starting places, but as you'll see in a moment, you can do better. But first, a great use for the one-click Grayscale button.

Continued

Step Five:

As I mentioned earlier, the hardest part of coming up with a great black-and-white photo is not the conversion process, it's figuring out which of your photos would look good as a black and white. Some photos, when converted to black and white, just look awful because it was their color that made them work (like the photo selected here). However, others might actually look much better as a black and white, but you don't know until you see them in black and white. That's what this tip is about—seeing them. Start with a collection of photos and view them in the Library's Grid view (as shown here).

Step Six:

Press Command-A (PC: Ctrl-A) to select all of the photos in this collection. Now, you're going to make virtual copies of all these photos (remember, virtual copies are just sets of instructions—you're not duplicating your JPEG or TIFF image file—so they take up virtually no space on your hard disk. Get it? *Virtually* no space for a *virtual* copy. Sorry, that was lame). So, go under the Photo menu and choose Create Virtual Copies (as shown here).

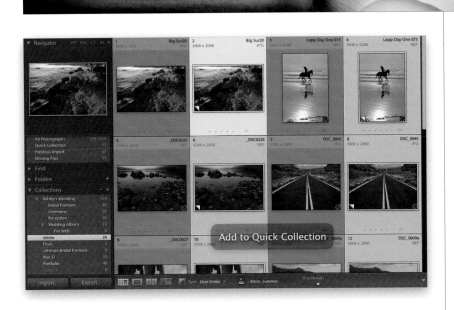

Step Seven:

Now, a virtual copy will appear right beside each of your original photos in the grid. When these virtual copies appear, they appear already selected (you can see they're all highlighted in the image shown here). While they're still selected, press the letter B on your keyboard to add these to a Quick Collection (as shown here).

Step Eight:

Go to the Library panel (in the left side Panels area) and click on Quick Collection, where you'll see all the virtual copies you made in the previous step (you can tell they're virtual copies because of the curled page icon in the bottom-left corner of each thumbnail). Now press Command-A (PC: Ctrl-A) to select all these photos, then go to the Quick Develop panel and click on Grayscale (as shown here). This converts all these color virtual copies to black-and-white photos, as seen here (okay, grayscale photos, but you know what I mean). You're not done yet, but you're almost there.

Continued

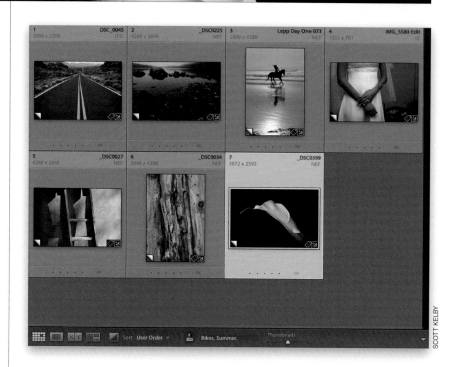

Step Nine:

Once they're all grayscale, deselect all the photos in your Quick Collection by pressing Command-D (PC: Ctrl-D). Now you can scroll through the photos looking for ones that just don't look good as black-and-white images (don't worry—they'll stand out like a sore thumb). When you find a photo that just doesn't look good in black and white, click on it and hit the Delete (PC: Backspace) key on your keyboard to remove it from your Quick Collection. Once you do this for a few minutes, you'll be left with just the photos that look good in black and white.

Step Ten:

At this point, you've probably got some pretty flat-looking black-and-white photos, but you can fix that in a moment. For now, you're just trying to determine which ones look good, and you're deleting the ones that don't. Once you're down to just the best ones, you can start tweaking them to make them look better. Double-click on one of these remaining virtual copies so it opens in Loupe view. Now it's time to add contrast and depth to your photo. In the example shown here, I increased the exposure, increased the Recovery amount, increased the shadows, and increased the contrast quite a bit—a recipe that usually helps flat-looking black-and-white photos (of course, I like really contrasty black-and-white photos, so you'll have to adjust the photo to your personal taste, which may be more or less contrasty than mine). Remember: Even though this is a virtual copy, you can turn it into a real photo by either saving it as a JPEG, TIFF, or PSD, or jumping over to Photoshop for further editing. Doing either one applies your instructions to create a "real" photo.

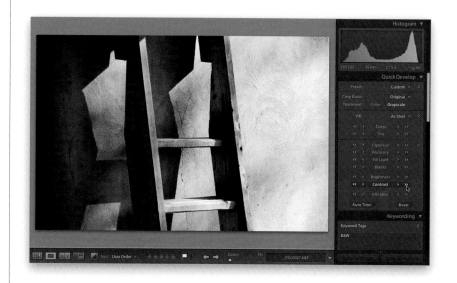

Step Eleven:

Now that you know which photos make great black and whites, you have a decision to make, do you: (a) go back to your original folder (with your color photos) and start converting the good ones to black and white, or do you (b) turn your Quick Collection into a permanent collection (because Quick Collections are temporary)? If you go with decision (a), you can Copy the settings from a selected virtual photo (Command-Shift-C on a Mac, or Ctrl-Shift-C on a PC), then go to the collection with your real color photo, click on it, and then Paste those copied edits onto it by pressing Command-Shift-V (PC: Ctrl-Shift-V).

Step Twelve:

If you decide to go the (b) route, press Command-A (PC: Ctrl-A) to select all the photos in your Quick Collection, then press Command-N (PC: Ctrl-N) to bring up the Create Collection dialog. Make sure the checkbox for Include Selected Photos is turned on and click the Create button. Now you've got a permanent collection with your black-and-white conversions. Remember, even though these are virtual copies, you can turn these into real copies when you either export them into Photoshop, or save them as a JPEG, TIFF, or PSD by choosing Export from the File menu. (*Note:* Don't forget that you still have virtual copies in your original collection, too. If you no longer need them, simply go back to that collection, select them, and press the Delete [PC: Backspace] key.) So there you have it—my trick for how to find the best candidates for black-and-white conversions, and what to do once you find them.

Better Black and White By Doing It Yourself

So the one-button grayscale method doesn't kick butt, and the built-in preset often makes things too light (plenty of detail mind you, because there's no shadow clipping whatsoever, but it doesn't have that rich contrast that makes us fall in love with a black-and-white conversion). Here's what I recommend: do it yourself. Well, you'll have some help in the form of the Grayscale Mix and its interactive controls, but because each photo is so different, the only way to get it just right is to do it yourself. So, this is pretty much like everything else in life.

Step One:

In the Library module, find the photo you want to convert into a black and white, and make a virtual copy of it by going under the Photo menu and choosing Create Virtual Copy, as shown here (the only reason to do this is so you can compare your do-it-yourself method with Photoshop Lightroom's two automatic methods side-by-side. Once you do this, you'll always create your black-and-white conversions by doing it yourself).

Step Two:

Press Command-D (PC: Ctrl-D) to deselect both photos, and then click on the original photo again (it's shown highlighted here on the left). Then go to the Quick Develop panel in the right side Panels area and click on the Grayscale button at the top right of the panel. This gives you the kind of flat-looking black-and-white conversion you see here. This is your Before photo.

Step Three:

Now, double-click on your virtual copy, and then press the letter D on your keyboard to take it over to the Develop module. In the right side Panels area, you'll see a panel named HSL/Color/Grayscale. Click directly on the word "Grayscale" and the Grayscale Mix appears, automatically converting your photo to black and white using the channel mixer sliders (which let you mix up to eight different color channels to create the best possible black-and-white photo). Now, if the black-and-white conversion you see here looks familiar, it should. That's because whether you click on Grayscale back in the Library module's Quick Develop panel, or at the top right of the Basic panel here in the Develop module, or you click on Grayscale in this panel, you get the same automated conversion.

Step Four:

This one-click conversion isn't a bad starting place, but to me it seems like it's always a bit flat. In fact, if you look at the histogram in Step Three (at the top of the right side Panels area), you'll see a big gap on the right side of the graph. A tiny gap is good—it means you've retained detail in your highlights. However, a big gap indicates a lack of highlights in your entire photo. So, a good way to build on this one-click conversion is to go to the Basic panel, and click on the Tone section's Auto button (shown circled here in red). This tends to adjust the photo so you get the maximum amount of highlights without clipping them and losing detail. So, go ahead and click on the Auto button, then look at your photo—it's now much brighter, but if you look at the histogram again, you'll see there's a very small gap between the end of the graph and the right wall, and that's a good thing.

Continued

Step Five:

If after clicking the Auto button, the highlights look a little hot to you (meaning the photo looks a little too bright), you can back off the highlight exposure a little by dragging the Exposure slider to the left, but I prefer to increase the Recovery amount by dragging this slider to the right. In our case, the sky looked a little too white, even though we weren't getting any highlight clipping warnings, and we could see in the histogram that the highlights weren't blowing out. By dragging this slider to the right, it brings back more gray into the sky while we still retain most of the brightness we gained by using the Auto Tone button.

Step Six:

If you're like me, and you like that really rich, high-contrast black-and-white image, then try going to the Blacks slider and dragging it to the right a little bit (as shown here), until the darkest areas of your photo (the deepest shadows of the rocks) are really dark and saturated. Now, there are those who believe that you should never let any part of your photo turn to solid black, even if it's a non-essential low-detail area like a shadow under a rock. I'm not one of those people. I want the entire photo to have "pop" to it, and in years of creating black-and-white prints, I've found that your average person reacts much more positively to photos with high-contrast conversions than to the flatter conversions that retain 100% detail in the shadows. If you get a chance, try both methods, show your friends, and see which version they choose. You might be surprised at the results.

Step Seven:
Rather than adding more contrast by just dragging the Contrast slider to the right, if it's a photo I really care about I'll go to the Tone Curve panel instead, so scroll down there. From the panel's Point Curve pop-up menu at the bottom, choose Strong Contrast (as shown here) to make your highlights brighter and your shadows deeper. If you'd like, you can tweak your curve by using the Highlights, Lights, Darks, and Shadows sliders to adjust your curve, but don't overdo it, because we haven't tweaked our photo using the Grayscale Mix yet (okay, we went there once, but we just accepted the Auto setting, and then left and went to the Basic panel).

Step Eight:
In the right side Panels area, go back to the Grayscale section of the HSL/Color/Grayscale panel. Click directly on the tiny target icon that appears in the upper-left corner of the panel, right below the panel header. Your cursor will change into a crosshair, and the target will be there too, but now it has an arrow on the top and bottom of it. This tool lets you adjust the Grayscale Mix sliders by clicking-and-dragging right in your photo. We'll start by making those trees in the top-right corner of the photo brighter. So, click-and-hold your cursor on those trees (as shown here).

Continued

Step Nine:

Now start dragging upward. Your cursor stays pretty much where it is, but you'll notice that the Green slider moves to the right as you drag upward, increasing the amount of green in the trees (even though this photo appears in black and white, it's still made up of color, so moving a color slider affects the tone in that area). Now, you might think, "Hey, big whoop—I know trees are green—I could've just grabbed the Green slider and slid it to the right myself." True, true (rats, where was I going with this? Oh, I remember!). But, while it's easy to assume that adjusting the Green slider would affect the green trees, it's quite a bit harder to choose which color slider will affect the rocks in the water, or the rocks out of the water. That's where this comes in really handy.

Step Ten:

Go ahead and take your cursor and move it over one of the rocks you want to make brighter (as shown here), then click-and-drag upward. If it looks too light, try dragging downward, and watch as the Red and Orange sliders move as you drag, adjusting the tones in that area. So, what you'll do now is look at any part of your photo that you're not happy with, move your cursor over that area, and click-and-drag (either upward or downward) to adjust that area. While you're doing this, keep an eye on the Grayscale Mix sliders and which direction they're going, but of course the most important thing is whether your photo is looking better because of the changes that you're making. If you make a move you don't like, immediately after the move, press Command-Z (PC: Ctrl-Z) to Undo the adjustment.

Step Eleven:
Here I clicked on a little bit of a darker rock, and dragged up, then down to see how it affected the rest of the photo. My goal is to make the photo as rich and saturated as possible, and in this case, dragging upward adjusted the Orange slider a bit, and I kind of like the overall look of the photo now.

Step Twelve:
When you've got it looking the way you want it (and I have to admit, besides the functionality of that tool, it's also fun to use. I enjoying clicking here and clicking there and seeing how it affects my photo. Of course, I would never admit that, so let's just keep that between us), press G to return to the Library module's Grid view. Here I pressed Shift-Tab to hide all the panels, and then I dragged the Thumbnails slider in the toolbar to the right until I could get the original conversion and my do-it-yourself conversion side-by-side as big thumbnails in the grid. This whole process just takes a couple of minutes once you've tried it once or twice, and it gives you full control over how your final photo looks. So, although I think that the one-click grayscale conversion is a good starting place, I also think that you can tweak things just a little and come up with a black-and-white photo you'll be really happy with. *Note:* If you like this conversion and think you might use it again, save it as a preset in the Presets panel in the Develop module's left side Panels area—then it's always just one click away.

Adding a Split Tone Effect to Your Black-and-White Photos

Once you've converted a photo to black and white, you might want to add a little tint to the photo to create a duotone or tritone effect. Photoshop Lightroom not only lets you do that, but it lets you apply a split-toning effect where you can apply one tint to the highlights, a different tint to the shadow areas, decide the saturation of each, and choose the balance between the two. In Photoshop, this is a pretty complicated little trick, but here in Photoshop Lightroom it couldn't be easier.

Step One:

Start by converting your photo to black and white using any of the methods I've shown so far (of course, you know I'm going to use the do-it-yourself method I just taught you in the previous tutorial, but I don't need to make the virtual copy this time, because now you know the score). So, click on the photo you want to add a split tone to, then press D to jump over to the Develop module (as shown here).

Step Two:

Start in the Basic panel by clicking on the Grayscale button, then click on the Auto Tone button. For some reason, it completely blew out this entire photo, clipping just about every highlight it could find, so I pressed Command-Z (PC: Ctrl-Z) to Undo it. Then I dragged the Exposure slider a little to the right to brighten the highlights, but because of that light sky in the background, I was already on the verge of clipping. I then increased the Recovery slider (to bring some lost highlights back), and dragged the Blacks slider to the right quite a bit to really saturate the photo. Unfortunately, it was too saturated, so I had to use a little Fill Light slider to bring back some of the lost detail in the shadows, and adjust the Brightness slider. Lastly, I went to the Tone Curve panel and chose the built-in Strong Contrast curve from the Point Curve pop-up menu.

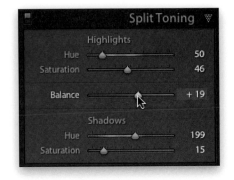

Step Three:
Now that you've got a decent-looking black-and-white photo, scroll down to the Split Toning panel (shown here). In the panel, you'll see there are Hue and Saturation sliders for both the highlights and the shadows, which lets you add one tint to the highlight areas, and a separate tint in the shadows. The Balance slider does just what you'd think it would—it lets you balance the color mix between the highlights and shadows (for example, if you had a cyan color in the highlights, and yellow in the shadows, and you wanted more yellow overall, you'd just drag the Balance slider to the right, as shown here).

Step Four:
Here's the thing: you probably get the whole Split Toning thing now, and you want to just grab the Highlights Hue slider and start dragging…so go ahead. I'll wait. What? Nothing's happening? Well, my impetuous young Jedi (yes, I used a *Star Wars* term in my book. It's not for me. It's for my friend Terry White. He has so little), the reason nothing happened is because the Saturation slider is set to 0 (by default), and you can consider that slider like a color tint volume slider. At 0, you don't hear (see) anything. So, I rec-ommend one of two things: (1) Start by dragging the Saturation slider to the right until it reads 25. That may well be more highlight tint than you need, but at least you'll be able to see the different hues when you drag the Hue slider, so it's not a bad place to start (you can always lower the Saturation amount later if you want). Now, I said there are two things, right?

Continued

Step Five:

The other thing (2) is to press-and-hold the Option key on a Mac or the Alt key on a PC, and then start dragging the Hue slider. You won't need to adjust the Saturation slider first, because by holding that key down as you drag, it gives you a preview of what your highlights would look like if the saturation were set to 100% (as shown here, which looks pretty harsh, but this is just to give you a preview of what the color looks like—thankfully, it's not the final effect). When you release the Option key, the saturation returns to zero again. So, use whichever method you're more comfortable with. But I will bet that using the bump-the-saturation-to-25% tip I mentioned first will give you a better idea of what your split toning will actually look like, because it's not so oversaturated. That's all I'm sayin'.

Step Six:

Now you can adjust the shadows. Start by increasing the Shadows Saturation amount to 25% (or use the Option/Alt method), and then drag the Hue slider until you see a tint you like for the shadows. I went with kind of a light bluish tint, which mixes pretty well with the yellows in the highlights.

Step Seven:

You can now adjust the balance between the two by using the Balance slider (shown circled in red here). In our case, I wanted a little more yellow, so I dragged just a little bit to the right until the whole photo took on a little more yellowish tint (as seen here).

TIP: Although split toning is most often done to black-and-white photos, it doesn't have to be. Try it with color photos to get some wild looks, or use it just in the highlights to make a gray sky bluer (drag the Hue slider to blue or cyan, then slightly increase the Saturation slider) or maybe make the grass greener.

Step Eight:

Let's say you like this particular split toning setup, and you think you might use it again on some different photos. This is the time to make a preset of those settings, so you can apply that exact same tint mix to other photos with just one click. Head over to the left side Panels area, and in the Presets panel, click on the + (plus sign) button to add a new preset. The New Develop Preset dialog will appear (seen here). First, click the Check None button to turn off all the checkboxes from the other Develop panel settings. Next, turn on just the Split Toning checkbox (as shown here), and click the Create button. Now those settings are saved as a one-click preset in your Presets panel (I named this one "Yellow/Cyan Split Tone").

Continued

Step Nine:

Now that you've got a preset saved, let's try applying it to another photo. Press G to go back to the Library module's Grid view, locate another photo you'd like to apply this effect to, click on it, and press D to open that photo in the Develop module (as shown here). By the way, you can access any presets you create in the Develop module from right within the Library module's Quick Develop panel, in the Preset pop-up menu at the top. All your Develop module presets will be listed in that menu, and you can apply any of them to selected photos in the Library module.

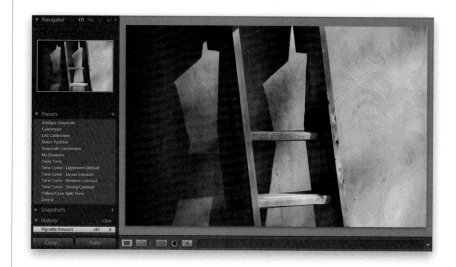

Step Ten:

Let's now convert that photo to black and white. Click on the Grayscale Conversion preset in the Presets panel, then head on over to the Basic panel and add in some extra Blacks, and then add a Strong Contrast point curve from the Tone Curve panel's pop-up menu to beef up the contrast. I added one more effect to this photo—the edge vignette effect I showed in the previous chapter (you can see the adjustments I made here in the Lens Corrections panel: I dragged the Lens Vignetting Amount slider almost all the way to the left to darken the edges of the photo, and then I dragged the Midpoint slider to the left quite a bit as well to soften and spread that edge darkening). Now we're ready for our split toning.

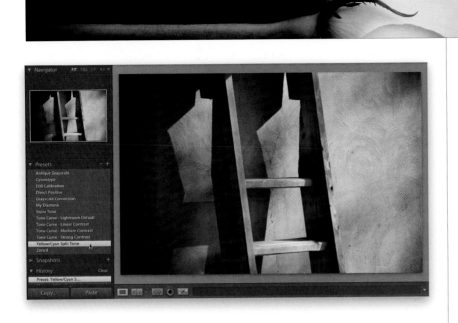

Step Eleven:

Go to the Presets panel and click on the Yellow/Cyan Split Tone preset, and the effect is applied to your photo immediately. If you need to change your balance, just go over to the Split Toning panel, and drag the Balance slider to the left (for more of the cyan shadow color) or right (for more of the yellow highlight color).

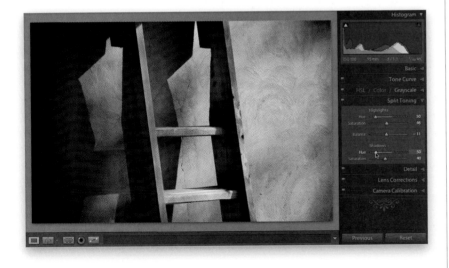

Step Twelve:

If you want a classic duotone effect instead, then all you have to do is give both Hue sliders the same number. For example, the Highlights Hue is set at 50 (a dark yellowish tint). Go down to the Shadows Hue slider and set it at 50 as well, and now you've got a duotone effect like the one you see here. So that's it—how to create your own split tone and duotone effects using the Split Toning panel.

Exposure: 1/125   Focal Length: 52mm   Aperture Value: ƒ/5.6

Slideshow
sharing your photos onscreen

It's kind of funny that in this digital day and age, we still use the term "slide show," even though traditional slides are nearly as outdated as records. For example, my 9-year-old son has never seen a record album. For him, music has always come from either CDs or iPods. Although I have many photographic slides, my son has never seen a real slide show using real conventional color slides. But it's not just him. I speak at conferences and tradeshows, and if I walked into the room where I was scheduled to speak and asked the class moderator where the slide projector was, he'd look at me like I was from Mars. Yet, Adobe Photoshop Lightroom still uses this term. So, today, in this very book I'm suggesting that not only should we, in the photography industry, use a different term for what was previously called a slide show, but I actually want to propose the new term. I have crafted a new word that I feel better represents the experience of viewing photographic images onscreen, and thus I'm quite certain this term will be quickly and unilaterally embraced by the worldwide photographic community. It's "flobotnor" (flow·bot·nore). So, once it's officially adopted (any day now, I'm sure), you'll see future releases of Lightroom where the Slideshow module will have been renamed the Flobotnor module. Of course, you'll have the satisfaction of knowing that not only were you there when it all happened—you helped shape modern history. These are amazing times, my friend. Amazing times, indeed.

Making an Instant Slide Show

Although one of Photoshop Lightroom's five modules is dedicated to helping you create your own custom slide shows, you can create an instant on-the-fly slide show almost anytime, within any module, by using Lightroom's Impromptu Slideshow feature. I use the Impromptu Slideshow feature during the initial sorting process because it lets me see any selected photos at full-screen size, which is great for checking sharpness and focus. Plus, while this impromptu slide show is running full screen, I can rate or flag any photo, so it's perfect for seeing "the big picture."

Step One:

The cool thing is—you can create one of these impromptu slide shows while you're in any module (even though I usually do mine in the Library module for the sorting reasons I mentioned in the intro above) by first going to the filmstrip and selecting just the photos you want to appear in the impromptu slide show (as shown here, where I've selected six photos in the filmstrip). If you want all the photos in the folder or collection you're working on to appear in the slide show, then click on any photo in the film-strip and press Command-A (PC: Ctrl-A), to select all the photos at once.

Step Two:

To start your slide show, go under the Window menu and choose Impromptu Slideshow (as shown here), or press Command-Return on a Mac or Ctrl-Enter on a PC. (*Note:* If you're thinking that Adobe should have named this feature something like "Quick Slideshow" or "Instant Slideshow," I just want you to know that there's no way Adobe's official Bureau of Non-Descriptive Naming was going to let that happen. If they named it something easy, then you would know what it does and they wouldn't get their year-end complication bonus, which incidentally, they've received every single year thus far without fail.)

Step Three:

Once you choose Impromptu Slideshow (or press that keyboard shortcut), the full-screen slide show begins using whichever slide show template you last used in the Slideshow module. If you don't like that look, go over to the Slideshow module and click on a different template in the Template Browser in the left side Panels area. That way, when you start your next impromptu slide show it will use that template instead. Now, once the slide show is running, you can rate your photos (using the 1- to 5-star rating system) by just typing in a number (1 to 5) as a photo appears. Depending on the template you choose, you may see your star ratings actually appear as an overlay in the top-left corner of your photo, but if not, you just have to trust that it worked.

Step Four:

When you get to the end of your selected photos, your slide show will automatically repeat (loop) until you stop it. To stop your slide show, press the Esc key on your keyboard. When you return to the Library module's Grid view, you'll be able to see the star ratings you assigned during the slide show (as seen here, where we have photos rated from two to five stars).

Slide Show Essentials (Plus How to Get the Right Photos Into Your Slide Show)

Well, the first step is figuring out which photos you want to include in your slide show, and easy ways to add photos to it and delete photos from it. Photoshop Lightroom gives you lots of different options, so we'll start here and build on it as we move through this chapter.

Step One:

If you want to make things easy on your-self, put the photos you want in your slide show into a collection first. That way you can easily add and subtract photos from your slide show, but per-haps more importantly, doing this lets you return to this particular slide show in the future with just these photos, and with your slides still in the same order. So, start by going to the Library module, to the Collections panel, and clicking on the + (plus sign) to create a new collec-tion. When the Create Collection dialog appears, enter a name (I chose "Portrait Shoot Slideshow"). Now drag-and-drop the photos you want to appear in your slide show onto this new collection (as shown here). *Note:* You can drag photos from just about anywhere into your slide show collection, even if they're in other folders, other collections, etc.

Step Two:

Now, once you've got all the photos you want in your slide show collection, click on that collection to select it, then go up to the Module Picker and click on Slideshow (or Press Command-Option-3 [PC: Ctrl-Alt-3]) to jump over to the Slideshow module (shown here).

Step Three:

All the photos in your collection are now in your slide show (you can see them all in the filmstrip). The first photo in your filmstrip is the first that will appear in your slide show, the second photo will appear second, and so on. If you want to change the order of your slides, just click-and-drag them into the order you want them. (In the example shown here, I clicked on the photo I wanted to appear first and dragged it to the first position on the left in the filmstrip.) So, go ahead and do that now—click-and-drag the photos into the order you'd like them to appear in your slide show. (*Note:* You can always change your mind, or the order, any time by clicking-and-dragging right within the filmstrip.)

Step Four:

The center Preview area shows you a large preview of how the first frame of your slide show is going to look. When you first switch to the Slideshow module, it displays your photos in the default slide show preset, which has a slight gradient in the background, the filename under the photo, a white border around the photo, a drop shadow behind your photo, and your custom Identity Plate appears in the upper-left corner (as seen in the previous step). If you want to try a different look, you can use any of the pre-made slide show templates that come with Photoshop Lightroom. For example, go to the Template Browser (in the left side Panels area) and click on the Crop To Fill template, which makes your photo fill the entire slide (as shown here). If you move your cursor over other presets, you'll see a preview of what they look like up in the Preview panel at the top left.

Continued

Step Five:

If you want to remove a photo from your slide show, you actually have to remove the photo from your collection. Luckily, you don't have to go back to the Library module's Collections panel to do that—just go down to the filmstrip and Control-click (PC: Right-click) on the photo you want to remove. When the contextual menu appears, choose Remove from Collection (as shown here). The photo will be removed from both your collection and your slide show. If you want that photo back in your slide show at some point, then you'll have to go back to the Library module, find the photo (in whichever folder or collection it was in), and add it back to your slide show collection. If this seems a bit clunky to you, then I'm glad to hear I'm not the only one.

Step Six:

Although we started by creating a collection, it's not absolutely necessary to do it that way, but without one it's much harder to control which photos wind up in your slide show. For example, if you're working with a folder rather than a collection (like our example here) and you delete a photo from your slide show, you're now also deleting it from your folder and from Lightroom itself (and from your computer if you click the wrong button). Another downside is this: every photo in the folder is added to your slide show—you can't choose which of those photos winds up in your slide show. Even though you can select individual photos in the filmstrip (as shown here), the Slideshow module simply ignores those selections and instead plays all the photos in that folder in order from left to right.

Step Seven:

Okay, now back to our portrait slide show. If you want a quick preview of your slide show, go to the toolbar and click the Preview button (it's a right-facing triangle—just like Play on a DVD or CD player, shown here). This plays a preview within the center Preview area, and although the slide show is the exact same size in that window, you're now seeing it without guides, with transitions, and with music (if you chose to add music, which we haven't covered yet, so you probably haven't, but hey ya never know). Once you hit the Preview button, it becomes a Pause button, so if you want to pause for a moment, click it. If you want to stop, press the square Stop button on the left side of the toolbar. *Note:* If you want to preview the effect of a full-screen slideshow, without going full screen, once the preview starts, just press the letter L twice to enter Lights Out mode. Even though it's just a preview, you'll get the benefit of the full-black background. To return to normal, press L again.

Step Eight:

Once you've seen the preview, you can do any last minute tweaking (like changing the order of the slides by click-ing-and-dragging them down in the filmstrip), and then it's time to see "the big show"—the full-screen version! To see it, you click Play in an entirely different place—at the bottom of the right side Panels area. Just click that Play button, and the default slide show, using your photos, starts at full-screen size (as shown here). Now, maybe it's just me, but I'm not a huge fan of the default slide show, and that's why in the next tutorial we look at how to create your own custom slide show, so it looks and feels the way you want it to.

Customizing the Look of Your Slides

The defaults are okay, but after you create a slide show or two with them, you're going to be saying stuff like, "I wish I could change the background color" or "I wish I could add some text at the bottom" or "I wish my slide show looked better." (*Note:* You're not saying you wish your photos looked better—you wish your slide show looked better.) Well, this is where you start to create your own custom look for your slides, so it looks just the way you want it, every time.

Step One:

Although you might not be wild about the pre-designed slide show templates Photoshop Lightroom comes with (okay, it's just me that isn't wild about them, but I was hoping you wouldn't let me take the heat all alone), they're great starting points for creating your own custom look. So, start by going to the Slideshow module, and in the Template Browser in the left side Panels area, click on Default to load the default Lightroom slide show look (seen here, which puts your photos over a gray background with a thin white border and a hard drop shadow, the filename below the photo, and your Identity Plate in the upper-left corner). So you know where your margins are, make sure the Show Guides checkbox is turned on in the Layout panel in the right side Panels area.

Step Two:

Now that we've got our starting point template loaded up, let's go ahead and hide that Template Browser for now because it's just taking up space—and we could use that space to make our slides much larger onscreen. So, press F7 on your keyboard to hide the left side Panels area, then F6 to hide the filmstrip, which gives you the clean, uncluttered look you see here. Not too shabby.

Step Three:

Since you've already got the default slide show template applied, you may as well use that as a starting place to create your own custom slide show. First, let's look at resizing your photos on the slide, so they're not taking up every inch of white space (photos either need to be full screen, or they need a decent amount of space around them so they don't look like they're being crowded, which is one of my complaints with the default slide show—the photo looks a bit cramped for space). To reduce the size of your photo on the slide, you just click-and-drag the margin guides inward, and the photo shrinks. Here, I clicked right where the lines intersect on the top right (shown circled here in red) and dragged inward, and you can see the photo now has some breathing room on the slide.

Step Four:

You can also resize your photo by going to the Layout panel (in the right side Panels area) and dragging the margin sliders (as shown here). When you move one margin slider, the rest move right along with it in unison because, by default, they're all linked together. If you'd like to move the margins individually, turn off the Link All box just below the sliders.

TIP: If you see a gap between the edges of your photo and the margin guides, you can fill that gap instantly with a very cool feature called Zoom to Fill Frame. Turning on this checkbox (found in the Options panel at the very top of the right side Panels area) increases the size of your photos proportionally until they completely fill the area inside the margins. Give this a try—you'll probably use it more than you'd think.

Continued

Step Five:

If you want to create more space below your photo (to create a fine art look for your slide), turn off the box beside the Top margin slider (as shown here), then drag the slider to the left. This does two things: (1) it shrinks the top margin, which moves your photo closer to the top, but because the size of the photo is determined by the placement of these margins, it also (2) increases the size of the photo (as the margins get closer to the edges of the slide, the photo has room to expand and vice versa). *Note:* If you want to hide those margin lines from view, just turn off the Show Guides checkbox in the Layout panel or press Command-Shift-H (PC: Ctrl-Shift-H).

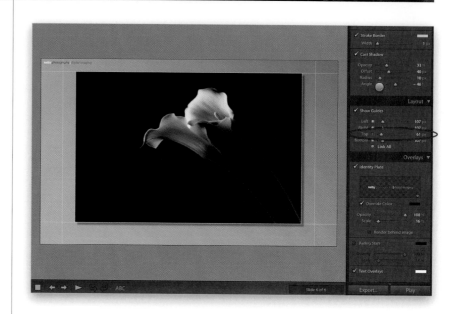

Step Six:

Okay, so our size is better, but we still have the filename appearing below our photo, and as you can see in the example shown in Step Five, it doesn't look real good. To hide the filename, just go to the Overlays panel and turn off the checkbox for Text Overlays (as shown here). This hides any text you have on the slide (with the exception of any text used in your Identity Plate), and in our case gives us a much cleaner look (seen here). If you wanted to add some text instead, you would click on the ABC (Add Text) button down in the toolbar (it's circled here in red). The only problem is your filename text is visible again if you do this, because clicking that ABC button turns Text Overlays back on. But that's easy enough to fix—just click directly on the filename text under your photo to select it, then press the Delete (PC: Backspace) key on your keyboard and it's gone.

Step Seven:

Let's go ahead and add some text, so click on the ABC button and a custom text field appears where you can type in your text (I typed "Calla Lilies on Black," and for a more elegant look I added one space between each letter and three spaces between each word). Press the Return (PC: Enter) key and this text appears on your slide. Next, click directly on your text and drag it right over to the middle of the slide (as shown here). To resize your text, grab any corner or side point and drag outward to make the text larger or inward to make it smaller. You can choose the font and font face in the Overlays panel (I chose the font Trajan Pro in a regular face for the text you see here, but if you don't have this font, choose one you think looks good).

Step Eight:

While you're in the Text Overlays section, you can also change the opacity by using the Opacity slider, and the color of your text by clicking on the color swatch to bring up the Colors panel (shown here, where I dragged the side slider down to make my white text a dark gray). Once you choose your color, you can close the panel. When your text edits are all complete, click outside the text box to lock in your changes. If you want to rotate your text, click on the Rotate Counter-Clockwise and Rotate Clockwise buttons in the toolbar. Now in our example, we created a line of custom text ("Calla Lilies on Black"), but you can have Lightroom automatically create text blocks with select EXIF data, or you can create your own custom presets of data you can add with one click.

Continued

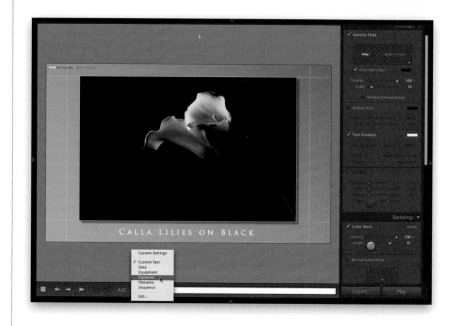

Step Nine:

When you click the ABC button to add text, a Custom Text field appears, but if you click-and-hold on the words "Custom Text" a pop-up menu appears with a list of EXIF data presets (shown here). For example, if you choose Equipment it creates a text block with the make and model of the camera you used to take the photo, along with the lens and aperture that you used. If you choose Exposure, you get a text block with the shutter speed and aperture used. However, what's really handy here is the ability to create your own presets with your own custom text. To do that, choose Edit from the pop-up menu.

Step Ten:

This brings up the Text Template Editor dialog (shown here) where you build your text template by typing directly in the large field at the top (to create custom text) or by having metadata automatically inserted for you by choosing the info you want included from the pop-up menus. In the example shown here, I clicked on the default blue pill-shape (named Custom Text; in braces on a PC) and hit the Delete (PC: Backspace) key, so I could type in "Kelby Photography" with a space after it. Next, I went down to the IPTC Data section, to where Copyright was chosen in the pop-up menu, and clicked Insert. Now, each photo's embedded copyright info will appear right after my studio's name (see the text preview directly above the text field). Once you've customized your text, click on the Preset pop-up menu up top, and choose Save as New Preset. Now when you click on that Custom Text pop-up menu in the toolbar you'll be able to choose your text preset from that menu.

Step Eleven:

Let's do a little more customizing to the look of our slide. Go to the Backdrop panel and turn off that light gray to dark gray gradient that appears as our slide's background. You do that by turning off the checkbox for Color Wash (as shown here). Although we're turning this feature off, you'll need to know how to use it in case you want to have a color wash (basically, a gradient) in other slide shows. When the checkbox is turned on, there's a clickable color swatch to the right of it, and that's where you choose the main color of your gradient (Lightroom uses the background color as the second color). The two sliders below that control the angle of your gradient, and the Opacity slider controls…well…the opacity. With the color wash turned off, my background color is now a light gray (as seen here).

Step Twelve:

You change your background color right in the same panel—just click on the gray color swatch to the right of the Background Color checkbox and the Colors panel appears where you can choose a different background color if you'd like (I'm okay with the light gray background already in place). Also turned on by default is your Identity Plate, which appears in the top-left corner of your slide (look at any previous step and you'll see it). You can: (a) hide it altogether by going to the Overlays panel and turning off the Identity Plate checkbox, or (b) if you like it on, in this same panel you can choose which Identity Plate to display (I chose a scan of my signature) or to edit it, what color it should be, its size and opacity, and you can click directly on it in your slide and drag it anywhere you'd like (as shown here).

Continued

Step Thirteen:

Well, now that we've added some text and chosen the Identity Plate, it's starting to get a little crowded down below the photo, so let's move it up a little to give the text some breathing room. Click on the bottom-right corner margin (at the point where they intersect, as shown here) and drag inward to move the bottom margin up and shrink the photo a bit (make sure your Identity Plate is anchored to the corner of the photo, so it will move too). Notice that the top margin stayed in place—only the bottom margin moved up, but since this margin controls the size of your photo, the photo got smaller too. Now you have room to move your "Calla Lilies on Black" text up quite a bit. The text looks a little big, so click on it to select it, then click-and-drag any corner inward to shrink the size.

Step Fourteen:

Now let's scroll up to the Options panel at the top of the right side Panels area. There's a thin white border around our photo, which works great (and is very necessary) whenever dark photos appear over a dark background (like the black background in the EXIF slide show template. If you used that background, this photo would blend right into the background), but in our case the background we have here is a very light gray, so we can get rid of the border by clicking on the Stroke Border checkbox to turn it off, which gives us the even cleaner look shown here.

TIP: The checkboxes in the right side Panels area are very small, and they make pretty tiny targets to hit directly, but you don't have to—you can click directly on the name of the command (like Stroke Border or Identity Plate) to toggle it on or off.

Step Fifteen:

This last one's just a personal preference, and that's to turn off the drop shadow. I dunno—in this instance it just looks a little cheesy to me, so I would turn it off by clicking on Cast Shadow in the Options panel. However, while we're talking about drop shadows (I know, we're talking about turning them off, but work with me, will ya?), there are four sliders that control the appearance of the drop shadow. You know what Opacity does, and the Offset amount is just how far away the shadow appears from the photo. However, Radius is the control for how soft the shadow is, and the softer it is, the farther it spreads. The last control is Angle, so you can choose which direction the light is coming from.

Step Sixteen:

Now you can click the Play button (at the bottom of the right side Panels area) and see your final customized slide show in full-screen mode without all the guides and panels (as shown here). Notice how clean and elegant it looks (it's that whole "less is more" thing)? One last thing: now that you've gone through all the trouble of creating a custom slide layout, you should save it as a slide show template so you can reapply it in the future with just one click (see the tutorial near the end of this chapter called "Saving Your Custom Slide Show as a Template").

Using a Photo as Your Slide Background

I don't want to say the background is as important as the photo, but it's important enough that if you don't use one that complements the photo, it can pretty much wreck your slide show. Luckily, Photoshop Lightroom gives you lots of control over how the backdrop (that's what Adobe calls it) behind your photos looks. Unfortunately, it doesn't come with a built-in good taste button, but if you stick with classic backgrounds (like black, white, or gray), you can have your backdrop support and complement your photos, instead of competing with them.

Step One:
Before we add a photo as our background, let's do a little setup: First go to the Template Browser and click on the template named Caption and Rating, then make sure your left side Panels area is hidden from view. Next, go to the right side Panels area and turn off the Text Overlays checkbox. In the Overlays panel section right above that, turn off the Rating Stars checkbox as well (so we don't see stars over our photo). Now we have the nice simple slide layout you see here.

Step Two:
Go to the filmstrip, find the photo you want to use as a background image, and drag-and-drop it right onto the Background Image well in the Backdrop panel (as shown here), and that image now appears as the background behind your currently selected photo.

Step Three:

By default, the Color Wash checkbox is turned on, so there's a slight gradient going over the photo. This might look great or it might look pretty bad—it just depends on the photo you choose, so as a general rule I go to the Backdrop panel and turn the checkbox off for Color Wash (as shown). You can see how much more crisp the background photo now appears without that gradient over it (compare the photo here with the one shown in Step Two).

Step Four:

If it seems like the background photo is competing with your slide photo (again, this depends on the photo you choose for your background, and the photos in your slide show), then you can screen the background photo by going to the Backdrop panel, to the Background Image section, and simply lowering the opacity (as shown here). This back-screened look is very popular, especially with wedding albums and slide shows.

Saving Your Custom Slide Show as a Template

Even though you've spent all this time creating a custom template, Photoshop Lightroom doesn't automatically save it, so if you go and choose one of the existing preset templates and don't save the one you just created—well, that layout you just created is gone. For good. Really. So, if you'd like to be able to save your custom slide show layout (so you can apply it in the future with just one click), you'll need to save it as a template. Then it will appear in the Template Browser and any time you want that exact same look, you just click on it.

Step One:

Go to the Slideshow module and create the look you want for your custom slide show layout. In the example here, I used the built-in EXIF Metadata template (found in the Template Browser in the left side Panels area), then I clicked on the text that was there and erased it one-by-one by hitting the Delete (PC: Backspace) key. Then I grabbed the margins and dragged inward to make the photo smaller, and went to the Layout panel, where I unlinked just the left margin by clicking on its link box, and dragged the slider all the way to the left to move the photo to the left and shrink it a bit at the same time. Then I moved the Identity Plate to above the top-left edge of the photo, and added a line of custom text below the bottom-left edge (I lowered its opacity to 55% in the Text Overlays panel).

Step Two:

Press F7 to make the left side Panels area visible, and click on the Add button in the bottom-left corner of the Template Browser (as shown here). This adds an unnamed template to the Template Browser, but the name field is already highlighted—all you have to do is type in a name (I chose "Black Bckgrnd w/Identity") and press Return (PC: Enter). That's it—you saved your layout as a template.

SCOTT KELBY

Step Three:
Now, before we go on, let's test our slide show template. In the Template Browser, first click on the Default template to change to that layout (by the way—if you hadn't saved your template already, it would be gone for good the moment you clicked on Default or any other template in the Template Browser). Press G to switch to the Library module, and in the Collections panel choose a different collection of photos. Now switch back to the Slideshow module and those photos will appear in the Default slide show layout (as shown here).

Step Four:
Here's where it all pays off: to switch to your saved slide show template, just go to the Template Browser and click on it. That's it—just one click and your custom layout appears (as shown here). If at any time you want to change your layout, just go to the right side Panels area and tweak to your heart's content. If you come up with a layout you like better than your previously saved template, just Control-click (PC: Right-click) on that template in the Template Browser and choose Update With Current Settings from the contextual menu that appears (as shown here).

TIP: To see a preview of any of the templates in the Template Browser, just hover your cursor over the templates in the list and look in the Preview panel up top. Then, if you see one you like, just click on it.

Adding Music and Choosing Your Playback Options

Now that you've created a custom slide show and saved it as a template, you're almost ready to present your slide show, but before you do you'll need to make a couple of quick choices in the Playback panel, including one that I really feel is critical, and that is to add some background music to your slide show. The right background music can make all the difference in a slide show presentation, and if you get a chance to see the top pros show their work, you'll find they always choose music that creates emotion and supports the images beautifully.

Step One:

Let's start by putting the photos in your collection in the order you want them to appear in your slide show (they display in order from left to right, so your left-most photo in the filmstrip will be the first photo in your slide show). To do this, just drag-and-drop them into the order you want right within the filmstrip. (In case you were wondering, I created that little medium gray logo strip that appears below the photo in Photoshop CS3, then I saved it as a JPEG and used it as my graphical Identity Plate. I didn't have to worry about getting the size just right, because there's a Scale [size] slider in the Identity Plate section of the Overlays panel.)

Step Two:

Once your slides are in order, go to the Playback panel near the bottom of the right side Panels area (shown here). We'll start by adding some background music, so turn on the Soundtrack checkbox (as shown here). Okay, that part was simple, but it's the next part—actually selecting which song will play behind your slide show—that takes some doing, and it's totally different on a Mac and a PC.

Step Three:

We'll start with the Mac version: In the Playback panel, to the right of Soundtrack, click-and-hold to bring up a pop-up menu (shown here) with a list of the music playlists you currently have installed in Apple's iTunes software (I told you this takes some doin'). Unfortunately, you can't just choose one song—you have to choose a playlist. So, what you really need to do is to launch iTunes, buy a song from the iTunes Store (they're only 99¢), and once it downloads, put that one song in a new iTunes playlist all by itself. If you own a CD with a song you think would make for some nice slide show background music, you can import that song into iTunes (right off the CD), and then make your one-song slide show playlist with that one imported song.

Step Four:

I often use a song for my slide shows called "Leola Kay" from a great CD by acoustic guitarist Todd Hallawell (it's really nicely done—very laid back and melodic. You can find it at toddhallawell. com). Anyway, I imported that CD, then created a new iTunes playlist, which I named "Slideshow Bckgrnd Music" (shown here), and then I dragged that one song—"Leola Kay"—into this play-list. That's pretty much the process. If you go back to Photoshop Lightroom and click on your playlist pop-up menu again, your new slide show playlist should now be one of the choices. If it's not, choose Refresh Playlist from iTunes at the top of the pop-up menu (seen in the previous step).

Continued

Step Five:

For PC users, you just have to find a song in MP3 format (you could import a CD as well), and put that one single song in a folder on your computer. Then, below Soundtrack, click on the Click Here to Choose a Music Folder link. A Browse For Folder dialog will appear where you can choose the folder containing your one MP3 song. I always preview my slide show at this point to make sure the background music fits with the photos, so press the Preview button in the toolbar (shown circled here), and your slide show will play in the center Preview area, and within a couple seconds of starting, your background music will start playing as well. Hey, this isn't the most elegant background music solution, but it beats the heck out of Adobe Bridge's background music scheme (there is none—you watch the slide show in silence. It's painful. Really).

Step Six:

If you'd like to see your preview larger, press F8 on your keyboard to hide the right side panels, which opens up more room for your slide show preview (as seen here). To pause your slide show preview, click the Pause button in the toolbar, and to stop it altogether, press the square Stop button. When you're done watching the preview, press the Esc key on your keyboard, then press F8 to bring your right side panels back.

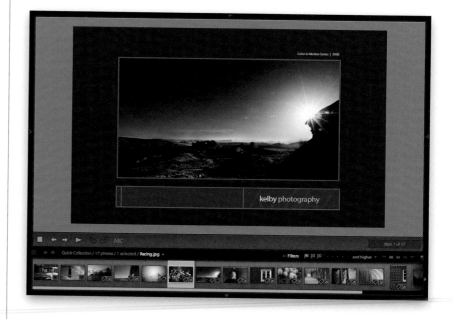

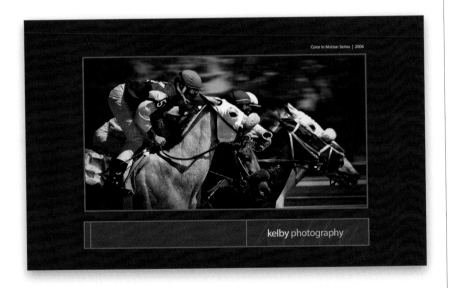

Step Seven:

The next set of controls in the Playback panel (the Slide Duration sliders) lets you decide how long each slide stays onscreen and how long the fade between slides lasts. I have to say, in this case the default settings are pretty decent and I rarely change them. At the bottom of the panel is a checkbox for playing your photos in a random order (I know, that was rather obvious, but I had to include it. Ya know, for my editors. They have so little).

Step Eight:

Once you're done tweaking the music and slide duration, then it's time to see the full-screen final slide show. For this, you don't click the Preview button in the toolbar—instead you click the Play button at the bottom of the right side Panels area. This displays your slide show full screen (as shown here) with your chosen music gently lilting in the background (that is, without a doubt, the first time I've typed or even used the word "lilting" in any context. Now that I see it in print, I clearly know why). You can also just press the Return (PC: Enter) key on your keyboard to start the full-screen slide show. To pause a running slide show, press the Spacebar, and to resume, press the Spacebar again. To exit the full-screen slide show, press the Esc key on your keyboard. By the way, you can add ratings, flags, and labels to photos as they appear in your full-screen slide show using the same shortcuts as always (Ratings: 1–5; Flags: P for Picks, X for Rejects; and Color Labels: 6–9).

Emailing Your Slide Show

If you want to show someone your slide show and they happen to be nearby, then no sweat—you can show it right in Photoshop Lightroom. But if they're not standing nearby (perhaps it's a client across town or across the country), you can email them a PDF of the slide show, which you create right within Lightroom itself. There are two limitations though: one is you can't control the length of the transitions (that's set by the PDF), and the second is you can't include the background music. That second one gets me, but I do have a workaround for some folks.

Step One:

To save your slide show as a PDF (which is ideal for emailing because it compresses the file size), go under the Slideshow menu and choose Export Slideshow (as shown here), use the keyboard shortcut Command-J (PC: Ctrl-J), or click on the Export button at the bottom of the right side Panels area. Doing any of these brings up the Export Slideshow to PDF dialog, shown in Step Two below.

Step Two:

Go ahead and name your slide show. In the bottom part of the dialog is a Quality slider, and the higher the quality, the larger the file size (which is a consideration when emailing), so I usually use a Quality setting of between 80 and 90. I also always turn on the Automatically Show Full Screen checkbox, so they see the slide show without any other onscreen distractions. The width and height dimensions are automatically inserted in the Width and Height fields, but if you need the images to be smaller for emailing, you can enter a smaller width or height and Photoshop Lightroom will automatically scale the photos down proportionally.

Step Three:

Here's the saved slide show as it appears on my Desktop, exported as a PDF file. The entire slide show, with 17 large-sized photos, is only 3.7 MB, which should email just fine (many email accounts have a 5-MB limit on attachments), so open your email software and include this PDF as an attachment.

Step Four:

When your client (friend, relative, parole officer, etc.) double-clicks on your PDF, it will launch the Acrobat Reader, and when it opens, it will go into full-screen mode and start your slide show complete with smooth transitions between slides. Now, of course there is no background music (as I mentioned in the intro on the previous page), but if you have Acrobat Professional, you can open the PDF document you created in Lightroom and add background music there that will play automatically when your client gets your PDF. Just keep an eye on the file size when you start embedding music. If it's a long song, it could really balloon your file size.

TIP: If you're planning on sending this PDF slide show to a client for proofing purposes, be sure to go to the Slideshow module first and make the filename text overlay visible before you make the PDF. That way your client will be able to tell you the name of the photo(s) they've approved.

Exposure: 1/125   Focal Length: 18mm   Aperture Value: $f/3.5$

Print
printing your photos

It could be argued that this is the single most important module of all Photoshop Lightroom's modules, because it's all about "the print." Everything we do is, ultimately, to produce a final printed image. In fact, one of my friends, the award-winning nature photographer Vincent Versace, has a saying he's quite fond of: "We are in service of the print." He must be right, because he's a brilliant photographer, and one heck of a Photoshop instructor, too. However, Vincent himself will be the first one to tell you he's a better chef than he is a photographer. Now, if you've seen any of Vincent's photography (some of his original prints go for upwards of $5,000 a pop), you know he's got to be one hell of a cook. Vincent has invited me over to his house for dinner on numerous occasions, but I've never gone. You know why? Because

I'm afraid Vincent will slip hallucinogenic drugs into my food. Why do I think that? It's because I think Vincent slips hallucinogenic drugs into his own food. Always. So, it only stands to reason that if he's cooking dinner, I'm going to wind up singing "Purple Haze" while staring intently at a ball of yarn. Maybe that's why everybody loves Vincent's cooking so much. By the time the main course comes around, they're all hopped up on crank and everything tastes yummy. Of course, I could be wrong. But if you get a chance to hear Vincent speak at a conference, see if you don't subscribe to my "don't eat the brownies" theory afterwards. However, I think Vincent's statement that "We are in service of the print" has some merit. Not that I really understand it, but I've noticed it really starts to sound good after a few appetizers.

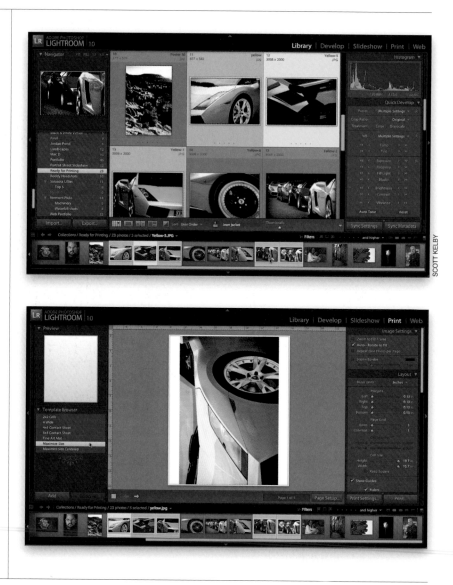

Printing Made Really, Really Easy

The Print module of Photoshop Lightroom is nothing short of brilliant, and I've never worked with any program that had a better, easier, and more functional printing feature than this. Adobe did a particularly good job in creating the printing templates that come with Photoshop Lightroom (I just wish there were more of them), but even if you don't love them, they make a great starting point for customizing and saving your own templates.

Step One:

Although I recommended creating a collection before you began to create slide shows or webpages, with printing it's not necessary. In the Library module, just look in any folder, collection, etc., then go down to the filmstrip and Command-click (PC: Ctrl-click) on just the photos you want to print (as shown here).

Step Two:

Now click on Print in the Module Picker up top (or press Command-Option-5 [PC: Ctrl-Alt-5]) to jump to the Print module. In the Template Browser in the left side Panels area, click on Maximum Size (this template positions your photo so it prints as large as possible on your selected paper size with the full image showing). In this instance, you can see that the paper is set for vertical (portrait) orientation, but the photo is horizontal (landscape), so Photoshop Lightroom automatically rotates your photo sideways so you get as big a print as possible.

Note: If text appears in the left corner of your photo, the good news is: (1) it won't appear on your actual print, and (2) you can turn it off by pressing the letter I (this feature is called Info Overlay). The info can be handy as it shows your curently selected paper size, printer, and number of pages.

Step Three:

While this rotating is part of the Maximum Size template, it's a checkbox that's turned on by default called Auto-Rotate to Fit, and you can turn it off by going to the Image Settings panel and turning off the checkbox (as shown here). Then your photo will try to fit horizontally as large as possible (which gives you the printing lay-out you see here). Now, before we go on, I just want to point out one of the coolest things about Lightroom's printing capabili-ties. If you look under the right corner of the Preview area, in the toolbar, you'll see a little info area that reads "Page 1 of 5 " (it's circled here in red). That lets you know that although you're only seeing one page right now onscreen, there are actually five pages that are queued up to print (your five selected photos down in the filmstrip).

Step Four:

To see the other pages that are queued up to print, use the Previous Page and Next Page buttons (right and left arrows) on the left side of the toolbar, circled here in red. If you click the right arrow, it takes you to the second page in the queue, so you can move through your five pages using the arrows. To return to the first page, click the square First Page button to the left of the arrows. This may not seem like that big a deal at first, but if you compare that to Photoshop CS2 or CS3 for example, you'd have to open five separate documents and then print each one of them separately, going through five successive print dialogs. But here in Lightroom, you can print as many or as few photos as you'd like, all with one click of one button. The next time you go to print five different photos in Photoshop, you'll get a whole new appre-ciation for Lightroom.

Continued

Step Five:

Also, adding more photos to print couldn't be easier—just go to the filmstrip and Command-click (PC: Ctrl-click) on any photo you want to add to your print queue (as I did here), and Lightroom instantly creates another page for it in the queue (take a look at the little info window now—it says "Page 1 of 6"). To remove a photo from the print queue, it's just as easy: go to the filmstrip and Command-click (PC: Ctrl-click) on any already selected photo to deselect it (Lightroom removes the page from your queue automatically so you don't print a blank sheet). So that's the scoop: selected photos will print on their own separate pages, and non-selected photos are just ignored.

Step Six:

Before we start changing the position of the photo on the page, we'd better choose how large a print we're actually going to print. This is done by clicking on the Page Setup button (which appears to the right of the info area in the toolbar—it's circled in red here). Click on that button, and the Page Setup (PC: Print Setup) dialog appears (shown here). There are basically three things you need to do here: (1) choose your printer from the Format For (PC: Printer Name) pop-up menu, (2) choose the paper size that you want to print on from the Paper Size pop-up menu (the current paper size shown chosen here is 16x20"), and (3) choose whether you want a tall (portrait) orientation for your page or a wide (landscape) orientation. So, go ahead and choose your printer from the pop-up menu (if your printer doesn't appear in the list, you need to install your printer's driver software).

Step Seven:

Here, I've chosen my Epson Stylus Pro 3800 as the printer I want to print to, and now it's time to choose the paper size. Although you can print 16x20" prints on the 3800 (you can actually print up to 17x22" cut sheets), let's go ahead and choose to print to a letter-sized page, as shown here (getting color inkjet paper that's only 8x10" is harder than you'd think—you usually have to special order it, as local stores generally only carry letter size, although all of their frames are generally for 8x10" photos. It's another one of the many unexplained mysteries of paper and printing. Don't get me started).

Step Eight:

Now click the OK button in the Page Setup (PC: Print Setup) dialog, and then take a quick look at the rulers (at the top and left sides of the center Preview area) to confirm that your page is now set up to 8½x11" (if Lightroom's rulers are not visible, just go to the Layout panel, down to the section for Show Guides, and turn on the Rulers checkbox, as shown), and while you're there, scroll up a little to the top of that panel and make sure the unit of measure shown is Inches (as seen here).

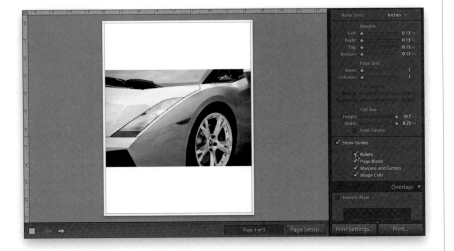

Continued

Step Nine:

Now that we've got the paper size selected, we'll look at how to resize the photo on the page, in case you don't want it to print at the maximum page size. First, let's switch to a totally different photo, and to do that, all you have to do is click on a different photo in the filmstrip. This deselects the five photos we had set up for printing, and now we have just this one photo ready to print at letter size, and since we haven't really modified any of the layout settings in the Maximum Size template we chose when we started, it tries to fit the photo as large as possible on the page (as seen here).

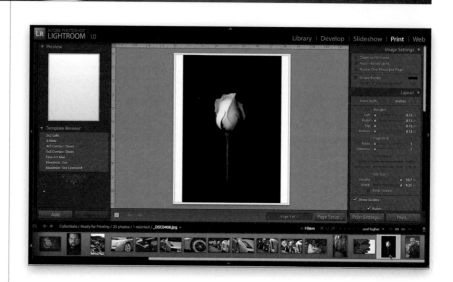

Step Ten:

If you wanted that photo of the white rose (I did convert it to black and white, but it started as a color photo of a real white rose) to be smaller on the page, you've got a couple of choices. Probably the easiest way is to go to the Layout panel, and in the section for Cell Size, drag either the Height or Width slider (doesn't matter which) to the left (as shown here, where I dragged the Width slider), and as you do it shrinks the size of the cell that surrounds the photo, which makes the photo smaller. (Lightroom puts each photo in a separate cell, kind of like a spreadsheet cell, which comes in real handy later when you want multiple photos to appear on each page, which Lightroom really excels at.) *Note:* The Margins sliders (also in the Layout panel) control how close your photo is allowed to get to the edges of the page.

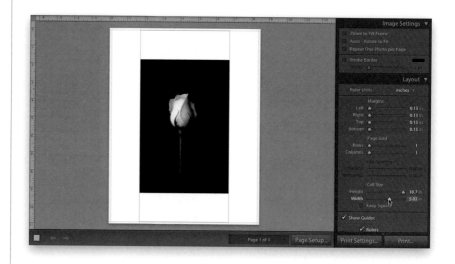

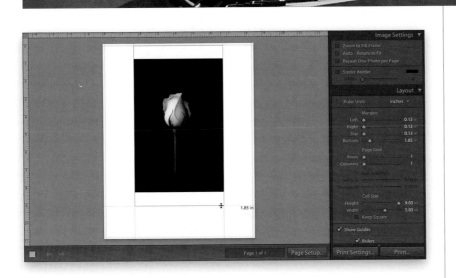

Step Eleven:

Once you shrink the size of the cell, and your photo is smaller, it's easier to see the margin lines that define the border of the cell (those margins were there in the previous steps, it's just that the photo was so close to the full size of the page, you couldn't see those margins as easily). You can adjust each margin individually (top, bottom, left, and right) by either going to the Layout panel and moving the Margins sliders, or by just clicking-and-dragging a margin, like I did here. So, to move your photo up higher on the page, go ahead and click on the bottom margin and drag it upward (as shown here). If you look over at the Margins sliders in the Layout panel, you'll see that the margin has been changed for the Bottom slider, but you did it by dragging directly on the margin rather than moving the slider.

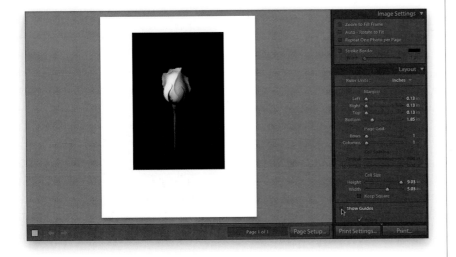

Step Twelve:

To see your final printing layout without seeing all the margin guides, either turn off the Show Guides checkbox near the bottom of the Layout panel (as shown here), or just press the keyboard shortcut Command-Shift-H (PC: Ctrl-Shift-H), which does the same thing. So, to recap the whole resizing thing: you're going to use the Cell Size sliders to resize the photo proportionally on the page, and you're going to use the Margins sliders (or you're going to grab an individual margin and drag it) to change the position of your photo on the page, moving it to the left, right, up higher, or down lower. Easy enough. Next, we'll look at how to print multiple photos on the same page.

Adding Text to Your Print Layouts

If you want to add text to your photo layouts, it's pretty easy as well, and like the Web and Slideshow modules you can have Photoshop Lightroom automatically pull metadata info from your photos and have it appear on the photo print, or you can add your own custom text (and/or Identity Plate) just as easily. Here's what you can add, and how you can add it:

Step One:

First, a little setup: We're going to use the same paper size (US Letter), but go ahead and click on a wide photo in the filmstrip. Make sure the Auto-Rotate to Fit checkbox is turned off, then grab the bottom cell margin and drag upward (as shown here) to move this photo up higher on the frame.

Step Two:

Now let's add some text. The easiest thing is to just turn on your Identity Plate, which is found in the Overlays panel (shown here). Just turn on the Identity Plate checkbox and it appears onscreen (for some reason, mine actually appeared upside down, so I had to click on the rotate button at the top right of the Overlays panel). Once your Identity Plate appears, you can click-and-drag it right where you want it (in this case, drag it down and position it in the center of the white wide-open space below the photo as shown here).

Step Three:

Although my existing Identity Plate looked good when I was using it on my Web gallery layout, I'm not too crazy about how it looks here. So go under the Identity Plate pop-up menu (it's that down-facing arrow at the bottom right of the Identity Plate preview window) and choose Edit to bring up the Identity Plate Editor (shown here). Highlight your existing text and retype your studio's name in all caps, but to add space between the letters, hit the spacebar twice between each letter and four times between words. I chose the font Gill Sans Light, but if you don't have that font, try Optima, Trajan, or even Arial.

Step Four:

Choose 14 as your point size, then click OK to lock in your changes. (*Note:* If you want to save this as a new Identity Plate, just reopen the Identity Plate Editor and choose Save As from the Custom pop-up menu.) Once your new Identity Plate appears, if you don't think the type is large enough, you can go to the Overlays panel, and in the Identity Plate section you'll find Opacity and Scale sliders. You can drag the Scale slider to the right to increase the size of your Identity Plate (as shown here).

Continued

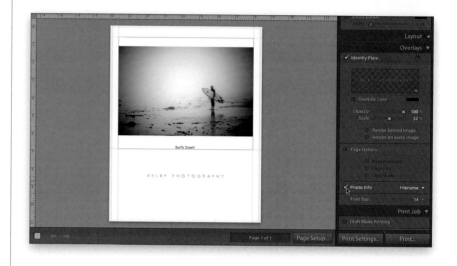

Step Five:

Besides adding your Identity Plate, you can also have Photoshop Lightroom pull text from your metadata (things like your exposure settings, camera make and model, the filename, or any of the caption info you added in the Metadata panel of the Library module). You do this in the Overlays panel, as well (you pretty much do everything to do with text in this one panel), by turning on the Photo Info checkbox (as shown here). By default, it displays the photo's filename, which will appear below the photo (as seen here). If you want to change the size of your text, right below the Photo Info checkbox is a Font Size pop-up menu where you can choose a larger size.

Step Six:

Besides the filename, you can choose a number of other automated settings by clicking on the pop-up menu to the right of Photo Info. For example, try Exposure, and now the exposure appears in that spot. Or, you can choose Edit to bring up the Text Template Editor (shown here) where you can create your own custom list of data that Lightroom will pull from each photo's metadata and print under your photo. In this case, I chose to add text showing the exposure, the ISO, the focal length of the lens, if any exposure compensation was used, and the model of the camera. Now, in a fine art print layout like this, I can't imagine why anyone would want that type of information printed beneath the photo. But you know, and I know, there's somebody out there right now reading this and thinking, "All right! Now I can put the EXIF camera data right on the print!" The world needs these people.

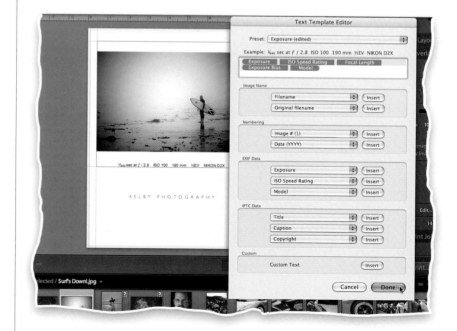

Step Seven:
The last bit of text info you can have appear on your print is the Page Options. For example, if you're printing multiple pages that are related (let's say you're printing out pages for a photo book you're assembling), you can have Lightroom automatically number those pages. In the Overlays panel, just turn on the checkbox for Page Options, then turn on the checkbox for Page Numbers (as shown here). Now, the page numbers will appear in the lower-right corner (seen here).

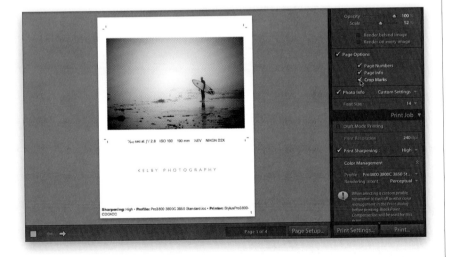

Step Eight:
If you're an "info hound," then you can have even more Page Options printed on your fine art gallery print (did I really just write that?). Just turn on the other two checkboxes under Page Options, and now your print settings (including your chosen level of sharpening, your color management profile, and your selected printer) and a set of crop marks (handy for trimming your photo after it's printed) will also be printed on the page (as shown here, where you've got every text option turned on—from the Identity Plate to the Photo Info to all three Page Options). If you were running tests comparing different printers, or color profiles, or cameras, I could see perhaps having this info on your final prints, but I trust you'll use more discretion when actually creating a fine art print to be hung on the wall. Hey…I'm just sayin'.

Printing Multiple Photos on One Page

Printing more than one photo on a page must be a lot harder than it looks because Photoshop Lightroom is the first program I've used that really does it well. Actually, its multi-photo setup is pretty ingenious, and once you see how easy and intuitive it is, you'll probably wind up printing more multi-photo pages than ever before. Here's how to make the most of it:

Step One:

Start by first clicking on the last template we used (the one called Maximum Size), then click on a different photo in the film-strip. Go to the Layout panel and make sure that you have the Show Guides checkbox turned on. The photo shown here is of one of my very best friends, Rod Harlan, taken during a two-day hands-on Photoshop Lightroom work-shop. The shoot was part of the class (I had the students do four different live shoots and then sort, process, and print their own photos all using Lightroom. I lit Rod with a Westcott daylight fluores-cent Spiderlite TD5 with a 2x3' softbox attached and a Westcott 6-in-1 reflector).

Step Two:

Now go to the Template Browser and click on the 2x2 Cells template (as shown here) to create a four-photo grid. This takes your photo and puts it in the upper-left cell, leaving you three identi-cal cells that are empty. (*Note:* As you move your cursor over templates in the Template Browser, a preview of each lay-out appears in the Preview panel at the top of the left side Panels area.)

Step Three:

If you'd like that same photo to be printed multiple times on this same page, just go to the Image Settings panel (on the top of the right side Panels area) and turn on the checkbox for Repeat One Photo Per Page, as shown here, and your selected photo will be repeated.

Step Four:

The template we used is for four photos on one page, but if you want more photos to fit on that page, just go to the Layout panel, and in the Page Grid section simply increase either the number of rows or columns (in the example shown here, I dragged the Columns slider over to the right just a little to add another column, which lets six photos fit on the page. Since I already had the Repeat One Photo Per Page checkbox turned on, it automatically added the photo in the two new cells).

Continued

Step Five:

If you were to add another row (by dragging the Rows slider just a little to the right), then you'd have nine photos on the page (as shown here). If you want to decrease the space between photos, then go to the Cell Spacing sliders and drag them to the left, which simply decreases the space between cells (as shown here, where the photos are fairly close together).

Step Six:

Nearly all of the same text features that you learned in the previous tutorial can be applied to these multi-photo layouts as well. For example, go ahead and turn on the Photo Info checkbox in the Overlays panel (as shown here), and the filename is added below each photo. Now, in the previous step we decreased the amount of vertical cell space between the photos, so to add a little space back in (now that you've added the filename below each photo), go back up to the Layout panel and increase the vertical cell spacing to 0.29 (as shown here).

Step Seven:

So that's pretty much the scoop on how to add more copies of your photo to your layout. Now, go ahead and turn off the Photo Info checkbox again (as shown here), then go to the Layout panel and drag your Columns slider back to 2, and your Rows slider back to 2, so we are pretty much back where we started (I could have just had you click on the 2x2 Cell template, but I did want you to see how easy it is to take away photos as well).

Step Eight:

Thus far we've looked at repeating the same photo multiple times on a page. What if you want four different photos? First, go to the Image Settings panel and turn off the Repeat One Photo Per Page checkbox. Then you just go to the film-strip and select the four different photos you want on your page by Command-clicking (PC: Ctrl-clicking) on the ones you want. Each cell will be filled with your selected photos (as shown here).

TIP: There's a feature we haven't talked about yet, and it's in the Image Settings panel up top—it's called Zoom to Fill Frame. Turning this checkbox on basically zooms in on your photo until it fills the frame as fully as possible, with no gaps on the sides, top, or bottom. You'd use this feature when you have smaller cells, or wider cells, and you want to try a totally different look, but avoid it on single photo pages because you may not have enough resolution to print that photo zoomed in that tight.

Continued

Step Nine:

So what happens if you select more than four photos? Lightroom just adds another page (or as many pages as you need) to accommodate the photos you've added. If you look in the info area at the right end of the toolbar, you'll see it now says "Page 1 of 2" and if you click the Next Page (right arrow) button in the toolbar, it will take you to that second page (shown here, where I selected three more photos). One tip for adding photos: photos are added in the order they appear in the filmstrip. In this case, all three of the photos I added came after the first four I had selected in the filmstrip, so they all wound up on their own new page without disturbing the first page I had already set up. Click on the Previous Page (left arrow) button in the toolbar to return to the first page.

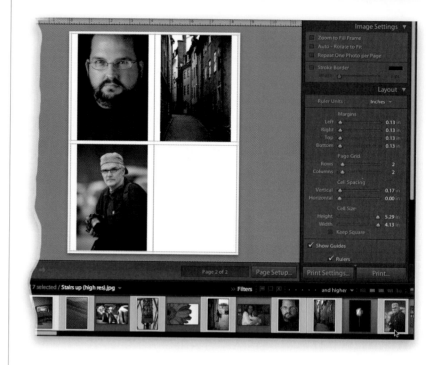

Step Ten:

Go to the filmstrip, scroll back to the left a bit and Command-click (PC: Ctrl-click) on a different photo that appears earlier in the filmstrip (as shown here, where I added a shot of a horse running on the beach). You'll notice that this shot now takes over the first position on the first page, and it shuffles all the other photos down one (click on the right arrow to see the second page—the photo that was in the third slot on mine [a shot of my buddy Dave Moser when we were shooting in Vermont] has moved to the last cell). So, the order you add photos in does matter (well, at least it can matter if you want particular photos on particular pages). If you want your photos to appear in a certain order, then put them in that order in the filmstrip first, knowing that the left-most photo winds up in the first slot, the next photo in the next, and so on.

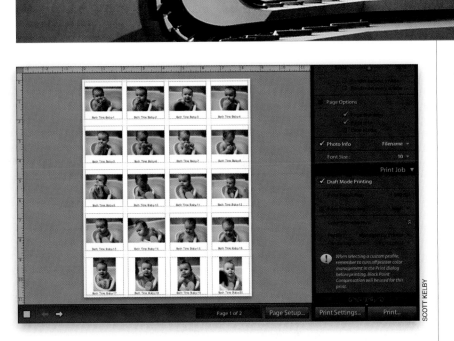

Step Eleven:

If you want to create a contact sheet of all the photos in a folder or collection, just go to the Library module, choose that folder or collection, press Command-A (PC: Ctrl-A) to Select All, then go to the Print module. In the Template Browser, click on 4x5 Contact Sheet, and your selected photos will fill the cells (as shown here), and as many pages will be added as necessary to include all your selected photos.

TIP: When you're printing contact sheets, you can take advantage of Lightroom's Draft Mode printing, which uses the cached previews (or built-in previews if necessary) for printing, rather than the high-resolution versions of the photos, so it prints in a fraction of the usual time, yet the print quality still looks great because the photos are so small. This Draft Mode Printing option is turned on by default when you choose any contact sheet template. You can turn this off/on at the top of the Print Job panel.

Step Twelve:

I saved my favorite multi-photo project for last. Select four photos in the film-strip, then go to the Template Browser, click on the 4 Wide template, and your four photos appear in this very slick wide layout. You can reposition any photo by just clicking-and-dragging it up or down right within the cell. The Identity Plate is turned on by default with this template (which looks good here), but go to the Layout panel and turn off the Show Guides checkbox (as shown here) to see this nice clean layout.

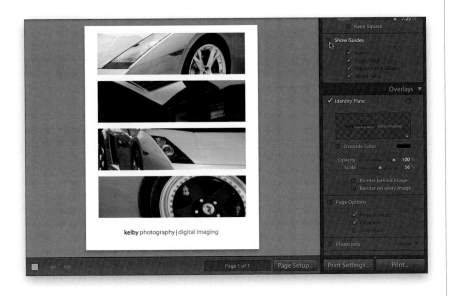

Continued

Step Thirteen:

For a nice variation on this effect, head back up to the Image Settings panel, and turn on the Repeat One Photo Per Page checkbox (as shown here), which gives you this very cool layout with the same photo repeated in all four cells. If you want to create a little more space between the cells (as I did here), just drag the Vertical Cell Spacing slider to the right and each cell gets shorter.

Note: There are two other options for how the Identity Plate is used in multi-photo layouts. If you choose Render on Every Image, it puts your Identity Plate right smack dab in the middle of each photo in each cell. If you choose Render Behind Image it prints on the background, as if it was a watermark (scale it up so it is slightly larger than your image).

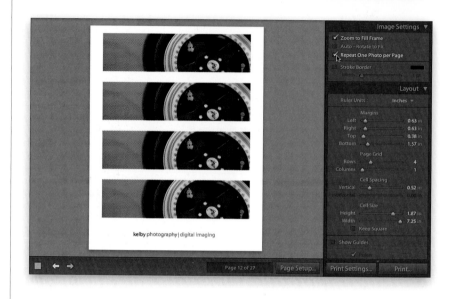

Step Fourteen:

Just to take this another step further (and show what can be done), let's try taking the same idea, but making the columns tall inside of wide (it's easier than it sounds). First, start by choosing the 4 Wide template, then go up to the Image Settings panel and turn off the Zoom to Fill Frame checkbox. Select four photos in the filmstrip. Go over to the Layout panel and in the Page Grid section, change it to 1 row and 4 columns to give you four tall columns (as shown here). To add some extra space between cells, go to the Cell Spacing section and drag the Horizontal spacing slider to the right to 0.19. Lastly, in the Margins section set the Left and Right margin sliders to 0.22, the Top slider to 0.37, and the Bottom slider to 2.73. Of course, the problem is the photos don't fill the cells the way they did with the wide layout, but that's a one-click fix.

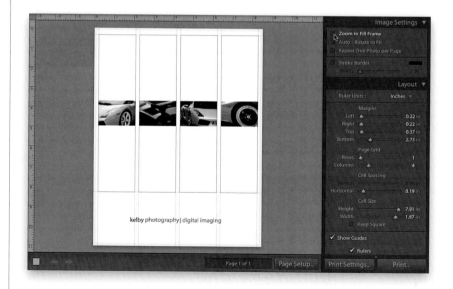

Step Fifteen:

To fill those cells, go up to the Image Settings panel and turn on the checkbox for Zoom to Fill Frame (as shown here), and Lightroom enlarges those photos until each one fully fills each cell to give you the look you see here. Now, you're probably thinking, "Didn't you have me turn Zoom to Fill Frame off back in Step Fourteen?" Yes, yes I did. But I had you do that so I could graphically illustrate what the Zoom to Fill Frame checkbox does. See, now you know what it does, and when to use it.

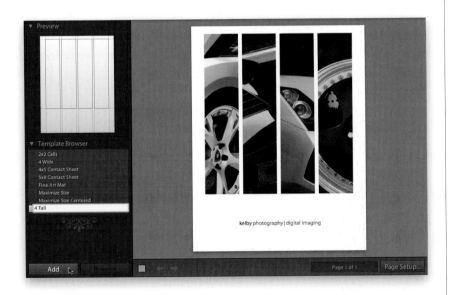

Step Sixteen:

Well, while you've got this new custom layout, let's save it as a printing template so next time you don't have to jump through all these hoops—you just click on the template and it's ready to go. So, go to the Template Browser in the left side Panels area and click on the Add button (as shown here), and when the new template field appears in the Template Browser, give your template a name (I named mine "4 Tall," as shown here). The nice thing is that when you save templates here in the Print module, they include the Page Setup dialog settings as well, so when you choose it, it knows to use a letter-sized page with portrait orientation.

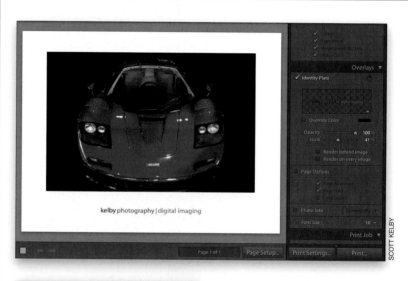

The Final Print Settings and Color Management

Once you've got your page set up with the printing layout you want, you just need to make a couple of quick choices in the Print Job panel so your photos look their best when printed. Here's which buttons to push, when, and why:

Step One:

Get the page layout the way you want it to appear when printed (in the layout shown here, I clicked on Page Setup and set my page to a wide [landscape] orientation and in the Layout panel, in the Margins section, I dragged the Bottom margin slider to the right a bit to give me a little extra room around my Identity Plate). Once all that's done, it's time to choose our printing options in the Print Job panel at the bottom of the right side Panels area.

Step Two:

Since you're printing one photo on a letter-sized page (and not a contact sheet with multiple small photos), you want to make sure the Draft Mode Printing checkbox is turned off. Now it's time to choose the resolution. The default print resolution is 240 dpi, which works fine for most color inkjet printing. (If, like me, you use Epson printers, then ideally you'd print at 360 for letter-sized or smaller, 240 for 13x19" prints, or 180 for 16x20" or larger. The larger the print size, the lower the resolution you can get away with.) In this instance, we're printing to an Epson Stylus Photo R2400 on an 8½x11" sheet, so highlight the resolution field and type in 360 (as shown here), then press the Return (PC: Enter) key.

Step Three:

Next is the pop-up menu for Print Sharpening, and I recommend clicking on that pop-up menu and choosing High (as shown here). Here's why: The default Print Sharpening setting is Low. This setting adds sharpening that is barely visible. It should be renamed "Off." The Medium setting is a little better, but should be named "Low," and the High setting should be renamed "I'm really more like Medium." Choose High and you'll get sharper prints, but I wish there was another setting (which they would probably name something like "Maximum Sharpening," but in reality it would be something more like "Medium Plus").

Step Four:

Now it's time to set the Color Management options. Start by choosing the printing profile. The default setting is Managed by Printer (shown here), which means your printer is going to color manage your job. Having your printer manage your color used to be a total joke, but with the advances in printing technology, it's not all that bad. However, you'll get better results by having Photoshop Lightroom assign a printer/paper profile. To do this, first go to the website of the company that manufactures the exact brand of paper you're going to be printing on. On their site, find the ICC color profiles they provide for free downloading that exactly match: (a) the paper you're going to be printing on, and (b) the exact printer you're going to be printing to. In our case, I'm printing to an Epson Stylus Photo R2400 printer using Epson's Premium Luster paper, so I would go to Epson's website, to the R2400 Drivers & Downloads page, download their ICC color profiles for Premium Luster paper, and install them.

Continued

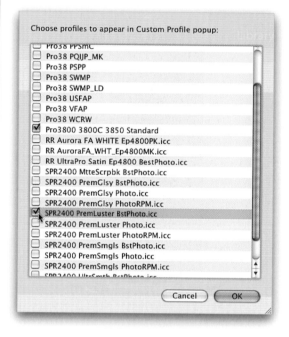

Step Five:

Once your paper/printer profile is installed, click-and-hold on the Profile pop-up menu (right where it says "Managed by Printer") and choose Other. This brings up a dialog listing all the profiles installed on your computer. Scroll through the list and find the paper profiles for your printer, then find the profiles for the papers you normally print on (in my case, I print primarily on Premium Luster and Velvet Fine Art), and turn on the checkboxes beside those papers. Since I also use an Epson Stylus Pro 3800, I included a profile for that as well. Once you've found your profiles, click OK to add them to your pop-up menu.

Step Six:

Now, return to that Profile pop-up menu in the Print Job panel, and you'll see your paper profiles for your printers are now available as choices in the menu. With the kind of photo we're printing (a red sports car), we probably don't want to print to a textured fine art paper like Velvet Fine Art, so instead choose the Premium Luster profile (abbreviated in your pop-up menu as SP [Stylus Photo] R2400 PremLuster BstPhoto.icc). Now you've set up Lightroom so it knows exactly how to handle the color for that printer on that particular type of paper. This step is really key to getting the quality prints we're all aiming for, because at the end of the day, it's all about the print.

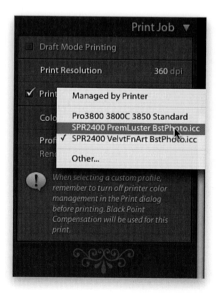

Step Seven:

Under Rendering Intent, you have two choices: (a) Perceptual, or (b) Relative (Colormetric). Theoretically, choosing Perceptual may give you a more pleasing print because it tries to maintain color relationships, but it's not necessarily accurate as to what you see tonally onscreen. Choosing Relative may provide a more accurate interpretation of the tone of the photo, but you may not like the final color as much. So, which one is right? The one that looks best on your own printer. Relative is probably the most popular choice, but personally I usually use Perceptual because my style uses very rich, saturated colors, and it seems that Perceptual gives me better color on my particular printer. So, which one should you choose? The best way to know which one looks best for your printer is to print a few test prints for each photo—try one with Perceptual and one with Relative—and when the prints come out, you'll know right away which one works best for your printer.

Step Eight:

Now you can click on the Print button that appears below the bottom of the right side Panels area (as shown here).

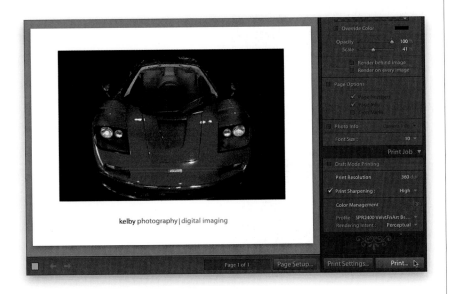

Continued

Step Nine:

This will bring up the Print dialog (shown here). Go to the section that controls printer color management (your pop-up menu choices may be different depending on your printer. On a PC, click on the Properties button to locate it), and turn the printer color management off (as shown here). Since you're having Lightroom manage the color, you don't want the printer also trying to manage your color, because when the two color management systems start fighting each other, nobody wins.

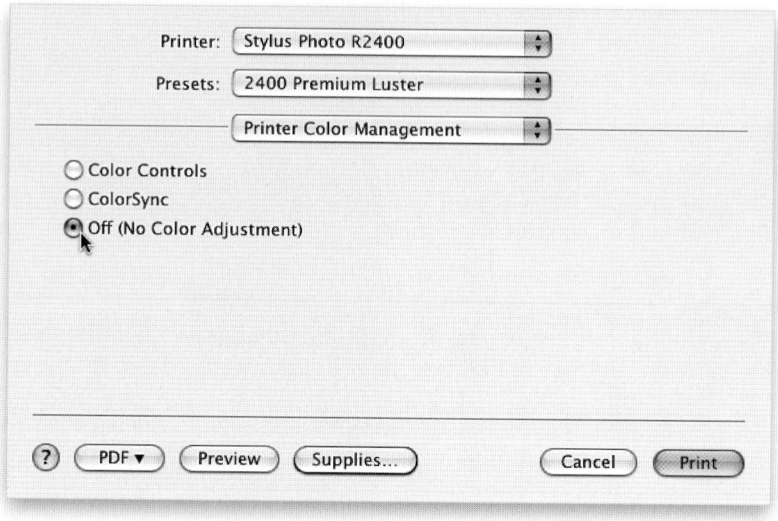

Step Ten:

Now switch to the Print Settings section (again, your pop-up menus may be different and on a PC, these will be in the Properties dialog for your printer), and for Media Type, choose the exact paper you'll be printing to from the pop-up menu (as shown here, where I chose Premium Luster Photo Paper).

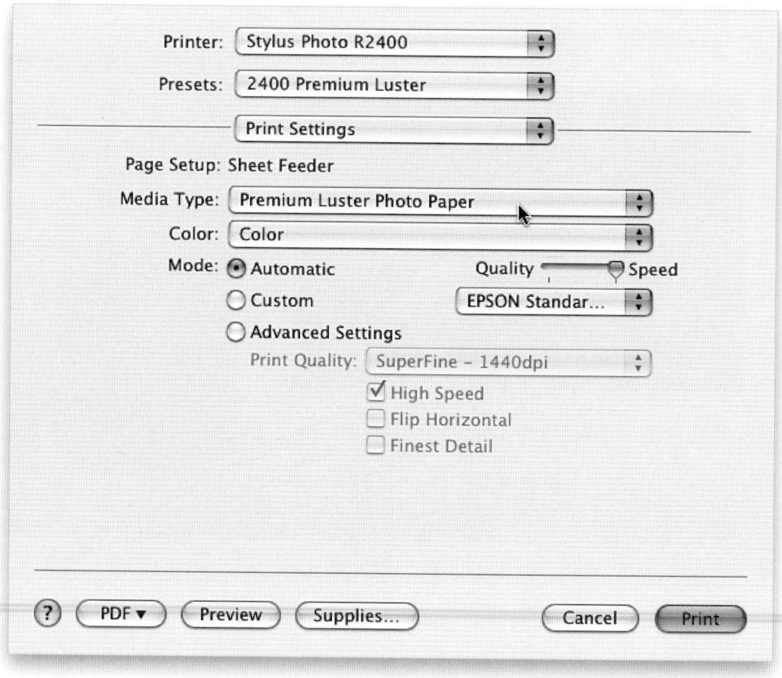

SCOTT KELBY

Step Eleven:

In that same Print Settings section, for Mode choose Advanced Settings, turn off the High Speed setting (if it's turned on), then choose SuperFine – 1440dpi as your Print Quality (again, this is for printing to an Epson printer using Epson paper. If you don't have an Epson printer...why not? Just kidding—if you don't have an Epson printer, you're probably not using Epson paper, so for Print Quality choose the one that most closely matches the paper you are printing to).

Step Twelve:

Click the Print button to close the Print dialog and send your job to the printer. Now all you have to do is wait for the printer to spit out your print and see how ya did. A couple of things to keep in mind: (1) If your print doesn't match your monitor, the most likely culprit is you haven't calibrated your monitor, and the best way to do that is with a hardware calibrator (they're now very affordable—look at the ones from X-Rite or ColorSync). (2) Don't be afraid to do a few test prints to determine which settings work best for your particular printer. And, (3) make sure you download the printer/paper profiles from the company that makes the paper you're printing on. Does it really make that big a difference? Yup, sure does.

Adding Cool Frame Borders to Your Prints

This is normally something that I would have gone to Photoshop CS2/CS3 for, but right before we went to press with this book, I started using this technique from Sean McCormick (from his Photoshop Lightroom blog at www.seanmcfoto .com/lightroom/) who showed how to use Lightroom's Identity Plate to get these pre-designed edges and borders onto your print. You have to do a little bit of prep work in Photoshop (it's easy) before you bring them into Lightroom, but once you do, then you can apply these frame effects any time you like. Kudos to Sean for sharing this one!

Step One:

We're going to start in Photoshop with prepping our edge file for use in Photoshop Lightroom. I downloaded the edge border you see here from iStockphoto.com (it cost me $4 for the high-res 300 dpi download, but you can download it free from this book's web-site). The edge comes flattened on the background, so to start, click the Magic Wand tool (W) within the black area in the center to select that area. Press-and-hold the Shift key and click on some of the outside edge areas to add those to our selection. Lastly, go under the Select menu and choose Similar to pick up any stray areas we missed. Then press Command-Shift-J (PC: Ctrl-Shift-J) to put this edge up on its own separate layer (as shown in the next step).

Step Two:

We need a hole cut out of this solid black edge graphic in the shape of a rectangle (so our photo can show through). So, get the Rectangular Marquee tool (M) and click-and-drag a rectangular selection that's almost as big as our edge graphic (as shown here), then press the Delete (PC: Backspace) key to knock a large rect-angular hole out of our graphic.

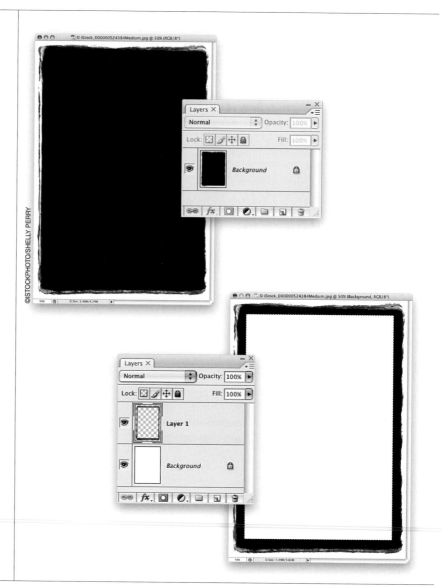

Step Three:

For this to work properly, our file can't have a solid white background or it will cover our photo when we bring it into Lightroom—instead the background has to be transparent. To do that, go to the Layers palette and drag the Background layer into the Trash (at the bottom of the palette) to delete it (prior to CS3, you had to unlock the Background layer first). That leaves us with just our edge border on a transparent layer. Now we can save it, so go under the File menu and choose Save As. When the dialog appears, you'll need to choose a file format that supports transparency (JPEG doesn't), so choose PNG as your format, give the file a name, and click Save (you'll probably get a notice that because this is a layered file, you'll have to save a copy of the file instead—no problem—just click Save).

Step Four:

All right, that's all the prep work in Photoshop—now back to Lightroom. Click on the photo you want to have an edge frame, then jump over to the Print module. In the Print module, in the Overlays panel, turn on the Identity Plate checkbox. Then, in the Identity Plate pop-up menu, choose Edit to bring up the Identity Plate Editor you see here. In that dialog, click on the Use a Graphical Identity Plate radio button (because we're going to import a graphic, rather than using text), then click on the Locate File button (as shown here), locate your saved PNG edge file, and click Choose (PC: Open) to load it into your Identity Plate Editor (you can see the top of our edge frame in the small preview window shown here).

Continued

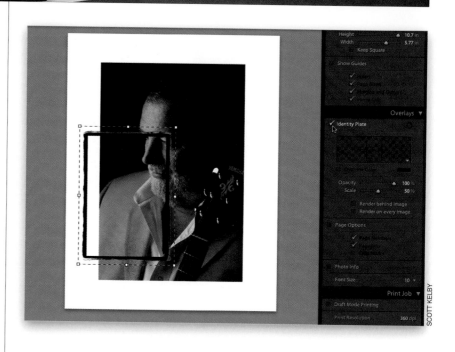

Step Five:

When you click OK, our edge frame will appear hovering over your print (almost like it's on its own layer). The size and position won't be right, so that's the first thing you'll want to fix (which we'll do in the next step, but while we're here, notice how the center of our edge is transparent—you can see right through it to the photo below it. That's why we had to save this file without the background layer, and as a PNG—to keep that transparency intact).

Step Six:

To resize your border, you can either click-and-drag a corner point outward (as shown here), or use the Scale slider in the Overlays panel. Once the size looks about right, you can reposition the edge by simply clicking-and-dragging inside the edge frame borders.

Step Seven:

When it's right where you want it, just click your cursor outside the border and it will deselect. The final photo with the edge frame border is shown here. Now, if you decide you want to keep this border and use it in the future—go back to the Identity Plate Editor and from the Custom pop-up menu at the bottom-left corner of the dialog, choose Save As to save this frame border as an Identity Plate you can use anytime to add a quick border effect.

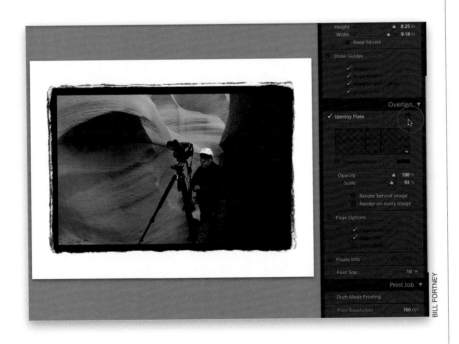

Step Eight:

We created a vertical frame, but how do you add this frame edge to a horizontal photo, like the one shown here (shot by my good friend Bill Fortney, when we were down shooting in Arizona's Antelope Canyon slots)? If you change your page setup to Landscape, the Identity Plate will rotate automatically. If you are printing horizontally in a Portrait setup, you can rotate the Identity Plate by clicking on the circular Rotate button that appears to the right of the Identity Plate checkbox in the Overlays panel (it's shown circled here in red). You'll probably have to resize and reposition the frame (as I did here) to make it fit just right, but now your single frame edge is doing double duty.

Web

getting your photos on the web

Okay, this is a weird chapter because it was originally the only chapter in the book just for Macintosh users. The reason why was simple. I'm a Macintosh user, and I wanted my Macintosh brethren to share a special bond with me—one that only came from having a special chapter that Windows users didn't get to enjoy. You see, in everyday computing life, Macintosh users get the short end of the stick. There's less Macintosh software, less Macintosh hardware, fewer Macintosh magazines, less Macintosh peripherals, and about a bazillion less games for the Macintosh platform. So, this was my cry for help—my personal crusade to somehow even the score by including a chapter just for Mac users. It was my way of striking back at the anti-Macintosh subculture that has for far too long held sway in the overall computing world and kept Mac users down. Well, it could be that, or it could've been the fact that the Windows version of Photoshop Lightroom didn't have a Web module until Beta 4, so there was no reason to make Windows users read this chapter. Ahh, you'd like it to be that wouldn't you? You'd like there to be some logical explanation—something that made perfect sense as to why this chapter was just for Mac users. Then it would perpetuate the Microsoft world domination scheme that has kept Macintosh users from having an Apple-branded two-button mouse for more than 20 years. You'd like that wouldn't you? Wait. Huh? Apple came out with a two-button Bluetooth mouse? Really? Oh. I didn't realize that. I'm so embarrassed. Really, this is so embarrassing. Forget this ever happened.

Before You Start Building Your Web Gallery, Do This First!

For a photographer, having a storefront on the Web has become more important than ever, and Photoshop Lightroom does a brilliant job of letting you effortlessly create professional-looking photo galleries to help promote your business and let your clients do their proofing on the Web. But before you click on the Web module and start throwing together your site, if you take one simple step first, it will save you a lot of time and frustration down the road (and by "down the road" I don't mean six months from now—I mean about 20 minutes from now).

Step One:
Although technically you can create a Web gallery directly from a folder or a Quick Collection, or even from the results of a search, you're way, way better off starting by creating a regular collection and turning that collection into your gallery. There are loads of benefits (besides the obvious organization of having just the photos you want in your Web gallery all in one place) but beyond that, adding photos, deleting photos, and reordering photos is just so much easier. So, go to the Collections panel (in the Library module) and create a new collection (for this example, just name it "Web Portfolio"), then drag the photos you want in your Web gallery into this collection.

SCOTT KELBY

Step Two:
Once the photos you want in your Web gallery are all in a collection, jump over to the Web module (you can click the link up in the Module Picker or press Command-Option-5 [PC: Ctrl-Alt-5]). When the Web module appears, you'll see the photos in your collection down in the filmstrip and arranged in the default Web gallery template in the center Preview area (like a slide show, they're added in order with the first photo on the left in the filmstrip being first, followed by the second photo, and so on).

SCOTT KELBY

Step Three:

Photoshop Lightroom comes with a nice collection of pre-designed Flash-based and HTML templates. Flash-based sites let everything happen on one page—your thumbnails and larger preview photos appear right on the same page, plus you get a smooth dissolve between photos. With HTML pages, each preview requires its own separate page (so you'll have a multi-page site), and there are no nice, elegant dissolves. They both work fine, it's just that Flash pages offer more features. Start by going to the Template Browser in the left side Panels area, and hovering your cursor over each template. As you move over a template, look up at the top panel (the Preview panel) and you'll see a preview of how that template looks (if you see a large, white, bold *f* appear in the lower-left corner of the preview, as shown here, that's a Flash-based template).

Step Four:

If you find a template that fits your style, click on it to apply that template, rather than using the default template shown in Step Three. I personally like the template named "Paper White" (shown here), which gives you a scrolling set of thumbnails on the left, and when you click on a thumbnail you get the larger preview on the right. There is also a button at the bottom of the template for hiding these thumbnails on the left and viewing the photos as a slide show. So, at this point go ahead and click on any template (the rest of the steps work pretty much the same on any layout, so you don't have to use Paper White if you don't want to. But if you do choose Paper White like I did, at that moment we will have formed a close and personal bond that can never be broken). Now you're ready to start customizing your Web portfolio.

Customizing Your Web Gallery

Now that you've got a template picked out as your starting place, customizing the site is incredibly easy. The long stack of right side panels might make it look like this is going to be a complicated process, but you'll be able to ignore most of those panels because Photoshop Lightroom allows you to do live editing, right on the page, so we'll only go to those panels on a few occasions. This live onscreen editing is what makes the process so easy, and even if you have no Web design experience whatsoever, you'll be able to create a great-looking gallery in about five minutes. Here goes:

Step One:

Okay, we're starting with that Paper White template we chose in the previous tutorial, and we're going to customize it. Since you've already chosen your template, you can hide the left side Panels area by pressing F7, which will give you a larger Preview area (as seen here). Now you can put your photos in the order you want them to appear on the site. The leftmost photo in your filmstrip will be the top photo in the thumbnails on your page. So in the filmstrip, drag the photos into the order you want them to appear (here I dragged a different photo into the first position).

Step Two:

Once your photos are in the order you'd like them, you can press F6 to hide the filmstrip, giving you even more room (notice how a fourth thumbnail is now visible thanks to the extra room?). Okay, let's start customizing: to change the text that appears on the page, you simply click directly on the text to highlight it, then type in your new text as I did here where I renamed the site title (in the upper-left corner) "kelby photography." This seems so much easier and more intuitive than going to the Labels panel in right side Panels area, and entering this in the Site Title field.

Step Three:

So basically, that's how we're going to customize most of this page—by clicking on text blocks and typing in new text, and then the text we enter is updated in the Labels panel (in the right side Panels area). Now, there's only one thing I actually do in that panel (which comes in Step Four), and the rest I do right on the page itself. So, go ahead and enter the information you want on your webpage by clicking on the text blocks, typing in your new text, and then hitting the Return (PC: Enter) key on your keyboard to lock in your changes. Here I've updated my page with the information I might put there for a client looking to find/choose one of my images for a magazine article.

Step Four:

If you look at my cursor in Step Three, you'll see that it's pointing at a line of text that says "email Scott" and when I move my cursor over it, it underlines because that's a live link to send me an email. Of course, you have to tell Photoshop Lightroom where to send email from this page, and this is the one time I do go to the Labels panel because you have to enter your email address there. Go down to the Web or Mail Link field and click to highlight the field. You want to leave the word "mailto:" alone and just replace the fake email address that's there with your email address (as shown here). So, when you're done it should read "mailto:youremailaddress@ whereever.com" (with no spaces between letters). Now when a visitor to your webpage clicks on that link, it will launch their email program, open a new email window, and your email address will already be entered in the To field.

Continued

Step Five:

Another thing you can do to customize your page is to have your Identity Plate replace the site title text that appears in the top-left corner (as shown here). To do that, just go to the Appearance panel and turn on the Identity Plate checkbox. Of course, if you have saved multiple identity plates, you can choose the one you want to appear on your page by clicking on the little down-facing arrow that appears in the bottom right of the Identity Plate preview window. This brings up a pop-up menu (shown here) with a list of your saved identity plates. If you need to temporarily change the size or color of your Identity Plate to suit this particular page (with its white background), choose Edit from that pop-up menu, and you can select the text and change its size or color (by the way, I changed the photo here 'cause I was getting tired of looking at that other one).

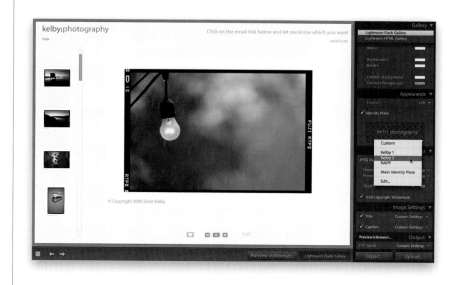

Step Six:

While we're in the Appearance panel, there is a pop-up menu where you can choose different layouts for your webpage. It's right above the Identity Plate section, and the default layout for this Flash-based gallery is Left (which describes where the thumbnails are located). Go ahead and click on the Layout pop-up menu and choose Scrolling. That gives you the layout you see here (all your text adjusts automatically), where the thumbnails appear across the bottom with your preview centered above them. Also try the Slideshow Only layout, which hides the thumbnails from view and gives you the largest image size for your photos. The fourth choice is called Paginated, and it puts smaller static thumbnails in rows (take a look at that one and see what you think).

Step Seven:

Besides just moving the location of the thumbnails, you can also choose their size and quality from the Output Settings panel. Click on the Thumbnail pop-up menu (shown here) and you can choose a size for your thumbnails (the default size is Large, but in the example shown here, I chose Medium and you can see how much smaller it makes the thumbnails). You can also control the size of the preview photo that appears when you click on a thumbnail from the Preview pop-up menu right below it.

Step Eight:

As you can see in the previous step, I changed the photo again—but this time I did it primarily so I could sneak a photo of my amazing wife and our sweet little seven-month-old daughter into the book. So, since they just happen to be onscreen right now (ahem), take a look in the bottom-left corner of the photo in Step Seven and you'll see my copyright info. Lightroom automatically pulls that info from the copyright metadata you added when you first imported the photos (providing, of course, that you did actually create a metadata template with your copyright and contact info back in Chapter 1. See, ya knew skipping that would come back to haunt you). Anyway, if you don't want that copyright info visible, you can turn it off in the Output Settings panel (as shown here). I also changed the Thumbnail size back to Large, as Medium looked a bit too small to me.

Continued

Step Nine:

In the Image Settings panel, you can add two lines of text below your preview photos (a title and a caption). You choose exactly which type of text is displayed from the two pop-up menus (the title text appears first and is slightly larger and bolder than the caption text). You can choose to have Lightroom automatically pull information from your photos' metadata and EXIF camera data and display it on one or both lines. For example, from the Caption pop-up menu, choose Exposure and it will find that info in the photo's EXIF camera data and display it (you can see it on the second line here). Another choice is to add your own custom text (as I've also done here. You can see it on the first line). The only problem is, that same exact text will now appear under every single photo in your gallery.

Step Ten:

If you'd like to have a caption automatically appear below each photo that describes the photo (rather than one static caption for every photo), then all you have to do is return to the Library module, and click on the first photo you want to add a caption to. Go to the Metadata panel in the right side Panels area, click in the Caption field, and then type in the caption you want to appear on your webpage, as shown here.

TIP: To remove a photo from your webpage, go to the filmstrip and Control-click (PC: Right-click) on the photo. From the contextual menu that appears, choose Remove from Collection. To add a photo to your collection, go to the Library module and drag the photo into your Web Portfolio collection. When you return to the Web module, that photo will automatically be added to your webpage.

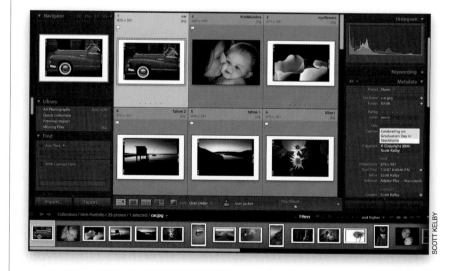

Step Eleven:

Now return to the Web module and go to the Image Settings panel. From the Title pop-up menu, choose Edit to bring up the Text Template Editor (shown here). If a token (Adobe's name for the blue pill-shaped info capsules [in Windows, this info is in braces]) appears in the Example field, click on it and press the Delete (PC: Backspace) key on your keyboard to delete it. Then, go down to the IPTC Data section in this dialog and to the right of the middle pop-up menu (where it says "Caption"), click the Insert button (as shown here). This tells Lightroom to pull the caption text automatically from the Metadata panel's Caption field in the Library module. You'll want to save this as a preset for later, so from the Preset menu at the top of the dialog, choose Save as New Preset. Give this preset a name (I chose Metadata Caption) in the New Preset dialog, and click Create. Then click the Done button in the Text Template Editor.

Step Twelve:

Go back to the Image Settings panel, and from the Title pop-up menu choose the new preset (Metadata Caption) you just created (as shown here). Now the metadata caption you added to this photo back in the Library module's Metadata panel will appear under the photo (as seen here). Lightroom will automatically gather and display this caption information for each photo you added that caption metadata to, so it's worth spending a couple of minutes adding those while you're in the Library module.

Continued

Step Thirteen:

If you want to change the colors of your web-page, go to the Color Palette panel (shown here), and click on the color swatch next to the area you want to change. This brings up the Colors panel where you choose the color you'd like for that area. To make your page look like the one shown here, click on the Header swatch and change the color to solid black. Then click on the Menu swatch and change it to a medium gray (be sure to change it to a shade lighter than the menu text, so that you can still read the text). Next, click on the Background swatch and choose a dark gray. For the thin border you see surrounding the thumbnail area and main preview area, click on the Border swatch and choose a light gray (you couldn't see this border before because it was the same white color as the background, and I'm sure that was by design. If you don't want to see that border, make your border the same color as the background).

Step Fourteen:

Now you can either save this new color scheme as your own Web template (just make the left side Panels area visible, and in the Template Browser click the Add button at the bottom), you can click back on the original Paper White template, or you can try a different template altogether by hovering your cursor over the different templates in the Template Browser (so you see a preview up in the Preview panel) and then clicking on one you like (here I clicked on the Flash-based template named Blue Sky and as you can see, it kept all of the text I entered in the previous template, and just changed the look and layout of the page. By the way, what you're seeing is another of the four layouts that Lightroom offers. This one is the Paginated layout I mentioned earlier, which puts three rows of thumbnails on the left side, with a larger preview on the right.

Step Fifteen:

Here's another customizing tip: if you need to add a lot more text (like detailed instructions for your client, or your full contact info with address, phone, etc.), you can add that to a webpage called "About these Photos." Your client can find this page by clicking on the View link that appears in the top-left corner of your page (shown here). They can choose that page, the Gallery page (the standard view with thumbnails), or the Slideshow view (with a larger preview photo but without any thumbnails) from the pop-up menu.

Step Sixteen:

To add your own text to this About These Photos page, you first click on the View link yourself and choose About These Photos from the pop-up menu (just like in the previous step). When the page appears, go to the Labels panel, then click once in the Collection Description field and start typing in your text. Now, here's the thing: I haven't been able to find a way to add paragraph breaks, so if you type in this field, it comes out as just one big blob of text. However, I also found that if you create your text in a word processing application like Microsoft Word (or any text editor), you can then copy-and-paste that text into this field and it keeps all the line breaks, bullets, etc., in place. So that's what I did here: I created the text in my Mac's built-in TextEdit application, then I copied-and-pasted the text right into that Collection Description field. One last thing: if you don't tell your client to click on that View link and choose About These Photos, they may never find this page. So you'll need to tell them, and you can do that in any of the visible fields on the site.

Continued

Step Seventeen:

So far, we've been customizing our Flash-based template (I switched back to our original Paper White template here, and clicked on the thumbnail for the third photo down), and in a moment we'll look at a couple of options that are different when customizing an HTML-based gallery. But before we get to that, if your Flash-based webpage is complete, before you upload it to the Web you should definitely preview your final webpage in your Web browser. That way, you can make sure it looks and works the way you want it to, and you'll get the exact same experience as the person (your client) viewing your webpage will have. To do that, you simply click the Preview in Browser button found in the toolbar below the Preview area (shown circled here in red).

Step Eighteen:

Once you click that Preview in Browser button, it launches your computer's default Web browser and displays the page you created in Lightroom (as shown here in Apple's Safari Web browser, where I clicked on the boat thumbnail on the left). The page should be fully functional, so try everything and make certain that the email link works, and that your email address is correct when it appears in the To field of your new email window. If everything's okay, you can jump right to the next tutorial in this chapter, which shows you how to upload your finished Web gallery to the Web. But before you do that, stick with me here another minute, as we'll look at what's different with an HTML-based gallery, and how to customize it (it doesn't take very long, since we covered a lot of the options already).

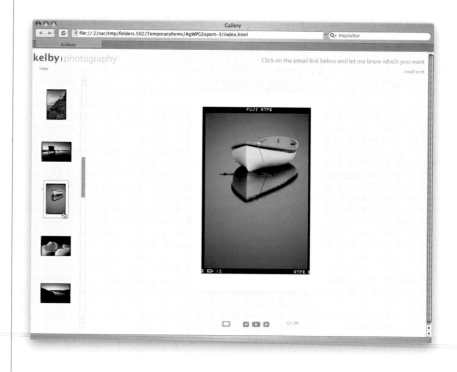

Step Nineteen:

Switching to an HTML-based layout is easy—you just click on an HTML template in the Template Browser. So, head over to the Template Browser and choose the HTML template named "Charcoal" (as shown here). This template gives you a 3x3 thumbnail grid (three columns across and three rows deep). That's only nine thumbnails on an entire page, and because of that it takes four separate pages to hold them all, but we will adjust that in a moment. For now, since our template choice has been made, go ahead and hide the left side Panels area.

Step Twenty:

You may have to re-enter some of your text on the page, so just click on a block of text right on the page to highlight it, then type in your new text. The text fields in the Labels panel and the Color Palette panel are pretty much the same as the ones we used earlier for our Flash-based gallery, so let's not go over them again. However, with HTML galleries you also now have some different options in the Appearance panel. The first thing to decide in this panel is how many rows and columns your thumbnail grid is going to have. If you look at the grid preview in the Appearance panel, you'll see that a 3x3 grid of squares is highlighted, representing your current thumbnail grid. Glide your cursor over this grid and as you do, the highlighted area on the grid expands (don't click yet—just move around over it and you'll see what I mean). Glide your cursor over to the right until two more vertical columns are selected (as shown here).

Continued

Step Twenty-One:

Once you've got five columns highlighted, click once on that grid to apply your new five-column layout. Now you're down to just three pages of thumbnails (this may be different for you depending on the number of photos in your gallery) and anyone viewing your site will see more of your work without having to dig down through four pages of photos (and many people won't dig down that far—they'll go to a page or so deep, and then they're gone). The more thumbnails you can get to fit comfortably per page, the better. So, go back to the Appearance panel and highlight a 4x4 grid instead (as shown here).

Step Twenty-Two:

When you click that 4x4 grid, it applies it to your page, and now you only have two pages of thumbnails, rather than the four pages we originally started with. Also in the Appearance panel, you can choose to add your Identity Plate, which I did here (but I had to choose Edit and slightly change the colors of my text to be seen easily on this darker background). There's also a Show Cell Numbers checkbox in the Appearance panel for turning off/on those larger numbers in each cell. I turned them off here so you can see what it looks like without them (compare this look with the cells in Step Twenty-One above). So, should you leave them on or off? Personally, I leave these cell numbers off if it's just an online gallery for friends or random Web visitors, but I leave them turned on for clients because then they can email me and simply write "I like number 8 and number 14."

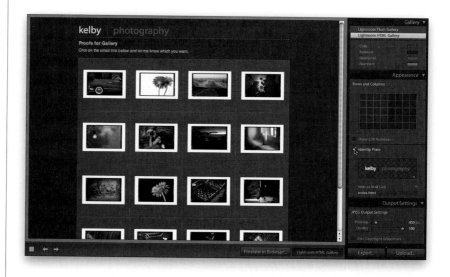

Step Twenty-Three:

When you click on a thumbnail, it loads a totally new HTML page with a larger version of your photo. You can control the size of this preview using the Preview slider in the Output Settings panel. The default size was around 420 pixels and it just didn't seem large enough to me, so I dragged the slider to the right until it reached the size you see here. Below that slider is a JPEG quality slider, and I usually set mine for 80, which gives a good balance between quality and file size. Also, if you go to the Image Settings panel, just like with the Flash-based galleries, you can add two lines of info. I chose a metadata caption preset like we made earlier to put the descriptive text below the photo, and then for the Title (above the photo) I chose Sequence, which shows which number photo of the total you're seeing.

Step Twenty-Four:

That's it for tweaking your HTML gallery. (HTML galleries don't offer less customization than Flash galleries—it's just that we already covered the options they have in common.) Of course, you'll want to preview your gallery in your Web browser to see that it looks and works the way you want it to. So, click the Preview in Browser button in the toolbar, and in a minute or two your gallery will appear in your Web browser (as seen here). If everything looks good, then it's on to uploading it to your Web server, which is covered in the next, and final, tutorial of this chapter. *Note:* Before I previewed this gallery, I turned the cell numbers back on, but then I went to the Color Palette panel, clicked on the color swatch beside Numbers, and made them darker so they wouldn't stand out so much.

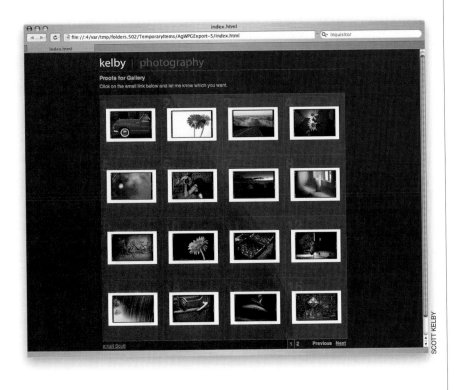

SCOTT KELBY

Putting Your New Gallery on the Web

The last part of this process is actually getting your new gallery up live on the Web. You can either export your gallery to a folder and then upload it yourself, or use the Web module's built-in FTP capabilities for uploading your gallery to a Web server. If you don't already have a company that hosts your website on their server, that will be your first order of business. Try Googling "Free Web Hosting," and in about two seconds you'll find loads of companies that are willing (read as: dying) to host your new site absolutely free.

Step One:

Now that your Web gallery is complete (as shown here, where I snuck yet another photo of my wife and baby girl in), you have two choices: (1) export the files to a folder on your computer and then use a separate FTP program to upload your files to your Web server, or (2) you can use the built-in FTP uploader in Photoshop Lightroom. We'll start with #2: let Lightroom do the work. Go to the Output panel, and from the FTP Server pop-up menu choose Edit (as shown here).

Step Two:

This brings up the Configure FTP File Transfer dialog (shown here) where you enter the name of your server, your username and password (these are given to you by your Web hosting company), and the exact path to the location of your homepage folder on the Web (again, this info is provided by your Web hosting company). Once you've entered this info, I recommend saving this as a preset (so you don't have to enter it again) by going up to the Preset menu and choosing Save as New Preset. Once it's saved, click the OK button (as shown). By the way, if you don't choose the Store Password in Preset option, when you do upload it will ask you for your password again.

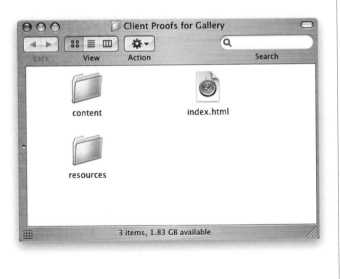

Step Three:

Once you've entered the FTP info and saved your preset, click on the Upload button (on the bottom right of the right side Panels area), and Lightroom will generate your webpage(s), optimize your photos for the Web, and upload the whole thing to your Web server so your new gallery is live on the Web (you'll see the progress bar in the upper-left corner of Lightroom's task bar). So, that's the "do it all in Lightroom" version. If you'd prefer to have Lightroom save the files for you, so you can upload them yourself (this is required by some Web hosting companies and almost all of the free hosting services, who have you do your uploading directly from a regular webpage rather than an FTP program), then you can ignore all the FTP stuff and click the Export button at the bottom of the right side Panels area. This brings up a Save Web Gallery dialog (shown here) where you name your exported gallery and choose which folder you want it saved in.

Step Four:

Once you click the Save button (shown in Step Three), Lightroom generates the webpage(s), optimizes the photos (just like with the FTP server version), and you can see the status in the top left of Lightroom's task bar. Once it's done, take a look in the folder you chose to save it in and you'll see three files: a webpage named index.html (which is your homepage), and two additional folders which contain your web-optimized photos and other webpages and resources your site needs (for Flash sites, the "content" folder will instead be named "bin"). You'll need to upload all three of these to your Web server for your gallery to go live on the Web.

Exposure: 1/30 | Focal Length: 86mm | Aperture Value: *f*/5.6

Wedding/Portrait Workflow

what to do, in what order, and when to jump to photoshop

So, you've been learning how to sort your photos, develop them, create slide shows, print, etc. But I think what's missing is just one single chapter that puts it all together, that starts with the photo shoot itself and leads you step-by-step through a Photoshop Lightroom and Photoshop CS2/CS3 workflow for wedding and portrait photographers, seeing everything as it happens up until the final print. But here's the thing: if I don't write that chapter, then I'm done—the book goes off to press on time, the publisher's happy, and I can take time off for a few days of really productive shoplifting. So, that was the plan. Stop writing now, and before you know it, I'd have a bunch of cool new stuff that I didn't have to pay for. Of course, you think I'm about to say something like, "But I couldn't leave you just hanging like that, so here is that chapter!" Sorry—I didn't do it. I'm not kidding. Oh, it was a fine idea all right, but honestly, I had a problem with it. The problem is: the workflow for wedding and portrait photographers is more in-depth than the one for nature, travel, and landscape photographers. So, I'd have to write not just one, but two complete workflow chapters. This would take an awful lot of time, and seriously cut into my routine of misappropriating consumer goods. But, in the end, I'm clearly a "fish" because I went ahead and wrote both chapters. The only upside is—I didn't have to pay for any paper, or coffee, or paperclips, or…

It All Starts with the Shoot

This workflow is for wedding or portrait photographers, and in our example we're going to start with a formal bridal portrait taken on the wedding day at the church. (An ideal time to shoot these formal portraits is three hours before the wedding. Not only can you set up lighting that you couldn't get away with during the actual ceremony, this will save everybody loads of stress, plus everything from the flowers to the bride's makeup will be fresh. Just make sure they know when they hire you that they need to be dressed and ready three full hours before the wedding starts.)

Step One:

For our example, we're going to focus on the formal bridal portrait. I used a simple, yet very effective and flattering lighting setup, which consists of just one flash (strobe) and a single round collapsible reflector on a boom stand, with silver on one side and gold on the other. I positioned the bride in the aisle, and set up my camera angle so I would capture some of the stained glass in the background (as shown here). If we just set up the softbox and fire the flash, we're going to get a very bright bride on an almost black background, so we need to set up the lighting and exposure so we keep some of the ambient light from the overhead lights in the church. (*Note:* It was quite dark in the church, so I lightened these photos for easier viewing.)

DAVE MOSER

Step Two:
Our flash has a softbox attached to the front to spread the light and make it softer (the softbox I'm using here is 2x3' in size, and is made by Photoflex). I'm going to position this softbox to the left of the bride with the height set to just above her head, aiming a little bit down at her (as shown here).

TIP: The closer you get the softbox to your subject, the softer the light will be, so position it as close to the subject as possible without seeing the softbox itself in your camera's viewfinder.

DAVE MOSER

Step Three:
With the softbox placed to one side, you're going to get directional light, which creates a nice loop lighting pattern, but you're going to wind up with shadows on the left side of her face. To lighten those shadows, I positioned the round reflector on the opposite side of the bride (on a boom stand) to bounce some of the light from the softbox back into those shadow areas. I positioned the reflector as close to the bride as possible without actually seeing it in my viewfinder (as shown here). Although the silver side of the reflector reflects more light, the gold side makes the reflected light warmer, and for a bridal portrait warmer is usually better, so after a few test shots I flipped the reflector over to its gold side.

Continued

DAVE MOSER

Step Four:

Here are the camera settings used for this segment of the shoot: The shots were taken with a Nikon D2Xs, with the camera's ISO at 200. I set the shooting mode to Manual, so I could set both the aperture and shutter speed manually. To get the ambient light in the church to appear in the shot, I had to lower the shutter speed to 1/60 of a second. I also lowered the power output of the flash to only around 25% because it was so close to the bride. I used a Nikon 70–200mm f/2.8 VR zoom lens, and I set the aperture to f/5.6 so the background would be a little out of focus, but not so much that you wouldn't be able to tell this was shot in the church. I set up my tripod about 20 feet back from the bride (for bridal portraits, I always use a tripod for maximum sharpness, which will come in handy when you print those large-sized prints later in this chapter).

Step Five:

Before you press the shutter, I highly recommend that you consider shooting tethered, which means you'll connect your camera directly to your laptop computer (using the USB or camera connector cable that came with your digital camera). The advantage is that once you take a shot, it appears at full-screen size right on your laptop (instead of just seeing it on the tiny LCD on the back of your camera). This makes a *huge* difference, especially when it comes to evaluating the lighting (which is why this works so well in a controlled environment like a studio or church). Shooting tethered is *much* easier than it sounds. Here's a step-by-step on how to set up to shoot tethered to your laptop: First, go under Photoshop Lightroom's File menu, under Auto Import, and choose Enable Auto Import.

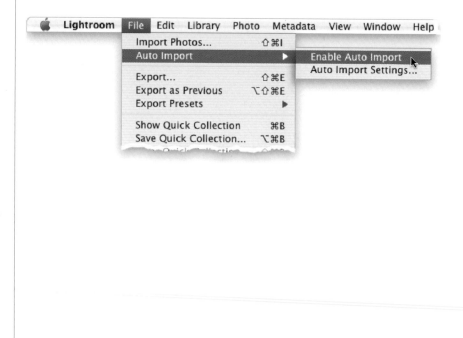

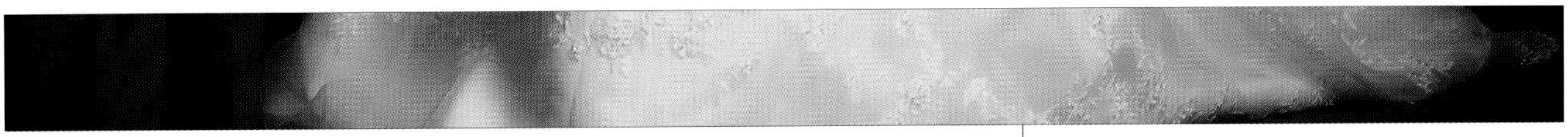

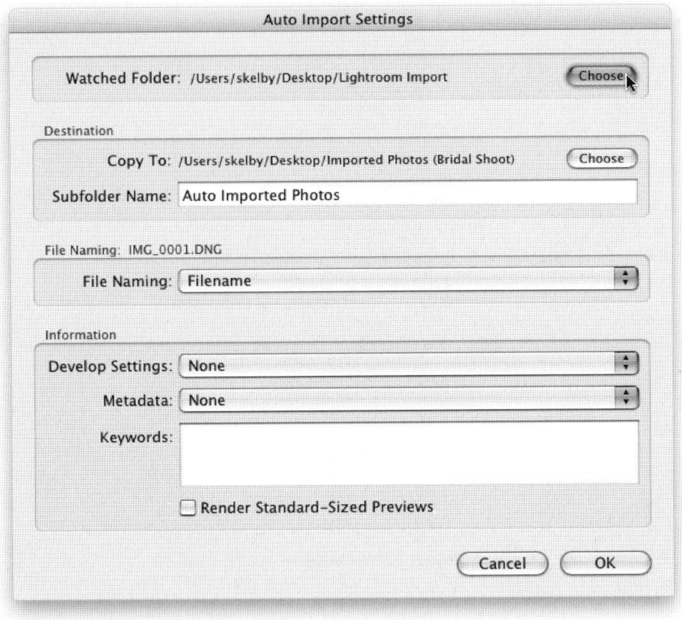

Step Six:
Now go under that same File menu, under Auto Import, but this time choose Auto Import Settings, and the dialog shown here will appear. You're going to create a watched folder, which is a folder that Lightroom keeps an eye on at all times, and any photo you put in this folder will be automatically imported into Lightroom using the settings you choose in the rest of this dialog. So, start by clicking on Choose at the top of the dialog, and then choose the folder that will be your watched folder.

Step Seven:
Then, in the Destination section, choose where you want your imported photos stored once they're imported. In the File Naming section, you can choose a custom name for each imported photo if you like, and in the Information section you can apply your personal metadata and embed keywords for easier searching later on. Once you've made these decisions, click OK. (For a more detailed description of this dialog, see Chapter 1.)

Continued

DAVE MOSER

Step Eight:

Next, set up your laptop right beside your camera (as shown here). I use a super light-weight, portable laptop stand called the Lizell QuickStand Workstation Plus (seen here), which I found at Skymall.com for $139. Worth every penny. Now take the USB cable that came with your camera, and plug one end into your camera's USB input and the other end into your laptop's USB port. By the way, another big benefit of shooting tethered like this is you can have the bride come over and look on-screen (as shown) once you've got a really nice shot. I've found this really makes the bride excited, more comfortable with the process, and more confident in you, the photographer, which translates into better, more natural-looking portraits.

Step Nine:

Now launch your camera manufacturer's software for shooting tethered (I shoot with a Nikon, so it's Nikon Camera Control Pro; for Canon users, it's EOS Capture). Go to the preferences dialog. In Nikon Camera Control Pro, you go under the Tools menu and chose Download Options (as shown here). When the Download Options dialog appears (or Canon's EOS Capture's preferences dialog appears), choose to save your captured photos into the exact same folder you chose earlier to be Lightroom's watched folder (as shown here).

Note: This process of going from your camera into your tethered software and then into Lightroom takes a few seconds (JPEGs appear much quicker than RAW images because of their file size). So what I do is view shots in Lightroom while I'm shooting test shots and the first few images, but once I get the lighting looking

the way I want it, and the proper exposure locked in, then I focus on the shooting and don't look at Lightroom all that much unless I change the lighting. It's easy to get sucked into staring at Lightroom instead of interacting with your subject, so be aware of the magical, yet distracting lure of full-screen photography.

Step Ten:
Now when you take a shot, it goes from your camera straight into your tethered software, and then it's immediately re-directed to your watched folder, which automatically imports the photo into Lightroom's library. Pretty slick, eh? There's only one problem: when your photo appears in Lightroom, it appears as a small thumbnail in the Library's Grid view, but we can fix that (next step).

Step Eleven:
To make this thumbnail appear at full-screen size (the whole reason why we shoot tethered), just drag the Thumb-nails size slider (shown circled here) all the way to the right so your thumbnail appears at full-screen size. (If you don't see this slider, click on the down-facing arrow below the bottom-right corner of the Preview area and choose Thumbnail Size from the pop-up menu.) To zoom in closer to check sharpness or detail, double-click on the photo. Now you're set up to shoot tethered directly into Lightroom. Remember, when shooting tethered like this, no images are saved to your camera's memory card—they go straight from your camera to your laptop.

Workflow Step Two: Right After the Shoot, Do This First

Once the wedding is over, before you head back to your studio to start the sorting/editing process in Photoshop Lightroom and Photoshop, you've got some absolutely critical "first things first" stuff to do, and that is to back up your photos, right now, before anything else. I actually back up while I'm still on location (using a LaCie Rugged All-Terrain 80-GB portable hard drive if I'm shooting tethered, or to an Epson P-4000 if I'm shooting with a memory card in the camera, because you can pop the card right into the P-4000 and back up directly). Here's the step-by-step:

Backing Up When Shooting Tethered:

If you shot tethered (directly from your camera to your laptop, using the setup in the previous tutorial), your photos are already in Photoshop Lightroom, but they're not backed up yet. These photos aren't in your watched folder any longer, they're in the folder you designated they should be saved into when you chose your Auto Import Settings in Lightroom (in our case, it was a folder named "Auto Imported Photos," as shown here).

So, go to that folder, and before you do any editing of any kind, back up that entire folder to either a CD/DVD or external hard disk.

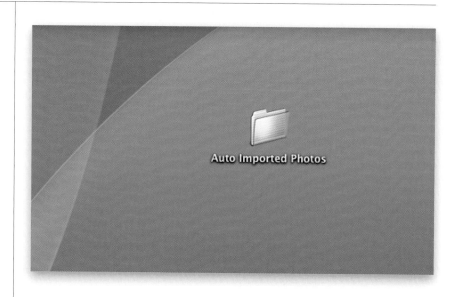

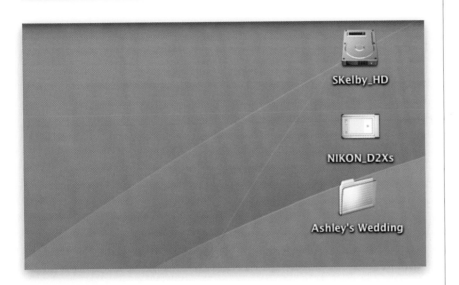

Backing Up When Shooting Normally (to a Memory Card):

The photos from the wedding shoot are still on your camera's memory card, so grab a card reader, plug it into your computer, drag all the photos on the card into a folder on your computer, and then back that folder up (to CD/DVD or an external hard disk) right now (before you do anything else). Once your photos are backed up, when you get back to your studio you'll need to import the photos in that folder on your computer into Lightroom (see Chapter 1 for a step-by-step on importing into Lightroom).

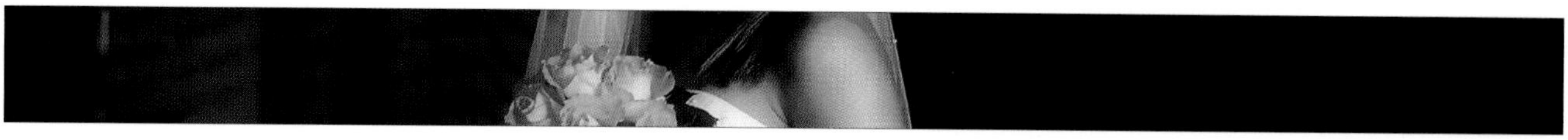

Workflow Step Three: Make Your Life Easier by Making Four Collections

Once your photos are imported into Photoshop Lightroom, they appear in the library right along with all your thousands of other photos. To make your sorting and editing life easier, I recommend that right now you create four collections: (1) a main collection with all the photos from the wedding, (2) the bridal/formals shoot, (3) the ceremony, and (4) the reception. If you're not shooting a wedding (you're shooting portraits instead), multiple collections can still make your life easier (i.e., a separate collection for different outfits, different lighting, other backgrounds, etc.).

Step One:

Okay, so all your wedding photos are imported and you see them there in the Library module. Before you do anything else, press Command-A (PC: Ctrl-A) to select them all. Then, go to the Collections panel on the left and click the + (plus sign) at the top right, which brings up the Create Collection dialog (shown here). Enter the name of the wedding, and turn on the Include Selected Photos checkbox. Click Create, and now all your photos from this wedding are in their own separate collection.

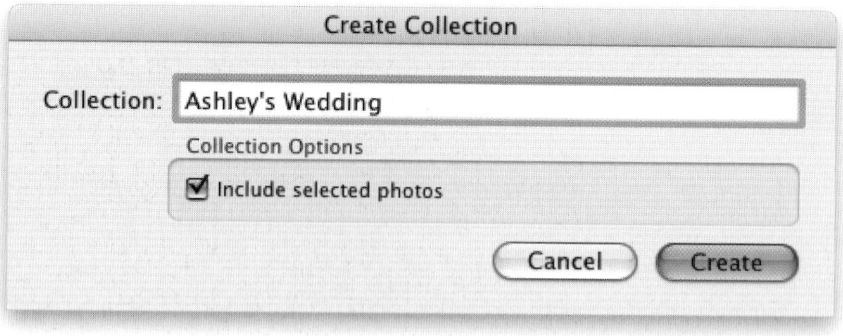

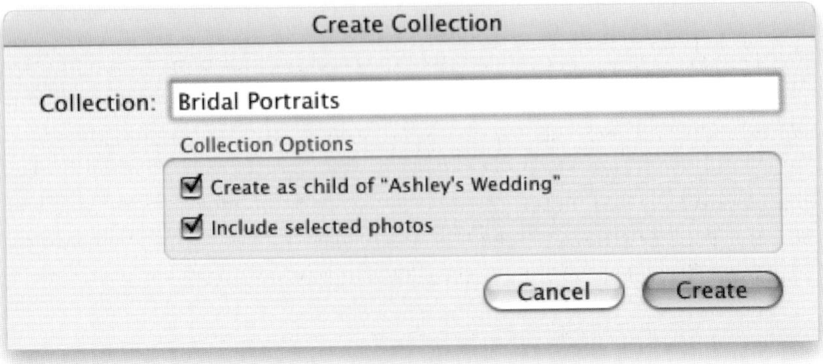

Create Collection

Collection: Bridal Portraits

Collection Options

☑ Create as child of "Ashley's Wedding"
☑ Include selected photos

Cancel   Create

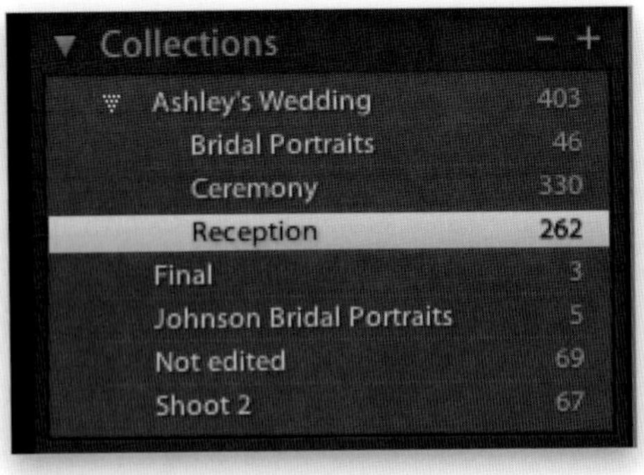

▼ Collections   − +
  ▽ Ashley's Wedding   403
       Bridal Portraits   46
       Ceremony   330
       Reception   262
     Final   3
     Johnson Bridal Portraits   5
     Not edited   69
     Shoot 2   67

Step Two:
Next, in that collection, find the first photo taken during the reception and click on it. Then scroll down to the last photo taken at the reception, press-and-hold the Shift key, and click on it to select all the reception photos at once. Create a new collection but this time when the Create Collection dialog appears, also turn on the checkbox for Create as Child of "Ashley's Wedding" (as shown here), then click Create. This new subcollection will appear listed under the main Ashley's Wedding collection (as shown in the Collections panel here). Select the ceremony photos and do the same thing, then do just the bridal portraits. Now, to quickly view just the photos from a particular part of the wedding, you're just one click away. It takes just two minutes, but saves hours.

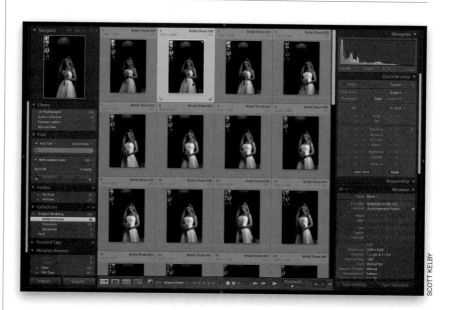

Workflow Step Four: Picking Which Photos Make the Album

Now comes perhaps the most fun part of the process—choosing which photos you, as the photographer, feel are candidates for making the final wedding album. Some photographers make the mistake of showing the bride and groom hundreds of photos and leave it up to them to choose which ones make it. Huge mistake. They're not trained as photo editors—you are. It's your job to presort the photos, so they see only the best images. That way, when they look at their album years from now, it will be filled with nothing but beautiful photos.

Step One:

We'll start by finding the best formal bridal portrait (you don't have to start there, but our shoot only included the formal bridal portrait, so that's where we're starting). In Photoshop Lightroom's Library module, in the Collections panel, under Ashley's Wedding, click on the Bridal Portraits subcollection. Now take a quick look through and delete any photos that obviously aren't going to make the cut (ones that are way out of focus, where the bride's eyes are closed, etc.). In our example, photo #2 won't make the cut, so click on it and hit the Delete (PC: Backspace) key. Remove these time-wasters now and your sorting process will go much faster (remember, you're not deleting the originals—you backed those up to CD/DVD or external hard drive).

Step Two:

Now we're going to choose the best shots from the first set of poses. Click on the first photo in the grid, then press-and-hold the Shift key, scroll down, and click on the last photo in this group that has a similar pose. Now all the photos with that pose are selected (as shown here).

TIP: To keep from having so many photos visible, you might want Lightroom to automatically stack photos together that have the same pose by using the Auto-Stack by Capture Time feature (see a step-by-step in Chapter 2).

Step Three:

Here's how I whittle things down from here. While the photos are selected, click on the Impromptu Slideshow Play button in the toolbar that appears below the grid. If you don't see a Play button, it's because you have it hidden. To make it visible, click on the downward-facing arrow on the far-right side of the toolbar and a pop-up menu will appear listing the controls you can have visible in the toolbar. Choose Slideshow (as shown here), and the Play button will now appear in your toolbar (you can see it circled in red in the capture shown here).

Continued

Step Four:

When you press this Play button, a full-screen impromptu slide show begins, using whichever slide show settings were last used in the Slideshow module. If you had background music selected, it will play during your impromptu slide show. (In the Slideshow module, I hid the white border around the photo and removed the drop shadow, as you see here.) As the slide show plays, when you see a photo that you like, press 4 on your keyboard, which sets the rating of the photo to four stars (with the default slide show, you'll see the rating appear in the upper left-hand corner, as circled in red here). Why not rate it five stars? You'll see in just a moment. So, that's pretty much it at this point—you watch the full-screen slide show and rate the good photos with a 4-star rating. When the slide show is complete, press the Esc key on your keyboard to return to the Grid view.

Step Five:

Let's say you rated 12 of these shots as 4-star photos. That's a lot to let the bride and groom choose from, so next I narrow it down even further by selecting the very best shots from these 12, and those will be the only ones of this pose I show to the bride and groom. I do this next round of cuts by first having Lightroom only display the 4-star photos. You do that by making the filmstrip along the bottom visible (I had it tucked out of sight), then to the right of where it says "Filters" you'll see five small dots. Click on the fourth dot, and now only 4-star and higher rated photos are visible. Now click-and-hold directly where it says "and higher" and choose Only from the pop-up menu, so now only your 12 4-star rated photos will be visible in the Grid view.

SCOTT KELBY

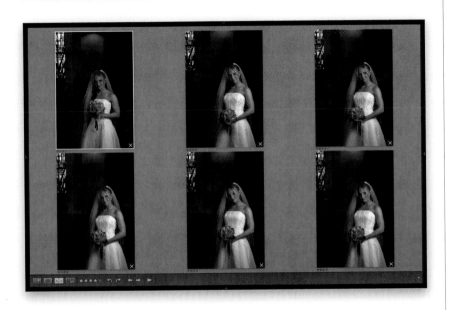

Step Six:

You can hide the filmstrip again to give you more viewing room. In the Grid view, click on the first photo of your 12, press-and-hold the Shift key, then click on the sixth photo (this selects the first six photos). Now press the letter N to jump to Survey mode (which gives you the side-by-side view of your selected photos). Press Shift-Tab on your keyboard, which hides all your panels and the filmstrip (as shown here), so your first six photos are displayed as large as possible on-screen and without the distraction of having the panels open.

Step Seven:

Now you're going to look at the six photos you're comparing onscreen, and when you find the weakest photo of the bunch, click the X in the bottom-right corner of that photo. This photo will be removed from the screen. Here I clicked on the little X on the first photo, and it was removed, leaving just the five you see here. Now remove the next weakest photo, and so on.

Continued

Step Eight:

When I removed two more photos from contention, it put these three onscreen at a larger size (the fewer photos you compare, the larger your images appear onscreen). Now, if you want to include any one of these in your final six, just go directly below the photo and this time click on the 5-star rating. The photo will be immediately removed (because you're displaying 4-star rated photos only and you just gave that one photo a 5-star rating). Don't worry—you didn't delete it—you just changed its rating. In this batch I chose two photos to make the final six. If you have three onscreen, and rate two of them as 5-star you'll be left with one 4-star image onscreen. So, now you can just press G to return to the Grid view.

Step Nine:

Now that you're back to the Grid view, you'll notice that there are only 10 photos visible (that's because your two 5-star rated photos are now hidden). Now select the last six photos (as shown here), then press the letter N to enter Survey mode again. You're going to do the same routine again—removing the weakest photos from contention.

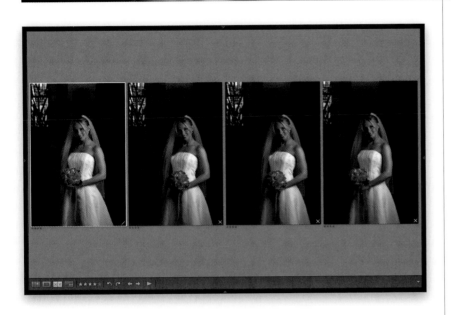

Step Ten:

After removing two photos from this bunch, I had these four left. In the four photos shown here, the second, third, and fourth photos look very similar, so I'm going to choose the best one of those three by making it 5-star rated (again, it will be removed from the Survey view). Now you can return to the Grid view by pressing G.

Step Eleven:

Now, make the filmstrip visible again, and in the Filters section on the right side click on the fifth star, so it's filtering to show only your 5-star rated photos. When you do this, you'll be left with the three absolute best bridal portraits, as chosen by an unbiased photography professional (that's you, by the way). If you want to quickly compare all three, just press the letter N on your keyboard and you'll see them displayed side-by-side (as shown here). That's my sorting process, and you'll continue this process for the next set of formal bridal poses, as well as for the shots in the Ceremony subcollection and the Reception subcollection (this process actually goes fairly quickly).

Continued

Step Twelve:

When you're done with finding the best photos in each of your three subcollections (Bridal Portraits, Ceremony, and Reception), go to the Collections panel and click on the main wedding collection (Ashley's Wedding) and make sure the filter in the filmstrip is set to 5-star Only. Now all the 5-star photos from all three subcollections will be visible at once (because you clicked on the main collection). Next, press Command-A (PC: Ctrl-A) to select all these 5-star photos then go to the Collections panel and click on the + (plus sign) at the top to add a new subcollection. When the Create Collection dialog appears, go ahead and name this subcollection (I named mine "Wedding Album"), turn on the checkbox for Create as Child of "Ashley's Wedding," and turn on the Include Selected Photos checkbox, then click Create to make a separate subcollection for the shots you're going to present to the bride and groom as serious candidates to make the final wedding album.

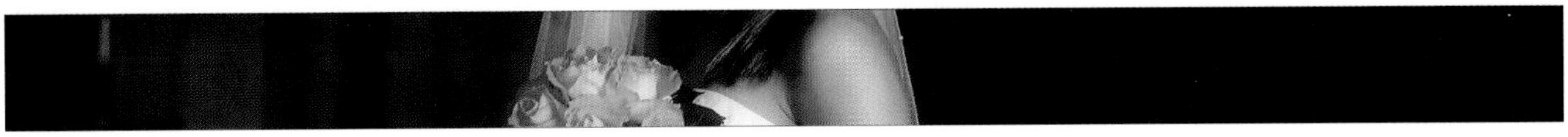

At this point, you've sorted the photos and put the best ones in their own separate subcollection called "Wedding Album." Now it's time to bring the bride and groom into your studio for a professional slide show presentation of the photos you've picked as wedding album candidates. This gives them the opportunity to narrow the field, and it gives you a chance to sell some large prints as well. Here's how to set your slide show up to give you, and your clients, the best possible experience.

Workflow Step Five: Presenting the Photos in Your Studio

Step One:
Well before the bride and groom arrive at your studio, we're going to do some customizing to make the experience more, well…customized. The first thing I recommend is to go to Apple's iTunes Store (for Mac and Windows—the software download is free, but iTunes formatted music will not work in Lightroom on a PC. So for PC users, you just have to find a song in MP3 format), and buy the song they used as their wedding song (individual songs are only 99¢ each, so it's a pretty small investment for the impact it adds to your slide show presentation). In the example shown here, the wedding song was "It's Your Love" by Tim McGraw and Faith Hill, so I bought and downloaded that song.

Continued

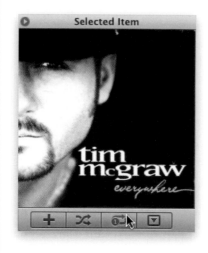

Step Two:

In iTunes, make a playlist for your slide show by clicking on the + (plus sign) in the bottom-left corner of the iTunes window. This adds an untitled playlist to your Source list on the left side of iTunes, and it's highlighted—ready for you to name it (I named mine "Ashley's song"). Now, in the Source list click on Purchased, then click-and-drag "It's Your Love" (or whatever song your bride chose) onto the Ashley's song playlist. Lastly, press the Repeat button twice (it's two over from the Create a Playlist button) so the song repeats if the slide show lasts longer than one playing of the song.

Step Three:

Now that you've got the music down-loaded and in its own separate iTunes playlist (PC users, save your MP3 in a folder on your computer), go back to Lightroom and click on your Wedding Album subcollection. Then click on the Slideshow module. When the Slideshow module appears, go to the Template Browser panel on the left side of the Slideshow module and click on Default. This brings up the template for the default slide show, which has a gray background, a white border around each photo, and a slight drop shadow. It also displays the file-name and your Identity Plate. If you haven't created a custom Identity Plate, then you'll see the name you registered the software in, in large white script letters in the upper-left corner (as shown here).

Step Four:
Now, if you have an "ego thing" going, you can leave this text set to your name or your studio's name, but if your goal is to customize the slide show so your bride and groom feel special (and more motivated to buy prints), then I recommend changing the text to their names. To do that, double-click directly on the floating text and the Identity Plate Editor dialog will appear (shown here). Highlight the existing text and type in your bride's and groom's names. Then, from the Custom pop-up menu at the bottom-left corner of the dialog, choose Save As, and name this Identity Plate "Ashley and Mark" so it doesn't replace your own Identity Plate (that way, when no one's around, you can bring the Identity Plate back that has your name on it, and play slide shows until it's time for your weekly therapy session).

Step Five:
There's another thing I'd recommend changing in the default slide show: hide the rating stars and the filename. You do that in the Overlays panel by simply turning off the checkboxes for Rating Stars and Text Overlays. That's it—they're hidden from view. If it were me (and in this case, it is), I'd also change the background color of the slide show to something more dramatic, like black. To do that, just go to the Backdrop panel (shown here) and turn off the Color Wash checkbox. Then at the bottom of that panel, click on the gray color swatch to the right of the Background Color checkbox and when the Colors panel appears, drag the slider on the right straight down until the background turns solid black (as shown here), then close the Colors panel.

Continued

Step Six:

I would change one other thing—the placement and size of the Identity Plate. It just looks too big, and you don't want it to distract from the photography. Personally, I like the way it looks centered under the photo, but you'll have to move the photo up a little in the frame to make room for your text. So, go to the Layout panel and drag the Left margin slider to the right to 121 pixels. This will change all the margins, since they are linked (the link boxes to the right of the margin names are turned on). Now, turn off the link box beside "Top" and drag the slider to the left until it reads 35 pixels (it's circled in red here). This moves the top margin, and your photo, upward, leaving room for your text below it. To get your text under the photo, you just click directly on the text itself and drag it right under the photo (as shown here). Once it's there, click-and-drag any corner inward to make your text smaller. When it comes to including text on a slide, less is more, so make it a bit smaller than you think it should be (remember, it will appear much larger in the actual full-screen slide show than it does here).

Step Seven:

The last thing left to customize is to apply the slide show music you downloaded into iTunes earlier. So, scroll down to the Playback panel (shown here), turn on the checkbox for Soundtrack, then to the right of the word Soundtrack, where it says Library, click-and-hold for a moment and all of your iTunes playlists will appear in a pop-up menu (as shown here). Choose the playlist you made for your clients (in this case, it was the playlist I named "Ashley's song") and now that becomes the background music for your slide show.

Note: On a PC, you'll click below the word "Soundtrack" to get a Browse For Folder dialog, where you can navigate to the folder that has your music in it.

Step Eight:
Now that you've totally customized your slide show, you don't want to have to do this all over again next week when you're working on a different wedding, right? Heck no (the word "heck" doesn't sound right here, but my editors are Amish, which makes you wonder how they can edit a technology book. Makes you stop and think, doesn't it?). So, just save this custom wedding slide show as a template, and next week the only thing you have to change are the bride's and groom's names and the wedding song. Go to the Template Browser on the left side and click on the Add button at the bottom. This creates a new template, so go ahead and name your new template (I named mine "Wedding Slideshow"). By the way, I'm well aware that I'm not going to win any awards for Most Original Name for Templates. I can live with that (for the most part). Now, next week when you're working on a different wedding, you just click on your Wedding Slideshow template, then you only have to change two things: the bride's and groom's names, and their wedding song.

Continued

Step Nine:

Now that you've customized the slide show and saved it as a template, let's put the slides in the order you want them by going to the filmstrip and clicking-and-dragging them into the order you want them to appear (the thumbnail on the far left will appear as the first slide, followed by the second from the left, and so on). In the example shown here, I'm dragging one thumbnail from later in the slide show and having it appear as the third slide by dragging-and-dropping it in right before the third slide.

Step Ten:

To remove a slide from your slide show, you actually have to remove it from your subcollection (because every photo in your subcollection winds up in your slide show). So, to remove a photo, on a Mac you'd go to the filmstrip and Control-click on the photo you want removed (on a PC you'd just Right-click on it), and a contextual menu will appear. Choose Remove from Collection to remove this slide from your slide show. This doesn't delete the file from your main library of photos—it just removes it from your Wedding Album subcollection. That photo will still appear in your main Ashley's Wedding collection if you change your mind later and want to bring it back.

Step Eleven:

Once the slides are in the order you'd like, I recommend running a quick preview slide show, so you can see if it looks the way you want it to. To do that you just press the triangular Preview button that appears on the left side of the toolbar, right above the filmstrip (as shown here), and a preview of your finished slide show will appear in the center of the Slideshow module window (as you see here). This preview shows you the slide show without the distracting border guides and/or rulers, plus you get nice smooth dissolves between slides, and your background music plays as well (see, that text looks pretty good at that smaller size, doesn't it?).

Step Twelve:

If the preview looks good, you're ready to bring in the clients to let them see the full-screen slide show. However, before they sit down to watch the slide show, there's one thing you might consider. I hate the fact that when your clients sit down in front of your screen, they're going to see exactly what you see here—the first photo in the slide show already displayed onscreen, but still at the smaller preview size with guides all around it. Even worse, they'll see all the little thumbnails of their photos, plus all of Lightroom's panels, and buttons, and other distracting stuff. This pretty much ruins that magic moment when they see their first image, presented professionally—full screen, with their wedding song playing softly in the background, and with nothing to distract them. So how do you keep from robbing them, and you, of this emotion-packed moment? I have a plan.

Continued

Step Thirteen:

Launch Adobe Photoshop CS2/CS3 and then go under the File menu and choose New. When Photoshop's New dialog appears, enter the same physical dimensions and resolution as the first photo that will appear in your slide show, and click OK. When this new blank document appears in Photoshop, press D to set your Foreground color to black, then press Option-Delete (PC: Alt-Backspace) to fill this new document with black. Now, go under the File menu and choose Save As. When the dialog appears, name your slide "Intro Slide," and save it as a JPEG document with a quality setting of 5. That's it—you're done in Photoshop (well, for now anyway). Now, back to Lightroom.

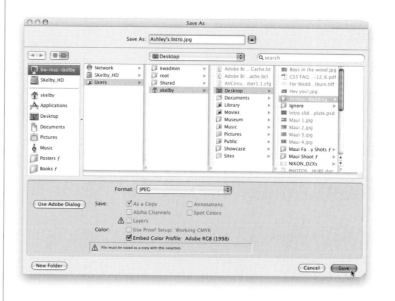

Step Fourteen:

In Lightroom, in the Library module, click on the Import button at the bottom-left corner of Lightroom's window. Find your intro slide, import it into Lightroom (it doesn't need any metadata or keywords added), then add this to your Wedding Album subcollection. After you import the intro slide, it won't appear in the Grid view because you probably still have your 5-star Only rating filter turned on. Set your filter to zero stars and your slide will now appear, but it will be the last slide, so go to the filmstrip and click-and-drag it to the first position so it shows up onscreen first. Now your slide show will start with this black intro slide, which not only adds a nice touch, it hides the first photo from being seen by your clients before the slide show starts, so you get the maximum impact. Lastly, Press Command-A (PC: Ctrl-A) to select all the photos, then set the star rating to None (you'll see why this matters later).

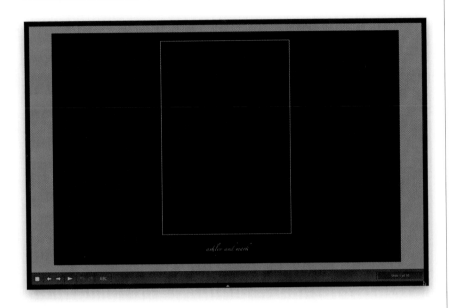

Step Fifteen:

Right before you bring your clients in to see your presentation, go to the Slideshow module, turn off the Show Guides checkbox in the Layout panel, then press Shift-Tab to hide all your panels. Press T to hide the toolbar, then press the letter F twice to expand Lightroom's interface to fill your screen and hide the menu bar across the top. Now you're ready to bring in the clients to let them see the slide show. All they will see onscreen is a blank slide with their names below the border (as shown here). Once they're seated, press Command-Return (PC: Ctrl-Enter) to start the slide show. The slide show plays full screen, the background music starts, and in a few seconds the first photo appears and your clients start to swoon. However, this isn't just to make them swoon—you have work to do.

Step Sixteen:

As the photos appear during the slide show, press the number 4 on your keyboard anytime it seems your clients really like a particular photo (this rates them as 4-star photos). Why just four stars? Because they'll want to see the slide show again, and once they've seen it once, you'll usually get more accurate feedback the second time. This time, mark their favorites by pressing 5 on the keyboard (to rate them as 5-star photos). Those 5-star photos are the ones that go in the final wedding album. If they don't want to see the slide show again after the first go-round of ratings, you'll just use the 4-star rated photos instead. (*Note:* When you rate the photos, nothing happens onscreen, but rest assured, it is rating each time you press a number key.)

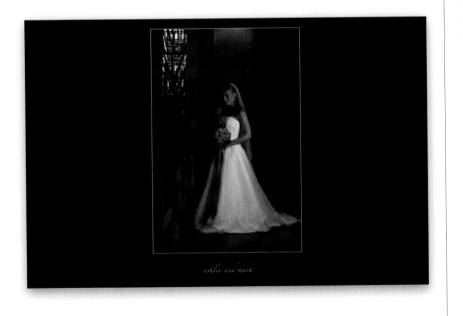

Workflow Step Six: Editing in Photoshop Lightroom and Photoshop

Once the slide show is done, there's a good chance that when it comes to "the money shot" (the bridal portrait), the bride and groom (now known as "your clients") would like some input from other members of their families, or close friends, or bridesmaids, etc. So, do you haul them all back to the studio one day for another round of proofing? Not if you can help it (and you can help it by the way), but first, we need to edit just those 5-star keepers and get them ready to be seen by lots of friends and family.

Step One:

In our hypothetical scenario, the bride couldn't decide which bridal portrait she liked and she wanted her mother, her best friend, and her sister to help her pick the perfect one, so here's our plan: we're going to process (fully edit) the shots she wants to choose from, then we're going to use Photoshop Lightroom to post them to our studio's website. That way, it saves them a trip to our studio again, and they can have as many friends and family members in on the final decision as they'd like. Then, when they agree on which image they want, they can email their decision right from the Web gallery we're posting. Start by going to the Library module and turn on the 5-star rating filter again, so just the photos that your client liked best (the ones that will definitely go in the final wedding album) appear onscreen (as shown here).

Step Two:

At this point, since all the other photos have been chosen by the bride and groom for the wedding album, we're just going to be concerned with editing the formal bridal portrait images. Click on one of the ones she can't choose between, then jump over to Lightroom's Develop module (as shown here).

Step Three:

When editing a photo in Lightroom, I usually start by correcting the white balance. Take the White Balance Selector tool (W), and click it on a neutral area in your photo (for more on setting your photo's white balance, see Chapter 4). In the example shown here, I clicked on a light-gray area on the bridal gown and it warmed the photo up a bit, which made the skin tones look warmer and more natural.

TIP: If I can't quickly see an area that's obviously light gray, I move my cursor over neutral areas (areas that obviously aren't highlights or shadows) searching for a reading (in the pop-up magnified pixel view) where the R, G, and B values are all nearly similar (although they're rarely all exactly the same—just get kinda close). Ideally, I also look for an area where all three numbers are somewhere around 70% (so it's a lighter gray area), but again, that's not always possible so don't sweat it. Once you find a neutral area, just click on that area to set the white balance.

Continued

Step Four:

In this particular photo, the photo looks a little underexposed to me, so to brighten the overall exposure, just click-and-drag the Exposure slider to the right a bit until it looks right to you. Next, I would drag the Blacks slider to the right a bit to darken the area behind her, and make her really stand out (after all, increasing the blacks a bit isn't going to affect the white in her dress). If after increasing the blacks, you think the bride looks a little too dark (her skin tone may have darkened), try dragging the Brightness slider to the right a bit, to open up the midtones (where much of the detail in the photo lies).

Step Five:

Of course, you could go on and tweak other settings (like the Tone Curve, Saturation, etc.), and in some photos that will certainly be necessary, but in this case I think the simple (but essential) adjustments we've made thus far are enough. Now, you've got other photos, taken under the same lighting situation, which also need to be adjusted. Here's the thing: you don't want to go back and do each one individually (that would take too long), so instead I would use Lightroom's built-in automation. First, return to the Library module, then press-and-hold the Command (PC: Ctrl) key and click on the other photos in your collection to select them (as shown here, where all five photos are selected, but the photo you just edited is the currently active image).

Step Six:
We're going to take the changes we just applied to our one photo and apply them to the other selected photos in just two clicks. First, click on the Sync Settings button at the bottom of the panels on the right side (shown circled in red here). When the Synchronize Settings dialog appears, just make sure the White Balance and Basic Tone checkboxes are turned on (it's okay if others are turned on—just make sure those are), and click the Synchronize button.

Step Seven:
In just seconds, all the other selected photos will now have the same white balance and exposure corrections you applied to the first photo. Using Lightroom's automation is a really critical step in keeping your workflow moving at top speed.

Continued

Step Eight:

Once you're done with your tonal changes here in Lightroom, it's time to "finish" the photos over in Adobe Photoshop CS2/CS3, so press Command-D to deselect all the photos. Then, click on the first photo you worked on and press Command-E (PC: Ctrl-E), which brings up the Edit Photo dialog (shown here). Click on the Edit a Copy with Lightroom Adjustments radio button, and click the Edit button. In a few moments a copy of your photo will appear in Photoshop CS2/CS3 (provided, of course, that you actually have either Adobe Photoshop CS2 or CS3 installed on your computer).

Step Nine:

There would be five edits I'd make to this particular photo in Photoshop (normally, I'd also do a decent amount of portrait retouching—removing blemishes, wrinkles, whitening teeth, etc.—but luckily our bride/model doesn't need any serious retouching). The first thing that stands out are the dark shadows on the left side of her face. To open them up a bit, I use a technique called "painting with light." Start by duplicating the Background layer (press Command-J on a Mac or Ctrl-J on a PC), then change the blend mode of this layer to Screen. This brightens the entire photo considerably. Press-and-hold the Option (PC: Alt) key and click on the Add Layer Mask icon at the bottom of the Layers palette (as shown here). This puts a black mask over the brighter layer, so the photo looks just like it did. Now, what you're going to do is set your Foreground color to white, get the Brush tool (B), pick a soft-edged brush, and paint over the left side of her face. Where you paint, the lighter version of her (the Screen layer) is revealed.

Step Ten:

Now, her face will probably look too light, so go to the Layers palette and simply lower the opacity of this layer until it looks realistic (in my case, I had to lower the Opacity to 40%). Okay, that takes care of the first issue, so you can merge that copy layer down into the Background layer. Next, I would use the Clone Stamp tool (S) to remove some of the distracting background elements (like the chairs) that appear behind and to the right of her. Go get the Clone Stamp tool, press-and-hold the Option (PC: Alt) key and click once to the left of the chairs to sample, then begin painting (cloning) over the chairs (as shown here) until they've been covered over by the black drapes. Once the chairs have been cloned over, you might want to remove any other furniture, tables, etc., but it's totally up to you (I pretty much cloned over everything on the right side, as seen in the capture in Step Fifteen).

Step Eleven:

Every photo needs sharpening, and I normally apply sharpening as the very last step I do. However, for formal bridal portraits I generally finish by adding a softening effect, and I've found that if I soften first, then try to sharpen, the sharpening isn't nearly as effective. So in this one instance, I sharpen before the softening. To be able to apply a good amount of sharpening without creating color problems, artifacts, and halos, go to the Image menu, under Mode, and choose Lab Color. Then, go to the Channels palette, and click on the Lightness channel (as shown here). Now, when you apply your sharpening in the next step, you're avoiding the color channels and just applying your sharpening to the detail areas.

Continued

Step Twelve:

Now that you've clicked on the Lightness channel, go to the Filter menu, under Sharpen, and choose Unsharp Mask. When the dialog appears, enter 120% for the Amount, 1.0 for the Radius, set the Threshold amount at 3 levels (as shown here), and click OK (I like these settings for providing a moderate amount of sharpening). You can see in the preview (shown at right) how it brings out the detail in the dress. Of course, it also gives the overall photo a nice crisp sharpness, especially in detail areas like the bride's eyes, her veil, etc. Now that your sharpening is complete, go back to the Image menu, under Mode, and choose RGB Color to return to our regular editing color mode.

Step Thirteen:

Now that we've sharpened, I'm going to use an edge vignetting effect that is great for darkening the areas around the edges of the photo, which helps to make it look like there's a soft light falling right on your bride. I use this effect on most of my portraiture, and it's particularly effective in wedding photos. You start by duplicating the Background layer again, then you change the blend mode of this layer to Multiply (as shown here), which darkens the entire photo. Now get the Rectangular Marquee tool (M) and click-and-drag out a large rectangle that almost touches the edges of the image (leave about 1" of space on all sides, like the selection you see here). Now, if you're using Photoshop CS or CS2, go under the Selection menu and choose Feather. If you're using CS3, instead go up to the Options Bar and click the Refine Edge button.

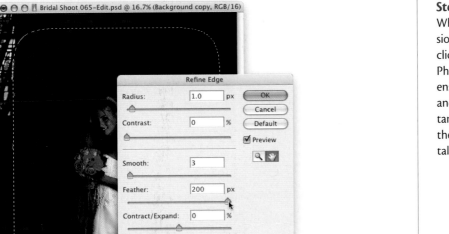

Step Fourteen:

When the dialog appears (for either version), set the Feather amount to 200 and click OK (the Refine Edge dialog from Photoshop CS3 is shown here). This softens the edges of your selection big time, and you can see the corners of your rectangular selection are now rounded (by the way, this is *not* the edge softening I talked about earlier—that's coming next).

Step Fifteen:

Once your selection edges are feathered, press the Delete (PC: Backspace) key on your keyboard (which knocks a large soft-edged hole out of the center of your darker layer, revealing the original lighter layer below), then press Command-D (PC: Ctrl-D) to Deselect. The end result is: the outside areas of your photo look darker, and the inside looks better lit (as seen here). Try this edge vignetting technique once, and I predict you'll use it again and again on most of your portraits. (Just as a side note, I often get emails about the photos I post on my blog, and the comments are often something like this: "How is it that your photos have a soft look, but at the same time, they look really sharp?" The trick is this edge vignetting technique you just learned.) Now, for the softening effect.

Continued

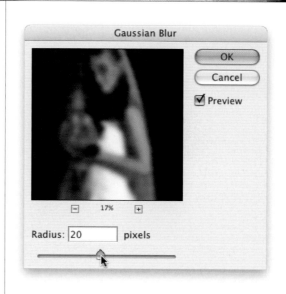

Step Sixteen:

Go to the Layers palette and choose Flatten Image from the palette's flyout menu. Now, duplicate the Background layer by pressing Command-J (PC: Ctrl-J) again. Next, go under the Filter menu, under Blur, and choose Gaussian Blur. When the dialog appears, enter a Radius of 20 pixels (as shown here) to put a major blur over the entire image. Now, I use 20 pixels because this was taken with a 12-megapixel camera. If you use a 10-megapixel camera, you can use 15 to 17 pixels. A 6-megapixel camera? Try 8 to 10 pixels. In short, no matter what the resolution of your camera, make sure your photo looks pretty darn blurry, like the one you see in the preview window of the Gaussian Blur dialog here.

Step Seventeen:

Now, this is going to seem really, really simple, but that doesn't diminish its effect (in fact, I for one particularly like it if a great effect is easy to create. I have had a similar conversation with my wife, who is just an amazing cook. Every time I tell her how wonderful dinner is, she has to dismiss it by saying, "Oh, it was so easy—it takes like two minutes." She's incredibly modest, but she's also one of those cooks who for some reason believes that nothing can taste really good unless it was an absolute pain in the butt to cook. However, I'd rather that when something tastes really great, it was really easy for her to make. In fact, the easier the better. Do you see where this is going? No. Oh well, back to the technique. By the way, I was able to babble on like this because the rest of this technique is so simple, I don't need much space). You now simply lower the Opacity of this layer to 20% (as shown here). I told you it was simple.

Step Eighteen:

Here's the final image, after all five edits in Photoshop. The softening looks pretty subtle here, doesn't it? It's supposed to. In fact, most people don't know I used any softening at all, but now go to the Layers palette and hide that top layer (click on the Eye icon beside the layer) and then look at the difference. Ahhhhh. See, it's much more powerful than you'd think, yet it's still subtle enough that most people won't realize the photo's been softened. They'll just think you're a master of soft light. That's why I love this technique so much. So, to recap: what kind of stuff do I leave Lightroom and jump over to Photoshop for? I do all my portrait retouching there (eyes, nose, skin, teeth, hair—you name it), I do all my sharpening in Photoshop, and any "painting with light" (using layer blend modes and layer masks), and of course anytime I need to make a selection, do an edge effect, apply one of a dozen filters, or work with layers in any way—I go to Photoshop.

Step Nineteen:

At this point, our edits in Photoshop are done, and it's time to head back to Lightroom. All you have to do now is flatten the layers, save the file, and close it. When you do that, the copy you edited is sent back to Lightroom with all the changes you made (the word "Edit" is now added to the end of the photo's filename, as shown here), and your original is still untouched.

Workflow Step Seven: Letting Your Clients Proof on the Web

Once you've got the photos edited, you're ready to show them to your clients for the final round of proofing (your photos should look even better now that you've developed them in Photoshop Lightroom and finished them in Photoshop). Now, you don't want to make your clients have to drive back down to your studio, but they wanted to get input from their other family members, friends, etc. So we're going to use Photoshop Lightroom to build a webpage where your clients can do this final round of proofing from right on their home computer.

Step One:

We start in the Library module by selecting the edited photos (I have six selected here because I edited one image two different ways) and then making a new subcollection from these selected photos (name it "Bridal Web Proofs" and make it a child of your Wedding Album subcollection). Then, click on the Web module button at the top right of the interface.

Step Two:

When the Web module appears, you'll see the photos in your new subcollection appear in the default HTML Web gallery layout (as shown here). You can use this style (which really isn't bad), or you can move your cursor over the built-in Web design templates in the Template Browser on the left side of Photoshop Lightroom and see if you like one of those better. As your cursor moves over these templates, you'll see a preview of each template in the Preview panel at the top left. If you see one you like better than the default template, click on it to select it, and your webpage will change to that style. Now, in our example, I'm going to choose the template named "Charcoal," which is pretty much just a darker gray version of the default template, but I like it better, so go ahead and click on that now.

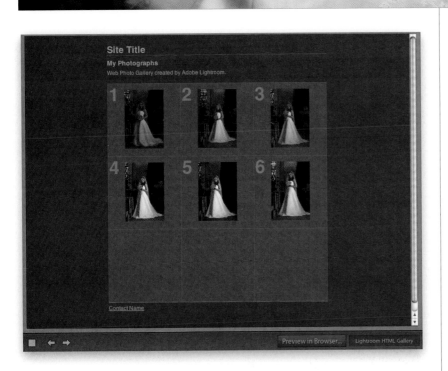

Step Three:

Here's a closer view of the Preview area, where you'll customize your webpage. There is a panel on the right side of the Lightroom interface which lets you customize the text on your page, but honestly, it's easier (and much less confusing) to just make your text changes directly on the page itself.

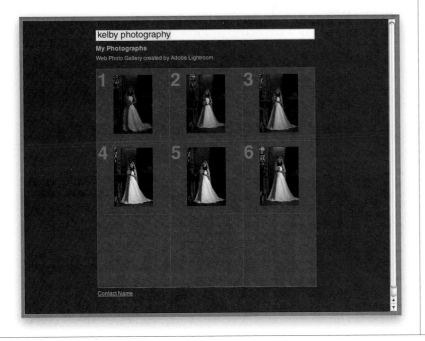

Step Four:

So, click your cursor directly on any of the placeholder text that's there, and that text highlights. Now just type in the text you want to appear on your page. We'll start with the site title. Click on the words "Site Title" and when it highlights, type in the name of your studio (in my case, it's "kelby photography").

Continued

Step Five:

Just below the rows of photos, there's a Contact Info link. Unfortunately, this is one bit of text on this page that you can't just edit by clicking, because it's not just text—it's a hot link to your email address, so for this you'll need to go over to the Labels panel on the right side of Lightroom. Near the bottom of this panel, you'll find a Contact Info field. Click on the words "Contact Name" to highlight the field, then type in your studio's name and the word "email." In the next field down (Web or Mail Link), click to highlight the field, but don't erase the word "mailto:" (that's HTML code Lightroom needs). Instead, just type in your email address directly after the word "mailto:" (as shown here), then hit the Return (PC: Enter) key to lock in your change.

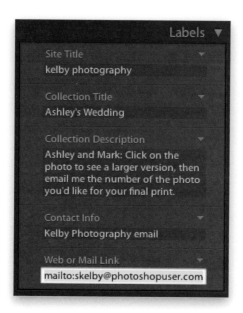

Step Six:

Now, on to the next thing we need to customize. When your client clicks on a photo, they will get a larger version, which is what you want. But in some of the HTML gallery templates, they'll also get all the EXIF camera data displayed directly below the photo like you see here (which you really don't want—the client doesn't need it and it's distracting). Luckily, we can get rid of all that, and replace it with something much more usable to you and the client.

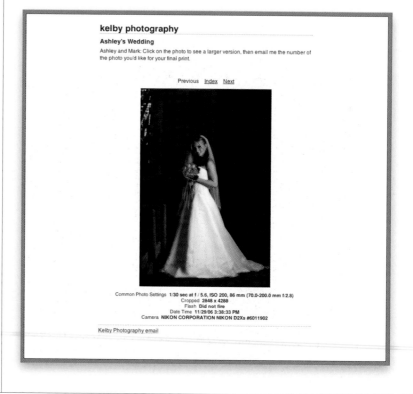

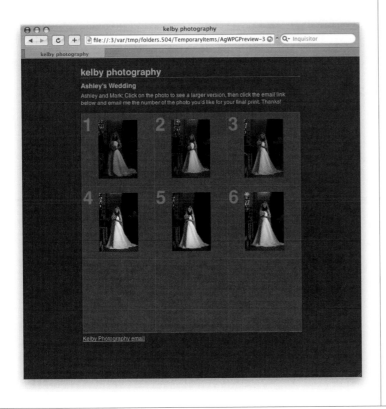

Step Seven:
In the right side panels, scroll down until you reach the Image Settings panel. There's a pop-up menu to the right of the Caption checkbox. Click on that pop-up menu and choose Sequence. This removes all the EXIF data, and instead simply displays the number of the photo, which you and your client both need (remember, they're supposed to email you with the number).

Step Eight:
That's really all we need to do to customize the webpage for showing our client, but you should always preview the page before you actually post it on the Web. To do that, click the "Preview in Browser" button that appears in the toolbar under the Preview area. When you do that, Lightroom builds a temporary HTML page and opens that page in your default Web browser (as shown here). This is a fully functional preview, so click on the photos and try the email link (it launches your default email software and creates a new blank email addressed to your studio, so all your client has to do is write "We like #5."). If it looks good, you're ready to post the page to a Web server. If you need to make changes, just close your Web browser, return to Lightroom, and make your changes. Then, I would preview the site once again. Once it looks the way you want (in the preview), you can move on to the uploading process.

Continued

Step Nine:

You can upload your Web gallery right from within Lightroom directly to your website using Lightroom's built-in FTP file transfer feature (see Chapter 9 for how to configure your FTP settings and save these settings as a preset so you only have to do this once—from then on you'll just choose your preset from the Output panel's FTP Server pop-up menu, as shown here). Now you can click the Upload button (seen here on the bottom-right side) and Lightroom will create your webpage and upload it to the server you designated.

Step Ten:

Once the page is up and live on your website (go there yourself and see that it did upload fully), you can call the clients or email them the link to their own personal bridal proof gallery. They can send the link out to friends, family, bridesmaids, etc., and look at these photos to their hearts' content until they come to a consensus as to which photo they want printed to 16x20". The instructions I entered at the top of the webpage tell them what to do, which is to simply figure out which number photo they like (they're numbered 1 to 6 automatically since there are six photos), and then click the email link at the bottom of the page to send their decision.

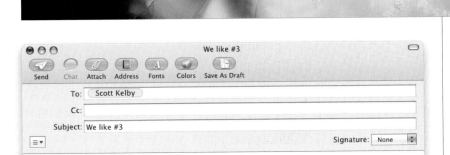

Step Eleven:

When your clients click the email link on your webpage, it launches their default email program and automatically fills in your email address in the To: field. Now all they have to do is enter a subject, tell you which number photo they want, and then you can take that info and run with it.

Step Twelve:

Okay, when your client's email arrives, you now know that the photo they want printed is #3, so go to Lightroom, and in the Library module click on your Bridal Web Proofs subcollection, then click on photo #3. Now, your photo was already edited and sharpened in Photoshop, so this baby is ready to print. Click on the Print module (as shown here) and in the Template Browser on the left side of Lightroom, click on the Fine Art Mat template to give you the page layout you see here.

Continued

Step Thirteen:

Now click the Page Setup button (just under the bottom-right corner of your Preview area), and when the dialog appears, choose your paper size (in this case, 16x20"). Now that your paper is properly sized, it is time to make any final adjustments to the margins (in the Layout panel) because it's almost time to print (for more on adjusting margins, see Chapter 8).

Page Setup

Settings: Page Attributes

Format for: Stylus Photo R2400

Paper Size: 16x20 Paper

15.95 in x 20.01 in

Orientation:

Scale: 100 %

Cancel   OK

Step Fourteen:

Now go to the Print Job panel (on the right side) and under Color Management you'll find a profile is already selected, and by default that profile is Managed by Printer. That's bad—you want Lightroom color managing your prints, so click on Managed by Printer and choose the printer profile that matches your printer and the exact paper that you're going to print on (for more on finding and installing printer profiles, see Chapter 8).

Print Job ▼

Draft Mode Printing

Print Resolution   240 dpi

✓ Print Sharpening :   Low ▾

Color Management   ⌄

Profile : SPR2400 PremLuster B... ▾
Rendering Intent :   Perceptual ▾

⚠ *When selecting a custom profile, remember to turn off printer color management in the Print dialog before printing. Black Point Compensation will be used for this print.*

Print Settings...   Print...

Printer:	Stylus Photo R2400
Presets:	Standard
	Print Settings

Page Setup:	Roll Paper
Media Type:	Premium Luster Photo Paper
Color:	Color
Mode:	○ Automatic
	◉ Advanced
Print Quality:	Best Photo

☐ High Speed
☐ Mirror Image
☑ Finest Detail

(?) (PDF ▾) (Preview) (Supplies...)   (Cancel) (Print)

Step Fifteen:

Now it's time to click on the Print button. When you do, the Print dialog appears (my print dialog for printing to an Epson Stylus Photo R2400 on a Macintosh computer is shown here). You've got some critical settings to choose here to make sure you get the best quality and that your color management is consistent (for step-by-step info on how to set these up, check out Chapter 8 again). Now, hit Print, sit back, and enjoy the prints. (*Note:* Although the clients asked for three prints, go ahead and just print one, then look at the print to see if the quality, color, and layout are exactly like you intended. If all is okay, then you can print the other two. If there's a discrepancy on color, chances are there's a color management problem [see Chapter 8 for the step-by-step setup].)

Step Sixteen:

So that's it—the entire workflow from the moment of original capture in the church to the final print, which in my case comes from my Epson Stylus Pro 3800, which I'm pictured holding here (well, I'm holding the print—not the printer itself. You knew that, right?). Now that you've learned my workflow for bridal or portrait shoots, you can modify it (take out parts, add in parts, etc.) to make it become your own custom workflow. The next chapter is for outdoor, landscape, and travel photographers, and even if that's not you, I highly recommend that you try that workflow as well (it's shorter and faster than the wedding workflow). You'll learn some things in that workflow that weren't covered here, and you may want to incorporate some of those steps into your own wedding/ portrait workflow.

DAVE CROSS

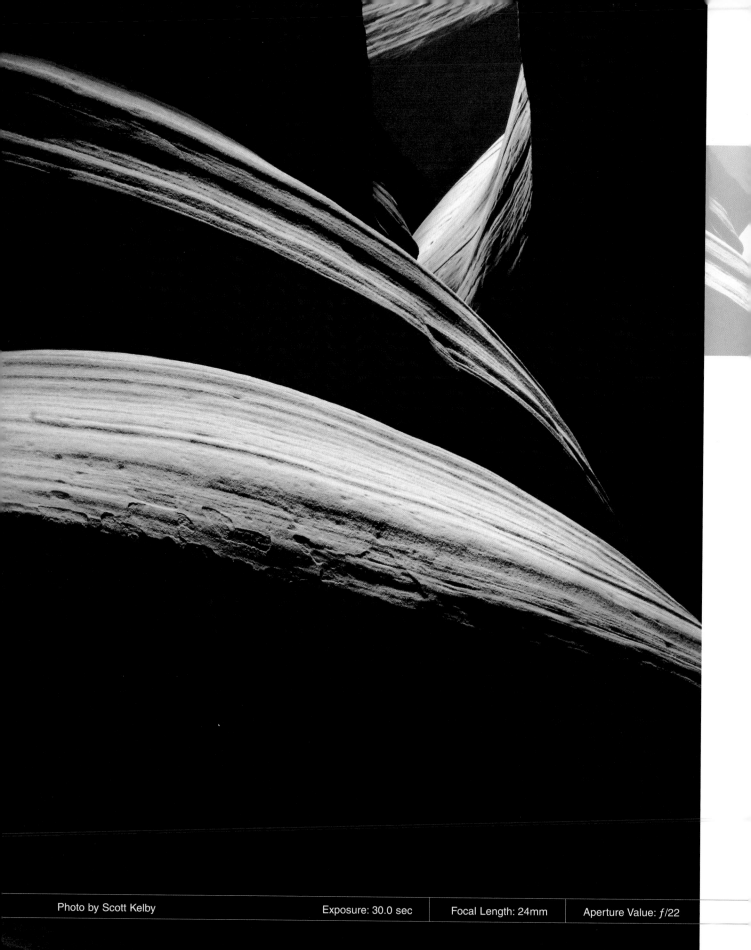

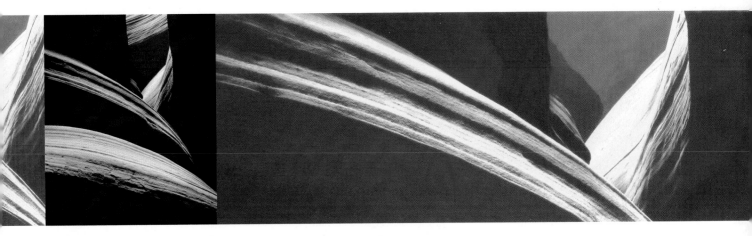

Landscape Workflow
working with outdoor and landscape shots

If you're an outdoor photographer, you probably skipped the Wedding/Portrait Workflow chapter, and came straight here. I want to urge you to read that chapter first, for two reasons: (1) Because if you own a really nice digital camera, mathematically it's just a matter of time before you're asked to shoot the wedding of a friend or relative. It's a lock. Trust me, people think that if you're good at shooting water rushing over a rocky stream, then you've got to be good at shooting people in a dimly lit church. So, you might as well learn that workflow now, because you'll want to do a decent job, and when the wedding couple's friends see your great wedding photos, you'll start to get calls to shoot their weddings, and before you know it, real wedding photographers (who do

this for a living) are cutting the brake lines in your car. And (2) the workflow for wedding photographers is different, but there are aspects that you might want to apply to your outdoor workflow. For example, in this workflow (which is actually my landscape workflow, but if you try it and like it, then it becomes "our" workflow, and from that moment on, you and I will share an unbreakable bond that will tie us emotionally and spiritually together for a lifetime. Or at least until you try a different workflow), we're not going to do any proofing on the Web, but for wedding photographers, that's big. So, read that chapter first, and you'll get way more out of this chapter. Plus, you'll be ready when your mechanic calls to tell you his daughter is getting married in a few months, and....

Workflow Step One: Importing and Organizing Our Shoot

With landscape photography, it's all about shooting in the best possible light, which only happens twice a day (around dusk and dawn). But sometimes the light is less than ideal, which makes us really take full advantage of Photoshop Lightroom's and Photoshop's ability to take lemons and make lemonade. By the way, I have no idea what that means.

Step One:

Our shoot takes place at Jordan Pond, just outside Bar Harbor, Maine, and we're there well before sunrise to get that wonderful first light (in the photo shown here, taken by the wonderful Laurie Excell [a.k.a. The Equipment Lady]). I wanted to get a low-angle view, so I set up my tripod right there on the rocks, with my buddy Rod Harlan setting up just a few feet in front of me. In the photo, I'm shooting a Nikon D2X set to RAW mode at 100 ISO. I started shooting with the Nikon 70–200mm VR f/2.8 lens you see here, but since the sky was kind of flat-looking, and the rocks in the foreground were so interesting, I switched to a Nikon super-wide-angle 12–24mm f/4 (I love this lens for landscape work). The rule of thumb I use for when to use a wide-angle lens is simple: If the foreground is interesting, I shoot wide angle. If the background or sky is more interesting, then I "go long" (by "long," I mean anywhere from 50mm up). To get the maximum sharpness from landscape shots, I: (a) always shoot on a tripod, (b) use a cable release to reduce camera shake caused by me pressing the shutter button, and (c) use mirror lock-up to eliminate any camera shake caused by the camera itself.

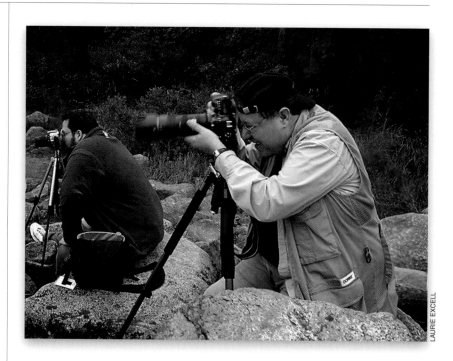

LAURIE EXCELL

SCOTT KELBY

Step Two:

I'm fairly paranoid about losing my original photos, so when I'm out in the field, before I even leave the shoot, I pop out my memory card and back up right there on the spot to an Epson P-5000 (it has CompactFlash and SD card slots built-in), which is a portable 80-GB hard drive with a huge, beautiful crisp LCD monitor (by the way, I've used the Epson P-2000 and P-4000, and they've been fantastic—never failed me—but the latest models are the P-3000 and P-5000). However, this is only temporary "in-the-field" storage. Once I get back to my studio, I plug my memory card reader into my computer (as shown here), connect my LaCie 500-GB hard drive, and have Photoshop Lightroom automatically make a backup copy of my photos to this hard drive as I'm importing (see next step). I then burn an archival-quality DVD for the long-term archiving of my photos. Remember, just because you're paranoid, doesn't mean they're not out to get you.

Step Three:

Now, let's import the photos from our landscape shoot into Lightroom. Go to Lightroom's Library module and click on the Import button on the bottom left. When the Import Photos dialog appears, make sure the Backup To checkbox is turned on so a second copy of your photos will be backed up to your external hard drive (as I mentioned in the previous step. See Chapter 1 for how to set up auto-backup during import). Enter your keywords, apply your personal copyright metadata template (how to set up your template is in also Chapter 1), and click the Import button.

SCOTT KELBY

Continued

Step Four:

Once the photos are imported, take a quick scroll through them. Each time you come to a photo that is obviously flawed (visibly blurry, totally blown-out highlights, etc.), press the letter X on your keyboard, which adds a tiny black Rejected flag in the upper-left corner of the photo's grid cell. Once you've gone through and flagged all your really bad shots (this takes two minutes because these really bad shots jump out at you), go to the Filters section on the top-right side of the filmstrip and click on the first flag icon from the left until just your Rejected photos are visible.

Step Five:

Next, press Command-A (PC: Ctrl-A) to select all your Rejected photos, and then hit the Delete (PC: Backspace) key on your keyboard (or choose Delete Rejected Photos from the Photo menu). This brings up one of those "Are you sure you want to do this?" warning dialogs (shown here). Click the Delete button, and they're gone! Getting rid of these now speeds up the rest of your process, saves room on your hard disk, and you don't keep getting bummed out by seeing your lame shots again and again.

Step Six:
Now you're going to look through the remaining photos and try to pick out the best of the bunch. For this process, you probably want to see the photos as large as possible on your screen, so start by pressing Shift-Tab (to hide the left and right panels, and the filmstrip), then drag the Thumbnails slider (still visible below the Preview area) to the right until two images fill your screen (as shown here). Now you can use the Right and Left Arrow keys on your keyboard to navigate your way through the photos. When you find a good one, press the letter P to flag it as a Pick, and then continue looking and flagging your best shots. (*Note:* If you prefer to see your photos full screen when making your picks, press the Impromptu Slideshow button below the Preview area for a full-screen slide show, and when you see a shot you like, press P.)

Step Seven:
Once you've flagged all your best photos from your shoot, press Shift-Tab again to make the side panels and the filmstrip visible again. Then click-and-drag the Thumbnails slider to the left so more of your photos are visible in the Preview area. Now we need to see just our Picks, so go to the Filters section and click on the third flag until the words "Picks Only" appear onscreen (as shown here). Now only your Picks are displayed. Select all these photos, then create a new collection just for these Picks (you can name it something like "Best of Jordan Pond"), and now those photos are just one click away. I'm going to choose one of these photos and develop it here in Lightroom, then finish it in Photoshop, and bring it back to Lightroom to print the final image.

Workflow Step Two: Processing Our Image in Photoshop Lightroom

We start by doing the essential processing of our RAW and JPEG photos in the Develop module of Photoshop Lightroom. RAW photos and JPEG photos are treated the same (as far as processing goes—there are no special sliders or adjustments available for RAW photos that aren't available for JPEG images as well).

Step One:

Click on the photo you want to process in Photoshop Lightroom, and then jump over to the Develop module. Since we're working on landscape photos, if you hide the left panels, you'll get a much larger view of the photo you're editing (as shown here). This shot was taken right before sunrise. The fog was rolling in, and we only had about 20 minutes to shoot, and then the fog became so thick all you could do was put your camera gear away. We remarked at the time how blue the morning looked, so I want to bring some of that back, and fix the underexposed exposure.

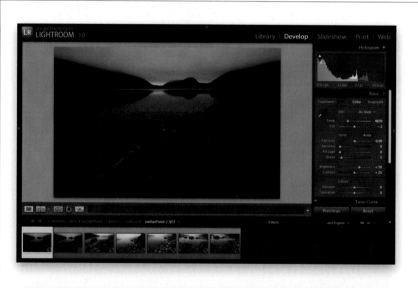

Step Two:

We'll start with the underexposure part: in the Basic panel, drag the Exposure slider to the right until the edge of your histogram graph (on the top of the right side Panels area) just starts to hit the right side wall of the panel. You've expanded the tonal range big time, which gives you a much better exposure, but you're also clipping off some of the highlights as well, so drag the Recovery slider a little to the right (as shown here) to bring back (recover) some of those lost highlights (which should leave a little gap between the end of the histogram and the right wall, as seen here).

Step Three:

To bring some of the blue back into the photo, drag the WB Temp slider to the left just a little bit, and the photo turns much bluer (as seen here). Next, to add more contrast, go to the Tone Curve panel and choose Strong Contrast from the Point Curve pop-up menu at the bottom of the panel. Now you can adjust the curve manually by moving the sliders or clicking-and-dragging the Targeted Adjustment tool up or down over the area in your image you want to adjust. In the example shown here, I would pull back the highlights a little (because the Strong Contrast curve starts to clip the highlights a bit) by dragging the Highlights slider a little to the left. Now click on the Targeted Adjustment tool icon in the top left of the panel to get the tool, move your cursor out over the photo, and then click-and-drag upward on the rocks on the left side to lighten that area.

Step Four:

If you looked near the bottom-right side of the photo, you'd notice that part of my camera bag snuck into the shot. So, I clicked on the Remove Spots tool (down in the toolbar), clicked over the left edge of my camera bag, and dragged to a nearby area of rocks. When you release the mouse button, it covers the problem. Do the same thing for the right side of my bag (you can see the circles where I dragged here). When it's totally hidden, click back on the tool icon in the toolbar. Next, let's keep the changes we've made and take the photo over to Adobe Photoshop for some finishing touches and sharpening. Press Command-E (PC: Ctrl-E) to jump over to Photoshop. In the dialog, choose the third option (as shown here in the inset), then click Edit to open a copy of your photo in Photoshop with the changes we made in Lightroom already applied.

for Digital Photographers

Photoshop

Jumping over to Photoshop to finish our photo editing would be a totally optional step, except for the fact that Photoshop Lightroom doesn't really offer professional-level sharpening. So you'll always wind up in Photoshop (if only for a few moments) to apply your sharpening. In our example, since we're already in Photoshop for sharpening, we're going to also add some finishing effects which boost the color and darken the edges. So, if you don't want these finishing effects added to your photo, just do the sharpening steps.

Step One:

Now that a copy of your edited photo is in Photoshop, we're going to apply a Lab Color move, which does an amazing job of pumping up the color in a photo. I learned this technique from color genius (and Photoshop Hall of Famer) Dan Margulis, but I came up with a simplified version for my book *The Photoshop Channels Book* and that's the version we're going to use here. It starts by going under the Image menu, under Mode, and choosing Lab Color (as shown here).

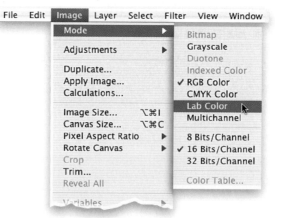

Image 7 Lab Mode
7 Apply Image

Step Two:

Go back under the Image menu, but this time choose Apply Image. (Apply Image lets you use blend modes on channels just like you would on layers. It's one of my favorite features for enhancing contrast and color.) When the dialog appears, change the blend mode to Soft Light (as seen here). Apply Image lets you choose from three totally different looks. You already see the first look, which is Lab channel. To see the other looks, go under the Channel pop-up menu and look at the "a" channel, then the "b" channel, and choose the one you feel looks the best. I chose the "a" channel because it kept the blue overall look, but brought out the red in the rocks (as seen here). Now click OK.

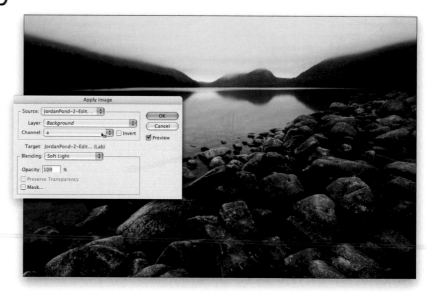

Step Three:

Now we can do some lightening in specific areas of the photo, using a layer blend mode and layer mask (sounds complicated, but it's easy). Start by duplicating your Background layer (Command-J [PC: Ctrl-J]), then in the Layers palette change the layer blend mode of this layer from Normal to Screen. This makes the photo much too bright (as seen here), but we're going to use that brightness to our advantage. We're going to hide that very bright version of our photo behind a black mask, and then we'll reveal just the areas we want to make lighter. You start by pressing-and-holding the Option (PC: Alt) key, then clicking on the Add Layer Mask icon at the bottom of the Layers palette (shown circled here).

Step Four:

This puts a black mask over the brighter version of your photo, completely hiding that version from view (if you look in the Layers palette shown here, you can see the mask added to the right side of your duplicate layer). You can now use the Brush tool to reveal parts of the brighter version just where you want it. So, press D to set your Foreground color to white, get the Brush tool (B), and with a large, soft-edged brush just paint over the tree line on both sides of the pond to make the trees brighter and bring them out of the shadows. You can also paint over any dark parts of the rocks, which not only makes them brighter, but because of the Screen mode it makes them a bit more colorful as well. If the effect seems too intense (and it probably will), just lower the opacity of this brighter layer in the Layers palette (as shown here, where I lowered the Opacity to 50%, which looks about right to me).

Continued

Step Five:

So far here in Photoshop, we've used the Lab Color trick to make the colors pop a bit, then we used a Screen layer and a layer mask to bring out some darker areas of the photo (the trees and some of the rocks). You can now merge your two layers together by pressing Command-E (PC: Ctrl-E), because now we're going to add the same edge-vignette effect that we added to the bridal portrait from the last chapter. So, press Command-J (PC: Ctrl-J) to duplicate the layer and change the blend mode to Multiply (to make the entire photo darker). Then get the Rectangular Marquee tool (M) and draw a rectangle that is about 1" inside the borders (as shown here).

Step Six:

Go under the Select menu and choose Feather (if you're using Photoshop CS3, you'd go under the Select menu, under Modify, and choose Feather there). When the Feather Selection dialog appears, enter 200 pixels, and click OK. Applying a feather greatly softens the edges of your rectangular selection, so we'll have a smooth transition between the darker edges around your photo, and the lighter version underneath.

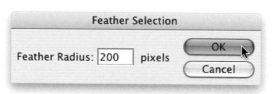

Step Seven:

Once the feather is applied (you can see how the edges of the selection are now rounded), just press the Delete (PC: Backspace) key on your keyboard, and it cuts a huge soft-edged hole out of the center of your darker Multiply layer, revealing the original photo beneath. What all this does is softly darkens the edges all the way around your photo, leaving the center area untouched. Now press Command-D (PC: Ctrl-D) to Deselect and press Command-E (PC: Ctrl-E) to merge this layer with the one below it.

Step Eight:

You may not remember, but we're still in Lab Color mode, which is handy because I prefer to apply my sharpening to just the Lightness channel. This is a very popular technique with pro photographers, because you're only applying the sharpening to the detail areas, not the color. So you avoid most of the problems caused by applying your sharpening directly to the RGB color image. In short, doing this lets me apply more sharpening. You start by going to the Channels palette, and clicking on the Lightness channel. (Ya know, this photo doesn't make a bad black-and-white image, does it? Before Lightroom, we used to use this technique to create color to black-and-white conversions, because the Lightness channel usually makes a nice black and white.)

Continued

Step Nine:

Okay, so now that we know why we use the Lightness channel, let's actually use it. After going to the Channels palette and clicking on the Lightness channel, go to the Filter menu, under Sharpen, and choose Unsharp Mask. When the Unsharp Mask dialog appears, enter Amount: 120%, Radius: 1, Threshold: 3, and click OK. (I use these particular Unsharp Mask settings for landscapes because it makes the photo nice and crisp without it looking oversharpened. In some cases when using this Lightness channel trick, I can actually get away with applying it twice in a row.) Now, go under the Image menu, under Mode, and choose RGB Color.

Step Ten:

Here's the photo after applying the Unsharp Mask, using the settings I showed above. Now, at this point, the colors in the photo look a bit oversaturated to me. I like really vibrant color in my images, but these seem really, really vibrant (two reallys is really too much). Luckily, this is easy to fix. Go under the Image menu, under Adjustments, and choose Hue/Saturation.

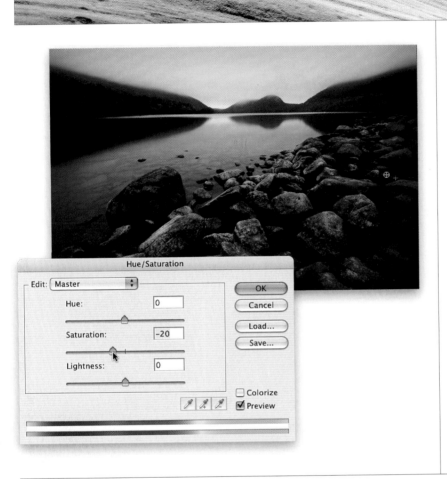

Step Eleven:

When the Hue/Saturation dialog appears, simply drag the Saturation slider to the left (as shown), which lowers the overall color saturation. I can't give you a specific number to hit, because how much you desaturate the color is really a personal call. In this photo, I lowered the Saturation amount to −20, which for me did the trick. Once the color looks better to you, just click the OK button.

Step Twelve:

That wraps up our edits in Photoshop CS2/CS3, so now we can return to Lightroom to create our prints. All you have to do to return this edited copy to Lightroom is close the photo, and (most importantly) save the photo. So, when you close the photo and a warning dialog appears in Photoshop asking if you want to save your changes, make sure you click on Save. That's it. Your copy, with all the changes you made in Photoshop, is sent back to Lightroom—a totally seamless trip to Photoshop and back.

Before

After

Workflow Step Four: Printing the Final Image

At this point, you've saved your changes in Photoshop, closed the window, and the copy of your photo is now back in Photoshop Lightroom (you'll find it in the filmstrip, right next to your original photo). Now it's time to print. Here you'll basically choose your printer and paper size, and turn on Photoshop Lightroom's color management.

Step One:

Your photo is edited and sharpened and now you're ready to print. So, click on the Print module and in the Template Browser on the left side of Photoshop Lightroom, click on the Maximum Size Centered template to fit your landscape on the page as large as possible. If your orientation is set to Portrait (as shown here, where your photo appears sideways), you'll need to click the Page Setup button (just under the bottom-right corner of the Preview area). When the Page Setup (PC: Print Setup) dialog appears, set your orientation to Landscape (as shown here), and choose your printer from the Format For (PC: Name) pop-up menu (in my case, it's the Epson Stylus Pro 3800). Then choose your paper size (in this case, 16x20") and click OK.

Step Two:

Now go to the Print Job panel (in the right side Panels area) and set your Print Resolution to 360 (ideal for Epson printers), set the Print Sharpening to High (as shown), then under Color Management click on Managed by Printer, and from the pop-up menu choose the profile that matches your printer and the exact paper you're going to print on (here I'm printing on Red River Ultra Pro Satin paper to an Epson 3800. For more on finding and installing printer profiles, see Chapter 8.

Step Three:

Click on the Print button at the bottom of the right side Panels area to bring up the Print dialog (my Mac OS X Print dialog for an Epson Stylus Pro 3800 is shown here). There are two important changes you need to make in this dialog (whether you're on a Mac or in Windows), and they are: (1) you need to turn off your computer's built-in color management, and (2) choose the proper Media Type (the exact paper you're printing on) and for Print Quality, choose the quality you want (depending on what I'm printing, and whether this is client work or not, I generally print on the second-highest quality setting). For more on choosing these options, see Chapter 8.

Step Four:

Now click Print (PC: OK) and before you know it you'll be holding your final color-managed print (as shown here. Of course, in this photo I'm holding the print, but in real life that will be you holding the print. You knew that, right?).

Where to Go Next for More Photoshop Lightroom Learning

So you've made it to the end of the book and now you can see how Photoshop Lightroom is going to change the digital photography workflow forever. Well, if you're hungry for more Photoshop Lightroom learning, I put together a page of different resources that I'm involved with, so even though you've finished the book, we don't have to stop learning about Photoshop Lightroom together.

Adobe® Photoshop® Lightroom™ Killer Tips **videocast:**
Each week my buddy (and my co-host of *Adobe® Photoshop® TV*) Matt Kloskowski hosts *Adobe Photoshop Lightroom Killer Tips*—a free tips and tricks video pod cast for Photoshop Lightroom users. Check it out at www.lightroomkillertips .com, where Matt also posts lots of cool Photoshop Lightroom news and tips. You can subscribe for free on Apple's iTunes Store and then watch it right from within iTunes.

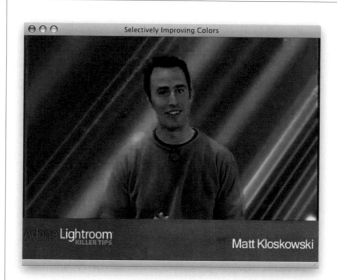

My Adobe® Photoshop® Lightroom™ LIVE! Seminar Tour:

I'm heading up a nationwide one-day Lightroom LIVE! seminar tour that heads to major markets across the U.S. The tour is sponsored by Adobe Systems, and produced by NAPP, and it starts with a live on-location bridal shoot, right there in the class, with full studio lighting and all the info on how we're shooting it, the equipment used, etc. Then we take these shots into Photoshop Lightroom as you see the whole step-by-step workflow unfold live in front of your eyes. It's kind of like a live version of this book, and at the end of the day, just like the book, we'll be outputting big, beautiful 16x20" prints of our bride. It all happens in one day, and there's never been a tour like it, so I hope you'll join me when we come out your way. For info, or to sign up, visit www.photoshopseminars.com.

The National Association of Photoshop Professionals (NAPP): The Photoshop Lightroom Authority!

This is the world's largest photography, graphics, and digital imaging professional association in the world, with nearly 60,000 members in the U.S. and 221 countries around the world. They were nice enough to support this book because, well…I'm their President. I started the organization nine years ago because there was no central resource for learning about Photoshop 365 days a year. Now, we're expanding our training to include Photoshop Lightroom, and besides publishing *Darkroom* magazine, we also produce the world's largest Photoshop event, The Photoshop World Conference & Expo, and we've added a full conference track, and a pre-conference workshop, just for Photoshop Lightroom users. Find out more at www. photoshop-world.com.

Index

"PhotoFrame is the only product that I use to create edge effects that look as if I did them in the darkroom. When it comes to adding border and edge effects to my images, PhotoFrame is simply the best."

Jim DiVitale

PhotoFrame Pro ③

Unleash your creativity.

— See your frame creations in real-time using interactive previews

— Thousands of new frames including film effects and traditional mattes and frames

— New Frame Browser makes it easy to find the perfect frame

— Apply textures to frames for even more creative options

Complete with thousands of professionally designed frames that can be combined to create infinite unique combinations, PhotoFrame lets you interactively design stunning border and edge effects in Photoshop.

on
onOne software

www.ononesoftware.com

expodisc

Professional Digital White Balance
Neutral or Portrait

Don't waste time fixing color.
Capture Accurate Color.

"The amount of time this saves you in Photoshop
is staggering, and it's so easy to use
- it takes just seconds, but saves hours.
An absolute must-have."

Layers, December 2006.
Scott Kelby

www.expoimaging.net

* frog not included

Image Copyright D. Maynard